A Functional Curriculum
for Teaching Students with Disabilities

A Functional Curriculum for Teaching Students with Disabilities

Volume IV
Interpersonal, Competitive Job-Finding, and Leisure-Time Skills

Michael Bender

Peter J. Valletutti

Carol Ann Baglin

pro·ed
An International Publisher

8700 Shoal Creek Boulevard
Austin, Texas 78757-6897
800/897-3202 Fax 800/397-7633
Order online at http://www.proedinc.com

© 1998 by PRO-ED, Inc.
8700 Shoal Creek Boulevard
Austin, Texas 78757-6897
800/897-3202 Fax 800/397-7633
Order online at http://www.proedinc.com

This book is designed in Bookman Light and Serif Gothic.

Production Manager: Alan Grimes
Production Coordinator: Karen Swain
Managing Editor: Christine Olson
Copyeditor: Suzi Hunn
Art Director: Thomas Barkley
Designer: Lee Anne Landry
Reprints Buyer: Alicia Woods
Preproduction Coordinator: Chris Anne Worsham
Editor: Debra Berman
Production Assistant: Claudette Landry
Production Assistant: Dolly Fisk Jackson

Printed in the United States of America

3 4 5 6 7 8 9 10 01

To my wife, Madelyn,
for her inspiring love for all children
and her tireless efforts to protect them.
—M.B.

To Audrey Smith Hoffnung,
who had faith in me at the very beginning
and who has always served
as a model of the consummate professional.
—P.J.V.

To my parents, Sally and Bill Hewitt,
who have helped me
through each stage
of my life . . .
for my whole life.
—C.A.B.

Contents

UNIT 3

Leisure-Time Skills
161

Preface

A Functional Curriculum for Teaching Students with Disabilities: Volume IV addresses the critical areas of interpersonal, competitive job-finding, and leisure-time skills. It expands the curricular areas covered in previous volumes, and like the other volumes its content has been impelled by several recent phenomena: (a) the changing perceptions of the nature of special education (e.g., inclusion, emphasis on a holistic approach, and the movement toward the development of independent living skills); (b) the identification of new and underserved populations (e.g., infants and toddlers, youth with attention-deficit/hyperactivity disorder); (c) modifications in service delivery (e.g., interagency cooperation and increased parental involvement); (d) recent federal legislation regarding education (e.g., P.L. 99-457, P.L. 101-476, and P.L. 102-119) and the civil and legal rights of persons with disabilities (e.g., Americans with Disabilities Act); and (e) reductions in targeted federal dollars.

The central problem, however, continues to be the nonproductive and, at times, destructive magical thinking engaged in by educators who believe that structural changes alone will automatically result in improvements in education. Unfortunately, many special students continue to receive an education that is not "special" whether they are placed in segregated or inclusive settings. Structural change that does not address the individual and special needs of students with disabilities or attend to the quality of instruction is merely cosmetic, not substantive. We consider this functionally oriented curriculum—if it is implemented by special education teachers, parents, and other trained personnel—to be a critical way of making the education of students with special needs an education that is truly special, regardless of the setting.

The first edition of this series, introduced in the 1970s, coincided with the movement for the educational rights of individuals with disabilities, as mandated by the landmark federal legislation P.L. 94-142. This was also the time when parent and advocacy groups, along with many other professionals, consolidated their efforts based on a collective mission not only to provide special education and related services to all children and youth with handicapping conditions but also to integrate them, whenever appropriate and feasible, in the public schools and the mainstream of society.

Instructional areas and emphases addressed by the first two editions, such as functional academics, interpersonal and social skills, and leisure education, represented a significant departure from the curriculum traditionally being taught in many special education programs. Of equal importance was the attempt to comprehensively and clearly identify appropriate instructional objectives, strategies, and resources that would promote independence, be age appropriate, be suitable for teaching in a natural environment, and be of lifelong functional value.

Much change has occurred since then. Evolving ideological currents have had a significant impact on guiding and determining the content of this expanded edition of the curriculum series. Several recent developments—the need for interagency cooperation, reduction in targeted federal dollars, emphasis on a holistic approach, the need for a competent core of human service professionals, and the movement toward independent living—have all resulted in major changes in this profession. For example, special education terminology has been modified. The word *handicapped* is no longer used to describe a person who is challenged by a disability. The rejection of the word *handicapped* has come about because the problems experienced by persons with disabilities are viewed as not being within the person him- or herself but rather as arising from social attitudes and perceptions and by society's failure to provide needed programs, services, and resources that will compensate for or minimize the effects of the individual's disability.

This change in terminology has been incorporated in the recent amendments to P.L. 94-142 (the Education for All Handicapped Children Act). These amendments—P.L. 101-476, the Individuals with Disabilities Education Act (IDEA)—reflect the changing concept of disabilities and the role of society in meeting the needs of individuals who have special needs. Of particular importance is the addition of the requirements for transition services, which focus on the successful movement of students from school to community, thus emphasizing the functional skills of independent living and community participation.

Moreover, the preferred descriptor, *disability,* should not be used as a label, as in "He or she is a 'learning disabled' or 'mentally retarded' child." Rather, as a way of accentuating the personhood of the individual, expressions should be used such as "the individual with learning disabilities." In this way, the disability is seen as merely one aspect or part of a total individual, thus minimizing the placement of undue emphasis on the disability by others and by the person him- or herself, while at the same time emphasizing the person in all his or her myriad dimensions.

The concept of the least restrictive environment (LRE) shapes the placement provisions of P.L. 94-142 and its subsequent amendments (P.L. 99-457) as well as P.L. 101-476 and its various state legislative counterparts. LRE led to the implementation of a continuum of educational placements and services—from placement in a regular or mainstreamed class as the least restrictive of possible environments to the most restrictive environment in a nonpublic residential setting. Central to individual placement decisions, however, was the fundamental premise that placement within this continuum should be shaped by the concept central to special education, namely, that the primary determinants are the individualized needs of the students, based on the idiosyncratic nature of their disability.

Although mainstreaming was, at its inception, identified as the least restrictive or the most normalized school environment, it has not always been successfully realized in practice. Too often, needed support services have not been provided to mainstreamed students and their teachers, and inordinate emphasis has been placed on location of service rather than on effective and efficient instructional practices. Teachers assigned to mainstreamed classes, more often than not, were ill-prepared pedagogically and psychologically to teach their students with special educational needs on either an individual or a group basis. Invariably, the curriculum was not modified to reflect the needs of those integrated special students who required instruction in practical knowledge and skills taught from a functional perspective and with a functional purpose. Functional curricular modifications, if they had been assiduously pursued, might have benefited the students without disabilities as well. Typically, the curriculum of the mainstreamed class is test driven and tradition bound, resulting in too much time wasted on the teaching of atomized and irrelevant knowledge.

Recently, however, the concept of mainstreaming has been redefined as part of the inclusion movement or the Regular Education Initiative (REI). The REI maintains that a dual system of regular and special education is unnecessary, inappropriate, and ineffective, and that students with disabilities, regardless of the severity of their disability, can and should be educated in the mainstreamed (regular) setting. This service delivery approach rejects the continuum-of-services concept and views all other alternate placements, except the regular or mainstreamed class, as too restrictive. The collaborative teaching movement emanates from the REI and attempts to respond to some of the problems that resulted from more restrictive placements and misguided mainstreaming. The collaborative approach requires regular and special teachers to work as a team as they plan instruction for and teach all the students (both those with disabilities and those who are not so challenged) in their assigned classes. As the collaborative approach is increasingly being employed, it will be necessary for all teachers, regular and special, to modify the existing regular class curriculum so that it addresses the adaptive behavior needs of all students, whether they have disabilities or not.

This curriculum, although meant primarily for teachers functioning within a special setting, has the additional goal of assisting collaborative teams of teachers as they analyze and modify existing curricula, subsequently design individualized curricula (Individualized Education Programs [IEPs] and Individualized Family Service Plans [IFSPs]), and cooperate with other human service professionals and related human service agencies to meet the life needs of regular as well as special students.

Curricular areas identified in this specific volume have also changed. For example, vocational education, often associated with skill development and traditional "shop" programs, is now often defined in terms of work readiness, supported employment, and career education. Curricula in the area of leisure education have also gained prominence—a justified development given that free time continues to increase for most people in our culture. The problem of meaningful utilization of leisure time, especially for older people with disabilities, is particularly acute because many are chronically unemployed or underemployed, and therefore not only have expanded free time but also lack the financial resources required for the productive use of that time.

Safety, as a curricular entity, has also gained increasing recognition, especially as more and more programs emphasize community-based education, which entails greater and more numerous threats to safety than the traditional, classroom-based approach. Safety elements should pervade all curricular areas, and therefore have been included in the lesson plans and learning activities of this edition.

Unserved, underserved, and increasing populations of children with disabilities continue to enter educational programs at a rapid rate. Some of this change is a result of recent legislative mandates, such as P.L. 99-457 (Education of the Handicapped Act Amendments). Part H, reauthorized as P.L. 102-119, IDEA Amendments of 1991, mandates the provision of comprehensive early intervention and family services for infants and toddlers and their families (birth through age 2). School programs are also now serving children and youth with disabilities who were not often identified in the 1970s and whose numbers have drastically increased in the 1990s. Examples include children with fetal alcohol syndrome (FAS) and those who have been damaged prenatally (or perinatally) through maternal substance abuse, the AIDS virus, syphilis, or gonorrhea.

Technology continues to play an increasingly important role in educational practice. The instructional use of the personal computer and other instructional technology (including interactive television) is increasing at a rapidly accelerating rate. The use of technology has proven to be of considerable assistance in planning (development of IEPs), in managing teaching (recording of formal and informal assessment data), and in communicating with parents (progress reports and report cards). The personal computer, with its capacity for miniaturization, adaptations, and peripherals, is also moving rapidly to address the habilitative needs of individuals with disabilities. In the near future, as a result of research with neuromuscular feedback and computers, we can expect some individuals who cannot walk—to walk. Other technological advances will make it possible for those who cannot see—to see in some fashion, and those who cannot hear—to hear in some way from implant devices and as yet unknown technologies. The use of assistive technology will also expand as continuing efforts are made to assist students in meeting the demands of an increasingly complex and demanding postindustrial society.

The role of parents (or parent surrogates) is essential to the implementation of this curriculum. Parental participation in decisions regarding placement, IEPs, IFSPs, and needed related services is essential to a holistic approach to educating exceptional children. The parental role in providing pertinent information to teachers should not be minimized, because parents can provide information that is essential for assisting in identifying goals and objectives, establishing educational and programming priorities, and determining areas of interest. Parents have a unique advantage in instructing their children in activities that are best introduced and practiced in the home setting and also in the community. Parents can also serve as effective carryover agents who provide practice sessions and reinforce newly acquired skills as the child performs them within his or her reality contexts.

Because of these various trends and factors, it seems appropriate to now produce an expanded edition of the curriculum. Teams of teachers, students, parents, clinicians, and other related service staff have been surveyed to find out what needed to be addressed. Our overriding goal continues to be the presentation of new information and material that will assist teachers, other professionals, and parents in facilitating the functional performance of children and youth with disabilities in the full variety of life situations and contexts. As in past incarnations, this curriculum assumes that the reader possesses a basic understanding of teaching methods and a fundamental level of expertise in analyzing educational tasks so that they may be used as a framework for evaluating the child's current level of performance and as a means of focusing on specific behaviors requiring remedial or instructional attention. Emphasis continues to be placed on teaching students in reality situations in the home, community, and workplace. Whenever home-based or community-based education is not feasible, teachers must provide realistic classroom simulations that offer students with disabilities opportunities to practice life skills in functional contexts and settings. The past successes of the original curriculum have supported our view that reality contexts can be effectively simulated in a classroom setting only if the entire behavior is demonstrated with all its applicable dimensions (psychomotor, affective, and cognitive) expressed as a total, integrated act.

Long-range goals and specific teaching objectives have been identified, in this edition, as "general goals" and "specific objectives" to indicate their relationship to the development and subsequent revisions of the Individualized Education Program (IEP) and the Individualized Family Service Plan (IFSP). Although we have provided readers with suggested activities viewed from an age and grade-level perspective, readers applying the curriculum must appreciate the essential relationship between informal and formal assessment data and the decisions they make as to the relevant goals and objectives to be addressed. Although specific objectives have generally been placed in their developmental sequence, known sequences have been considered only if they make functional sense. Developmental milestones and traditional educational tasks have been deemphasized and eliminated from this curriculum if the identified behavior does not contribute to functional success for the intended population (e.g., drawing a geometric shape or matching wooden blocks of different colors). Furthermore, developmental profiles are less important as children get older, whereas they are central for infants and toddlers.

The curriculum is intended as a guide not only for individuals with disabilities but also for individuals who may be experiencing learning problems but who have not been classified as having a disability. In fact, many high-level goals and suggested activities are included to encourage program implementors not to have restricted or limiting views. There are many nondisabled students and adults, students and adults with mild disabilities, and students and adults with no formally defined disability who are functioning at a lower-than-expected level who would also benefit from the activities in the curriculum. These high-level goals and suggested activities are also meant to guide mainstreamed and collaborating teachers in their modification of regular curricula, which should do much to make inclusion more successful for both the students who have disabilities and those who do not.

This new volume has been designed as a guide to preservice and inservice teachers and other professionals who work directly as service providers to children and adults with disabilities. Parents, surrogates and foster parents, and other family members, as well as service coordinators (case managers), house parents in group homes/apartments or other alternate living arrangements, and counselors in activity centers and workshops should find this curriculum valuable as they interact with and instruct the individuals with whom they work and/or live.

The original curriculum also has had wide acceptance and use as a text for preservice teacher candidates and inservice teachers taking courses in curriculum development and teaching methods in special education at the undergraduate and graduate levels. The current expanded edition has been updated to reflect the present needs of students taking these courses, especially as they interact in diverse practica experiences with previously unserved and underserved populations of individuals with disabilities.

The lists of Selected Materials/Resources attached to each unit are relatively brief because many of the essential materials needed in teaching a functional curriculum are the ordinary materials of life that are invariably found in the home, school, community, and workplace, and because well-designed and well-presented teacher-made materials are usually more appropriate, better focused, and more motivating to students.

The Suggested Readings appended to each unit list not only recent publications but some older, classic materials as well. These classics have been included because they retain their immediacy and appropriateness and thus should not be automatically eliminated from lists of relevant professional literature out of a passion for newness.

This volume of the curriculum continues to provide information and suggestions that have proven to be of value in the past. The suggested activities provided, a direct response to user recommendations and reviews, have been separated into two major categories: Teacher Interventions and Family Interventions. Further, four distinct age/grade levels for each of these interventions have been developed to reflect content deemed appropriate for the following levels: infant and toddler/preschool, primary, intermediate, and secondary. The suggested activities for the infant and toddler/preschool level are meant to meet the functional needs of infants and toddlers (birth through 2 years) and preschool children (3 through 5 years). Additionally, attention needs to be directed to the several alternative settings for teaching children, especially where infants and toddlers are concerned, because they are frequently educated in their own homes and in day-care settings.

Finally, this volume of the curriculum, like the other volumes, does not address all the dimensions of a functional curriculum, because to do so is neither practical nor possible. It does not provide all the possible instructional activities that are applicable or would be interesting and motivating to students and adults with disabilities. It does, however, provide a structure and format from which a creative professional can extrapolate additional instructional goals and objectives, design learning activities, and suggest possible responses to the multitude of challenging questions that will arise from the actual implementation of the curriculum.

Acknowledgments

The development of this volume required collaboration with many education and health care professionals as well as the input of numerous parents. We would like to specifically acknowledge the contributions of Susan Harryman, RPT, and Priscilla Roberts, LPTA; Lana Warren, OTR/L; Marilee Allen, MD; Yvonne Caruso, RN; Margaret Morris, CCC-SLP; and the following parents, who regularly commit their energies to the education and support of the many children who will benefit from these curricula: Madelyn Bender, Kathy Cooper, Mona Freedman, Michelle Grant, Joyce Bergstein, and Robert Stephens.

As always, the support of office professionals is invaluable. Of particular importance in this project was Carolyn Savage, administrative assistant and mother.

Sheréa Makle, publications specialist, selected and inserted the graphics, and refined many formatting inconsistencies.

General Goals

UNIT 1. INTERPERSONAL SKILLS

I. The student will function as optimally as possible in diverse interpersonal and social situations.

II. The student will function as optimally as possible in diverse interpersonal and social situations that depend on effective oral communication skills.

III. The student will refrain from engaging in disturbing, distracting, destructive, and self-destructive behavior.

UNIT 2. COMPETITIVE JOB-FINDING SKILLS

I. The student will acquire those skills necessary to competitively apply for work.

II. The student will acquire those skills that allow him or her to get ready for work.

III. The student will acquire those skills that allow him or her to go to work.

IV. The student will follow work rules and policies.

V. The student will demonstrate appropriate interpersonal skills in the workplace.

VI. The student will understand his or her compensation for work and develop a bill paying and savings plan.

UNIT 3. LEISURE-TIME SKILLS

I. The student will participate in play activities and choose from a variety of games of leisure.

II. The student will engage in sports and activities of physical fitness.

III. The student will participate in camping and diverse outdoor activities.

IV. The student will use information from the study of nature to engage in relevant leisure activities.

V. The student will identify activities and opportunities to use as hobbies.

VI. The student will select craft activities to engage in leisure and hobby activities.

VII. The student will engage in performing and visual arts.

VIII. The student will seek a variety of entertainment and cultural opportunities.

Introduction and Curriculum Overview

A primary purpose of special education is to help students with disabilities lead successful and personally fulfilling lives now and in the future. A functional curriculum is designed to prepare students to function as independently as possible in an integrated society (Wheeler, 1987). A broad range of skills, therefore, must be included in the design of a functional curriculum for students with disabilities. It is axiomatic that the more severe the disability, the greater the educational need and challenge, and, thus, the more comprehensive the curriculum.

In addition, the skills needed by individuals with disabilities continue to expand as society becomes more complex. Moreover, with the renewed and increasing emphasis on inclusion and mainstreaming, it is imperative that curricula taught in these settings address the needs of students with disabilities who, given the nature of the traditional curriculum, are less likely to be expected to develop functional skills in these mainstreamed settings. Traditional ways of developing content for students with disabilities, such as through the watering down of the regular curriculum, do not work. If new entrants to the regular education mainstream are to be successfully integrated into the school and community, their programs must be modified in functional, real-life ways. In essence, *life is the curriculum.*

According to Gast and Schuster (1993), "A functional curriculum is a primary *external support* for children with severe disabilities" (p. 471). Gast and Schuster have identified a number of principles that should be observed in the development and implementation of a functional curriculum. These authors believe that the designer/instructor should:

> focus on teaching skills that are chronologically age-appropriate and immediately useful to the learner. Use ecological inventories and compile a community catalog of current and future environments that are important to the students. Define goals based on the prior step. Prioritize goals based on their potential for enhancing independence. Task analyze the skills needed to perform successfully. Conduct a discrepancy analysis to determine what the student can and cannot do. Use principles of applied behavior analysis. Provide instruction in integrated and community settings. (p. 471)

The need for acquiring functional skills has become the cornerstone for most programs involved in teaching special populations. Fortunately, for some mainstreamed students with disabilities, the principles and contents of this approach are increasingly being incorporated into regular educational programs.

DEFINING THE FUNCTIONAL APPROACH

The functional approach to educating students with or without disabilities is based on a philosophy of education that determines the format and content of a curriculum and that requires an instructional methodology emphasizing the application of knowledge and skills in reality contexts (Bender & Valletutti, 1985; Valletutti & Bender, 1985). Some authorities view this approach as being different from the developmental approach in that its emphasis is on teaching age-appropriate skills that are immediately applicable to diverse life settings (Gast & Schuster, 1993). Patton, Beirne-Smith, and Payne (1990), on the other hand, have posited: "The functional curriculum is a hybrid of the developmental and the behavioral curricula. It attempts to incorporate the best features of the two. Insofar as it emphasizes teaching interrelated classes of behavior and generalization within task classes, it is developmental, but it is behavioral in its emphasis on teaching skills that the infant or child needs now or will need" (p. 298). According to Kirk and Gallagher (1989), "Over the years, from research, common sense, and experience, a philosophy of teaching students with multiple and severe handicaps has evolved. Today our objective is to teach functional age-appropriate skills within the integrated school and nonschool settings, and to base our teaching on the systematic evaluation of students' progress" (p. 467).

Educators using the functional approach identify life skills, specified as instructional goals and objectives, and then seek to facilitate a student's acquisition of these skills. It is adult referenced in that it is a top-down approach, identifying behaviors essential to successful adjustment as a functioning adult rather than having a bottom-up design with its child-oriented focus (Polloway, Patton, Payne, & Payne, 1989). It fosters the development of skills that increase autonomy, as in self-care activities, and encourages constructive codependency, as in cooperative enterprises and mutual problem solving in the home, school, community, and workplace. It endeavors to make the individuals to whom it is applied as successful as possible in meeting their own needs and in satisfying the requirements of living in a community. It also strives to make the individual's life as fulfilling and pleasurable as possible (Cegelka & Greene, 1993).

The functional approach determines the nature of the instructional process. It requires that specified skills be taught in reality contexts. That is, skills are to be taught directly through typical home, school, or community activities, or, if a natural setting is not feasible, indirectly through classroom simulations (Brown, Nietupski, & Hamre-Nietupski, 1976; Polloway et al., 1989).

Conducting an ecological inventory has been suggested as a strategy for generating a functional curriculum that is community referenced. The steps involved in this process include identifying curricular domains (e.g., vocational and leisure), describing present and future environments, prioritizing the activities pertinent to these environments, specifying the skills needed to perform these activities, conducting a discrepancy analysis to determine required skills missing from the student's behavioral repertoire, determining needed adaptations, and, finally, developing a meaningful IEP (Brown et al., 1979).

A functional curriculum identifies *what* is to be taught, whereas the functional approach to instruction determines *how* a skill is to be taught. Whereas a functional curriculum is, in most cases, absolutely essential to instructional programs employed in special classes or special schools, it can also be particularly valuable to teachers of mainstreamed or inclusive classes. These teachers must make functional adaptations to existing curricula if life skills are to be addressed, despite the restrictions imposed by rigid adherence to the subjects traditionally found in school curricula. Teachers, therefore, must analyze the academically driven goals and objectives of traditional curricula and identify their potential practical applications.

DEVELOPING A FUNCTIONAL CURRICULUM

An analysis of the social roles that people play as children, adolescents, and adults can serve as the foundation for designing a functional curriculum (Bender & Valletutti, 1982; Valletutti & Bender, 1982). Social competency is thus primary in a functional curriculum. "Social competency dimensions are critical to the child's acceptability in the classroom, peer relationships, the efficiency and success of academic efforts, current life adjustment, and future social and vocational success" (Reschly, 1993, p. 232). Closely allied to the concept of a life skills curriculum is the concept of social competence, often referred to as "adaptive behavior." *Adaptive behavior* refers to the individual's effectiveness in meeting the demands and standards of his or her environment based on age and the cultural group to which the individual belongs (Grossman, 1983). According to Drew, Logan, and Hardman (1992), "Adaptive skills are necessary to decrease an individual's dependence on others and increase opportunities for school and community participation" (p. 257). Drew et al. specified that "adaptive skill content areas for school-age retarded children include motor, self-care, social, communication, and functional academic skills" (p. 258).

Curricular models based on the concept of career education emphasize effective participation by the individual in all of life's "occupations." Career education, thus, requires an educational program that starts early in the school career and continues into adulthood (Clark, 1979). Brolin's (1986) Life-Centered Career Education (LCCE) model identifies 22 major competencies needed for effective functioning in school, family, and community. These skills are divided into three domains: daily living, personal/social, and occupational. Cronin and Patton (1993) have produced a life skills instructional guide for students with special needs. This guide provides information that addresses the importance of life skills instruction and insight as to how to identify major life demands and specific life skills. Professional sources such as these yield a wealth of information on ways of integrating real-life content into the curriculum.

Developers of reality-based curricula, whether identified as functional, life skills, adaptive behavior, or career education, must examine the situations faced by members of society and specify the behaviors expected of them as they function at different stages in their lives. The long-range orientation of education, however, requires that competencies needed by adults be given programming priority.

Functionally oriented curricula must have an adult-outcomes emphasis. This is especially true for those students with disabilities and their nondisabled peers for whom a higher education is neither desired nor appropriate. Adult-outcomes curricula have abandoned their vocational myopia and now deal more comprehensively and realistically with the many elements needed for successful personal and social adjustment in adulthood (Cronin & Gerber, 1982). Students categorized as having diverse learning and behavioral disabilities, as well as students who are at risk for school failure who have not been so classified, are more likely to be stimulated by learning activities that emphasize their present and future problems, needs, and concerns. Regardless of age or grade, students should be prepared for the challenges of life after they graduate or leave school.

If the social-role perspective is accepted, then teachers, parents, counselors, and other trainers must decide which competencies should be included in a curriculum with such a nontraditional approach. This task is not an esoteric or an insurmountable one, however. Through an examination of their own lives and the lives of other adults, educators can easily identify what life skills should be included in a functional curriculum. Moreover, listening and attending to the writings of the students themselves, especially during the adolescent years, will also prove a superb source of functional instructional goals and objectives (Polloway et al., 1989).

The process of selecting the goals and objectives and establishing the functional priorities of a life skills curriculum requires the designer to eliminate those traditional academic tasks that have little or no value. The determinant of inclusion is whether the skill in question is needed or may be needed by the individual now or at some time in the person's future. Patton, Beirne-Smith, and Payne (1990) have suggested that the selection should be governed by an objective's adaptive potential and its direct and frequent application to the individual's environment, the likelihood of its successful acquisition, its potential for improving the quality and level of services available to the individual, and its impact on the reduction of dangerous or harmful behaviors.

Once the functional curriculum has been developed, the student's IEP or IFSP must be formulated based on this general curriculum, with attention devoted to the establishment of instructional priorities. Priorities are determined, in part, on the basis of answers to the following questions:

- Will the acquisition of a skill with less-than-obvious functional relevance lead to the later development of a key functional skill? For example, will it be important to teach an individual to hop and skip because these movements will be incorporated in games, sports, and other leisure activities, such as dancing?

- Is the skill of practical or current value to the individual as he or she functions on a daily basis?

- Will the skill be needed by the individual in the future? A skill that is immediately needed must be assigned greater priority than a skill needed in the future. Age appropriateness is always to be honored whether it applies to the choice of suitable instructional materials or to establishing instructional priorities.

- Has the individual demonstrated an actual need for the development of a particular skill? Teachers, support personnel, and other instructors need to observe the individual to identify the areas in which he or she is experiencing difficulty and utilize these observations in setting programming priorities.

- Has the individual expressed the desire to acquire a specific skill? Students will often ask for needed assistance in acquiring a skill that has psychological importance. These self-identified needs should never be ignored and often will determine educational priorities.

- Do the parents believe that the acquisition of a particular skill will increase their child's adaptive behavior or performance in the home?

- Will the individual's acquisition of a specific skill improve his or her performance in school- and home-related tasks?

- Does the skill have survival value? Clearly, teaching a person how to cross a street safely has greater priority than teaching a youngster to chant or sing a nursery rhyme.

- Will the development of a particular skill facilitate the acquisition of skills pertinent to the goals of other human service professionals who are providing related services? (Valletutti & Dummett, 1992).

On the basis of the responses to these questions, and with essential input from parents and relevant human service professionals, teachers and trainers must develop the student's IFSP or IEP with its stated instructional priorities.

FUNCTIONALITY AS AN INSTRUCTIONAL PROCESS

In order to teach in a functional way, instructors must ask the questions, "Under what circumstances is this skill applied?" and "Why and when is this skill needed?" The answer to either question determines the functional scenario that structures the instructional plan and process. For example, if the short-term instructional objective is, "The student draws water from the sink," the response to the questions "Under what circumstances . . . ?" or "Why and when is this skill needed?" may be, "when washing vegetables in preparing a meal," "when filling ice cube trays," or "when getting water to fill the fish tank." The responses to either of these two questions provide the creative vision out of which the lesson should emerge. The lesson might then involve making a meal for guests in which a salad is prepared and ice cubes are made for the meal's accompanying beverage.

Once the circumstances under which a skill is typically practiced have been identified, teachers, parents, and other instructors, if possible, should provide instructional activities in the skill's usual setting or, at a minimum, in its simulated setting. Whenever the realistic setting for a skill's application is the home, teachers must make the student's parents part of the instructional team by helping them to be effective teachers of their children, assisting them in carrying out functional "homework" assignments, such as doing simple household cleaning and home repairs. Teachers, of course, have primary responsibility for skills that are best developed in the school setting, such as teaching cognitive or academic skills in their functional applications. The community setting is the shared responsibility of both parents and teachers.

Whenever it is not possible to practice a skill in its reality context, learning experiences should be provided in classroom simulations. Instructional materials and equipment in a functional and functioning classroom also must be reality based. Furniture, decorations, appliances, and materials typically found in the home must then be found in the classroom as well. To simulate the community, the school might set up a mock traffic pattern in the gymnasium to practice safely crossing streets, establish a supermarket to practice shopping skills, and assign classroom duties as work tasks that mirror jobs available in the community.

THE SCOPE OF THE FUNCTIONAL CURRICULUM

A functional curriculum, if it is to meet the needs of students with disabilities, should be formulated in terms of the social roles people are required to play. Suggested instructional activities should be designed to assist students to fill these roles as successfully and productively as possible even when the curriculum is organized around traditional subject areas, and even when it is arranged around skill areas such as vocational, leisure, motor, communication, and interpersonal skills. Included among these roles are the individual as a

- socially competent person who works cooperatively with others for mutually agreed upon goals.
- capable student who learns from others, and, as a helper, assists others to learn.
- contributing member of a family unit.
- successful member of his or her own personal community (e.g., as a neighbor and friend).
- responsible and responsive citizen of the general community.
- skilled consumer of goods and services and participant in financial transactions.
- productive worker.
- skillful participant in diverse leisure-time activities.
- competent traveler who moves about the community while meeting all other social roles.

DEVELOPING INSTRUCTIONAL PLANS

Instructional plans serve as the blueprint for coordinating and teaching functional skills. In this curriculum, activities are presented in terms of Teacher Interventions and Family Interventions. Subsumed under these interventions are four age and grade-level designations appropriate to teaching different age groups of children and youth with disabilities: infant and toddler/preschool, primary, intermediate, and secondary.

With its annual goals and their short-term objectives, the curriculum serves as the framework for systematically observing and assessing the student's performance in terms of both process and product. Evaluation occurs as the learner functions on a daily basis in natural settings and as he or she responds to structured and simulated activities. These observations, supplemented by more formally acquired data, aid in selecting what goals and objectives are to be placed, for example, in the student's IEP. Once these decisions are made, lesson planning can commence as follows:

- Lesson planning begins, based on instructional insights acquired from assessment data, with the selection of a priority *annual goal* and its associated *specific objective* from the student's IEP.

- Following this selection, a pertinent *lesson objective* is then constructed. The lesson objective, like the short-term instructional objective, is student oriented and has the dual purpose of structuring the instructional sequence and suggesting the assessment strategy and its performance criterion level. Toward these ends, a lesson objective has three key elements:

  - Clarification of the stimulus situation or conditions: "When given . . ." or "After being shown . . ."

  - Specification of a desired response: "The student will . . ."

  - Establishment of a performance level: "He will do so in four out of five trials" or "She will do so without assistance."

- Next, *materials and equipment* are listed even though a complete list is not really known until the total plan is developed. This segment is placed in the beginning of the plan, however, for ease in reading when the instructor skims the plan immediately prior to its implementation.

- The *motivating activity* is stated. Identifying an appropriate motivating activity may be a challenging task because it is not always easy to identify age-appropriate motivating activities that will capture the attention and encourage the involvement of the different age groups of students with disabilities who are functioning at depressed levels.

- *Instructional procedures* are then enumerated. These are instructor oriented and are sequenced in logical steps arising out of the motivating activity and leading to assessment. The instructional procedure itself is divided into four steps: initiation, guided practice, independent practice, and closure. Evidence that teaching is taking place must be carefully articulated in each of these steps. Demonstrations, assistance, and problem-solving challenges are ways of ensuring that instruction is occurring.

- The *assessment strategy* to be employed is then specified. This procedure should reflect the desired response and performance criteria indicated in the lesson objective. It is instructor oriented and should specify the method to be used in recording observational data.

- At this point, a proposed *follow-up activity* or *objective* is written to ensure that the sequence of instruction is honored. The hoped-for follow-up activity or objective is composed in positive terms because it can be pursued only if the student successfully meets the plan's lesson objective. If the learner fails to meet the lesson objective, a remedial lesson plan must be written on an ad hoc basis (because it is not possible to predict the reason for failure, especially given that the lesson was designed and taught with the likelihood of instructional success).

- A concluding section, *observations and their instructional insights*, is appended. This section is included in the instructional plan as one means of recording student data and for identifying one's insights as to programming implications for later reference and for use in completing checklists, writing progress reports, and designing and modifying the student's IEP.

Then, introductory information should be provided at the beginning of the instructional plan, such as the following:

- topic area
- name of the designer of the plan
- required time for implementation
- student(s) for whom the plan is intended
- relevant background information on the involved student(s)

Finally, an instructional (lesson) plan should be written in a simple and direct way and be relatively free from jargon so that parents, teacher aides, volunteers, and other appropriate instructors can readily understand it and implement it.

References

Bender, M., & Valletutti, P.J. (1982). *Teaching functional academics to adolescents and adults with learning problems.* Baltimore: University Park Press.

Bender, M., & Valletutti, P. J. (1985). *Teaching the moderately and severely handicapped: Curriculum objectives, strategies, and activities. Vol. 1: Self-care, motor skills and household management.* Austin, TX: PRO-ED.

Brolin, D. E. (1986). *Life-Centered Career Education: A competency-based approach* (rev. ed.). Reston, VA: Council for Exceptional Children.

Brown, L. F., Branston-McLean, M. B., Baumgart, D., Vincent, L., Falvey, M., & Schroder, J. (1979). Using the characteristics of current and subsequent least restrictive environments in the development of curricular content for severely handicapped students. *Journal of the Association for the Severely Handicapped, 4,* 407–424.

Brown, L. F., Nietupski, J., & Hamre-Nietupski, S. (1976). The criterion of ultimate functioning and public school services for severely handicapped students. In M. A. Thomas (Ed.), *Hey don't forget about me: Education's investment in the severely, profoundly, and multiply handicapped* (pp. 2–15). Reston, VA: Council for Exceptional Children.

Cegelka, P.T., & Greene, G. (1993). Transition to adulthood. In A. E. Blackhurst & W. H. Berdine (Eds.), *An introduction to special education* (3rd ed., pp. 137–175). New York: HarperCollins.

Clark, G. M. (1979). *Career education for the handicapped child in the elementary classroom.* Denver: Love.

Cronin, M. E., & Gerber, P. J. (1982). Preparing the learning disabled adolescent for adulthood. *Topics in Learning & Learning Disabilities, 2,* 55–68.

Cronin, M. E., & Patton, J. R. (1993). *Life skills instruction for all students with special needs: A practical guide for integrating real-life content into the curriculum.* Austin, TX: PRO-ED.

Drew, C. J., Logan, D. R., & Hardman, M. L. (1992). *Mental retardation: A life cycle approach.* (5th ed.). New York: Merrill/Macmillan.

Gast, D. L., & Schuster, J. W. (1993). Students with severe developmental disabilities. In A. E. Blackhurst & W. H. Berdine (Eds.), *An introduction to special education* (3rd ed., pp. 455–491). New York: HarperCollins.

Grossman, H. J. (1983). *Classification in mental retardation.* Washington, DC: American Association on Mental Deficiency.

Kirk, S. A., & Gallagher, J. J. (1989) *Educating exceptional children* (6th ed.). Boston: Houghton Mifflin.

Patton, J. R., Beirne-Smith, M., & Payne, J. S. (1990). *Mental retardation* (3rd ed.). Columbus, OH: Merrill.

Polloway, E. A., Patton, J. R., Payne, J. S., & Payne, R. A. (1989) *Strategies for teaching learners with special needs.* (4th ed.). New York: Merrill.

Reschly, D. J. (1993). Special education decision making and functional/behavioral assessment. In E. L. Meyen, G. A. Vergason, & R. J. Whelan, *Challenges facing special education* (pp. 227–240). Denver: Love.

Valletutti, P. J., & Bender, M. (1982). *Teaching interpersonal and community living skills: A curriculum model for handicapped adolescents and adults.* Baltimore: University Park Press.

Valletutti, P. J. & Bender, M. (1985). *Teaching the moderately and severely handicapped: Curriculum objectives, strategies, and activities. Vol. 2: Communication and socialization.* Austin, TX: PRO-ED.

Valletutti, P. J., & Dummett, L. (1992). *Cognitive development: A functional approach.* San Diego: Singular Publishing Group.

Wheeler, J. (1987). *Transitioning persons with moderate and severe disabilities from school to adulthood: What makes it work?* Menomonie: University of Wisconsin Materials Development Center.

Interpersonal Skills

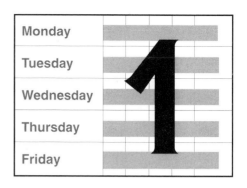

Monday	
Tuesday	
Wednesday	
Thursday	
Friday	

Instructional activities designed to promote the successful functioning of students with disabilities in diverse interpersonal and social situations are at the heart of a functional curriculum. The development of effective interpersonal and social skills requires teaching those behaviors that will help students become socially competent, that will facilitate their acceptance by society, and that will make their lives as productive and as personally satisfying as possible. Socially competent individuals are able to successfully satisfy their needs and achieve their desires through skillful interpersonal and social interactions. The essential goal of this section of the curriculum, therefore, is to facilitate the ultimate successful functioning of the individual as a competent adult member of society, functioning within his or her home environment, the general community, and the workplace.

We began the search for relevant educational goals and objectives by individually visualizing an "idealized" adult who possesses the totality of social skills needed to function optimally in diverse interpersonal relationships and situations. We then discussed and analyzed these reflections to arrive at a collaborative portrait of this hypothetical individual.

From the collaborative portrait, we then observed students with learning and behavioral disabilities across the life span in an attempt to identify both interpersonal skills and key deficits in performance, especially those deficits that contributed to these students' rejection by persons without disabilities and that resulted in continuing failure, frustration, loneliness, isolation, and unhappiness. Once we identified and confirmed interpersonal deficits by a review of relevant professional literature (see Suggested Readings) and through dialogue with professional colleagues, especially those who are currently providing direct services to individuals with disabilities, our next step was to view each of the deficits from a life span perspective, starting with the preschool and culminating in the adult years.

The underlying organizational principle, once pertinent instructional goals and objectives were identified, was to suggest learning experiences that should be provided as early as possible in the lives of students with disabilities, preferably during the critical preschool years. This emphasis on early experiences is based on the conviction that teachers and family members too often fail to provide early experiences that, although subtle in nature, will serve as a foundation for desired higher level performance. For example, parents and teachers may begin working with the key interpersonal skill of dressing and grooming oneself according to the social situation by simply verbalizing to the very young child the reason for their choice of garments. A teacher or parent might say, for instance, "I put on my work pants and am wearing my work gloves because I am going to work in the garden and don't want to dirty my dress clothes." Even if the very young child does not understand all (or even any) of the words of a message, it is highly probable that, with the message's repetition in similar social contexts (social language learning), with accompanying and consistent environmental props and clues, the groundwork is being established for eventual language comprehension and the acquisition of key social skills.

In a life skills curriculum designed to foster the development of a person capable of functioning as optimally as possible in the cultural mainstream, most activities (whether or not they are designated as specific interpersonal skills) will have an interpersonal dimension, whether they involve interactions with members of a household, family members, friends, neighbors, or coworkers. Therefore, interpersonal elements must be considered each time an instructional plan is envisioned and when it is implemented. All areas of a functional curriculum require teachers, family members, and other trainers to integrate pertinent interpersonal and social competencies with whatever skill is being taught, even when the interpersonal aspect is not as patently obvious as when one deals with the development of oral communication skills. For example, lessons dealing with the facilitation of fine and gross motor skills require the integration of interpersonal elements. Fine motor skills, while they often may be performed by the individual operating alone, also may

1. be stimulated by the requests of others.

2. require the assistance of others.

3. be performed in concert with others, as in a work-related task.

Gross motor skills may be enhanced by the person when alone, as in personal physical fitness activities, but are more likely to be enjoyed when engaging with others in active games and sports.

The acquisition and maintenance of positive and supportive relationships is a key factor in enhancing the quality of life for each individual, disabled or not. Too often, unfortunately, people with disabilities are shunned, in large part, because they lack the interpersonal skills that make other people happy or content or at least comfortable in their presence. Whenever possible, teachers, family members, and other caregivers must provide students with real experiences in which desired interpersonal behaviors are demonstrated in the natural course of their lives and in structured learning experiences that students are encouraged to replicate in their own lives. When actual experiences are not practical, role playing becomes a critical instructional alternative that can help illustrate and vivify essential interpersonal skills. Teachers, family members, and other trainers who implement an interpersonal and social skills curriculum from a functional perspective must be skillful in role playing, especially when facilitating the development of interpersonal competency.

General Goals of This Unit

I.   The student will function as optimally as possible in diverse interpersonal and social situations.

II. The student will function as optimally as possible in diverse interpersonal and social situations that depend on effective oral communication skills.

III. The student will refrain from engaging in disturbing, distracting, destructive, and self-destructive behavior.

GOAL I.

The student will function as optimally as possible in diverse interpersonal and social situations.

SPECIFIC OBJECTIVES

The student:

❏ A. Plays by him- or herself without disturbing or distracting peers and adults in his or her immediate environment.

❏ B. Plays cooperatively with others and shares toys, treats, materials, and games and takes his or her turn when appropriate.

❐ C. Behaves in an acceptable manner when dealing with peers and adults in diverse interpersonal and social situations.

❐ D. Practices good sportsmanship during play and in other leisure-time activities and accepts responsibility for his or her actions.

❐ E. Controls his or her temper when angry while expressing anger in an appropriate way.

❐ F. Responds positively to constructive criticism.

❐ G. Copes with rejection and ignores or expresses his or her annoyance in constructive ways if belittled or ridiculed.

❐ H. Dresses and grooms him- or herself according to the social situation.

❐ I. Works cooperatively with others in group projects and work situations in a supportive and facilitative manner.

❐ J. Completes assigned tasks and otherwise fulfills assigned duties and obligations.

❐ K. Arrives on time to scheduled appointments/meetings and attends regularly when attendance is required or expected.

❐ L. Returns borrowed materials, equipment, money, and other items.

❐ M. Reciprocates for the kindnesses and generosity of others.

❐ N. Behaves in an acceptable manner with people of all ages, of both sexes, and from different cultural groups.

❐ O. Respects the property, privacy, and civil rights of others.

❐ P. Participates in projects of benefit to the community.

❐ Q. Obeys all pertinent rules, regulations, and laws.

SUGGESTED ACTIVITIES

Specific Objective A

The student plays by him- or herself without disturbing or distracting peers and adults in his or her immediate environment.

Teacher Interventions

Infant and Toddler/Preschool Level.   Identify a toy or object in which the student has shown interest. (Note: The student might enjoy playing with boxes, pots and pans, or another nontoy item instead of a commercially produced toy.) At an appropriate time, provide the student with the object or toy of interest, and encourage him or her to play without your direct supervision or participation. Reward the student for playing quietly and appropriately.

Primary Level.   Set aside a time for free play in which you encourage the student to play a quiet game or quietly with a preferred toy. Explain to the student that people often like to be by themselves. Tell the student that, while he or she is playing quietly, you are doing important paperwork and appreciate that he or she is playing quietly.

Intermediate Level.   Teach the student a variety of arts and crafts activities, paper-and-pencil games, and solitaire card games. Explain that there will be times that he or she will (a) be alone, (b) want to be alone, or (c) be with a person or persons who wish to work or be by themselves and not be disturbed by those around them. Role-play each of these three situations, and reward the student for engaging in a quiet activity without causing any disturbance or distraction. Follow up by involving the student, along with one or two of his or her peers, in working on various *learning station* activities.

Secondary Level.   Engage the student in the suggested activities for the Intermediate Level. Add, as a fourth situation, a role play involving *work stations* in which the student and his or her peers are doing separate work assignments, perhaps as part of a production line.

Family Interventions

Infant and Toddler/Preschool Level.   Ask the parents to observe their child to determine the toy or material in which their child appears to be interested. Tell them to praise the child for playing by him- or herself in a quiet, nondistracting manner.

Primary Level.   Ask the parents to set aside times of the day when each family member is engaged in a quiet activity appropriate to his or her interests or household responsibilities. Tell them to speak to their child about the need for *quiet times* when people can either do required tasks or engage in quiet leisure-time activities.

Intermediate and Secondary Levels. Ask the parents to assign to each member of the household (including themselves) household tasks that can be done alone and that each one in the family (including the youngster) is capable of doing without supervision. Encourage them to praise each family member for completing his or her assignment without disturbing anyone else.

Specific Objective B

The student plays cooperatively with others and shares toys, treats, materials, and games and takes his or her turn when appropriate.

Teacher Interventions

Infant and Toddler/Preschool Level. Select several toys in which the student has shown interest. Engage him or her in joining you in playing with these toys. Shortly after the free play has begun, and the student is playing with his or her own selected toy in parallel play with you as you are playing with your own toy, indicate in some way that you wish to exchange toys. Reward the student for making the exchange with little or no protesting.

At snack or meal times, demonstrate sharing treats. Begin by sharing your treats (e.g., two small boxes of raisins) and saying, "One for you and one for me!" Follow up by giving the student a treat that he or she is to share with you at a later time. Proceed in this way, until he or she begins to share with a classmate and then with several classmates.

Primary Level. Repeat some of the activities suggested for the Infant and Toddler/ Preschool Level. This time, however, concentrate on sharing with peers.

Expand the activity to include playing table and card games in which turns must be taken. Make certain that the student understands *when* his or her turn is. Praise him or her for waiting for his or her turn to play with a toy or move in a game.

Intermediate Level. View various sports events on television and comment on the taking of turns by the teams or individual participants (e.g., batting order and innings in baseball and serving in tennis). Follow up by engaging the student in a variety of table games (e.g., checkers or dominoes) and sports activities.

As an example, involve the student in a basketball game in which the team that did not score the basket gains possession of the ball and a game of table tennis in which the players take turns serving. Emphasize that the taking of turns is a basic part of games and sports.

Also, give the student his or her turn in doing preferred classroom tasks such as passing out materials for a craft project. Point out examples of how and when you share materials with other teachers and how the teachers take turns, for example, in such responsibilities as bus duty.

Secondary Level. Involve the student in a work simulation in which the workers must perform a task that has to be completed in an exact sequence (e.g., assembling and then packing an item). Discuss what might occur if the group did not do the work in the right order, that is, if each member did not take his or her turn at the appropriate time. If you demonstrate the incorrect pattern, make certain that the student understands that you are deliberately making a mistake so that he or she is less likely to imitate the incorrect pattern.

Also, demonstrate the concept of taking turns through the rotation of classroom tasks and duties. For example, "It was your turn last week to wash the chalkboards. It is now [classmate's name] turn to wash the chalkboards. This week, it is your turn to clear the tables after lunch."

Family Interventions

Infant and Toddler/Preschool Level. Encourage the parents to engage their child in a play activity involving two preferred toys (or play materials) with one other family member. Tell them to make certain that sharing is an integral part of the play.

Primary Level. Tell the parents to demonstrate to their child how sharing is part of many household behaviors (e.g., sharing food at snack and meal times and sharing household responsibilities). For example, "Brother sets and clears the table, Daddy washes the dishes, Mommy dries the dishes, Sister puts the dishes away, and you wipe the table clean. We all must do our *share* of the work."

Intermediate and Secondary Levels. Encourage the parents to point out examples in the community when people take turns (e.g., waiting in line at a supermarket bakery counter or in a bank). Tell them to point out also when players take turns in sports events and when workers take turns doing a job that requires a step-by-step procedure (e.g., one salesperson rings up an item being purchased and then a second salesperson puts the purchase in a bag and staples the receipt to the bag).

If one or both parents are able to take the youngster to their places of employment, encourage the parents to do so and to point out instances of workers sharing and taking turns in step-by-step procedures.

Specific Objective C

The student behaves in an acceptable manner when dealing with peers and adults in diverse interpersonal and social situations.

Teacher Interventions

Infant and Toddler/Preschool Level.   Engage the student in a variety of play activities involving interaction with a peer in manipulating and using toys and playing simple table games. Reward the student for behaving in an acceptable manner. Gradually increase the number of students in the group until the student is successfully interacting with a small group of his or her peers.

After the student has begun to play successfully with toys and games with a small group of his or her peers, engage the student in group activities (at his or her level of understanding) involving heightened interaction with peers, such as circle dances ("Ring-Around-the-Rosy"), acting out action poems and finger plays, and low-activity games such as Simon Says.

Primary Level.   Engage the student in a variety of activities with his or her peers. Include such activities as class parties, games and sports, arts and crafts activities, and other activities that require cooperation and collaboration. Monitor to make certain that the student is engaging in acceptable behaviors such as sharing, taking turns, acting courteously, speaking at acceptable levels, and refraining from aggressive or destructive behaviors.

Involve him or her in activities in which the student must interact with adults working in the school. Review the various jobs of the people who work in the school. Follow up by providing the student with opportunities to interact with these adults, for example, delivering a message to a teacher, arranging for the school secretary to speak to the class, visiting the nurse's suite, and interviewing the librarian.

Intermediate Level.   Take the student for trips into the community where he or she must engage in safe behaviors (e.g., crossing streets) and courteous behavior (e.g., moving through store aisles and waiting in lines). Make certain to stop unsafe and inappropriate behaviors immediately (and reprimand if the behavior is unsafe or occurs frequently), and explain why the behavior is unsafe or inappropriate. Follow up by modeling the appropriate behavior and asking the student to imitate the appropriate behavior.

Secondary Level. Take the student to various settings in the community, including shopping centers, to observe how workers behave with coworkers and supervisors and how service workers interact with customers. Discuss the behavior appropriate to the roles people must fulfill as they interact with each other.

Engage in diverse role plays in the classroom in which the student practices and demonstrates appropriate behavior in a variety of social and work situations.

Family Interventions

Infant and Toddler/Preschool Level. Ask the parents to engage their child in interactions with other children in the family and with children of neighbors and friends. Remind the parents to closely monitor their child's behavior so that appropriate behaviors are reinforced and inappropriate behaviors stopped and reprimanded if they are unsafe or persist.

Primary Level. Tell the parents to take their child to playground and park facilities and to encourage their child in interactions with other children playing there. Remind the parents to closely monitor the behavior of their child so that appropriate behaviors are reinforced and inappropriate behaviors stopped and reprimanded if they are unsafe or persist.

Intermediate and Secondary Levels. Tell the parents that when their youngster is expected to or is planning to attend a wedding, baptism, bar or bas mitzvah, or other religious event, to be sure to discuss the nature of the event and the behaviors expected of participants. Tell them to simulate these events through role plays prior to their actual occurrence.

Ask them to provide their youngster with experiences in a variety of situations, especially those where the expected behavior is in stark contrast to the acceptable behavior in a dissimilar situation. For example, they should help their youngster differentiate appropriate behavior at a friend's birthday party with the appropriate behavior during a hospital visit or a funeral.

Specific Objective D

The student practices good sportsmanship during play and in other leisure-time activities and accepts responsibility for his or her actions.

Teacher Interventions

Primary and Intermediate Levels. When the student demonstrates good sportsmanship, praise him or her for being a "good sport." Concentrate both on being a gracious winner and an accepting loser. Whenever he or she behaves in an unsportsmanlike manner, discuss why the behavior is unacceptable and use the expression "poor sport" to further emphasize the inappropriate behavior.

Involve the student in establishing class rules, as well as the rewards for compliance and the consequences of noncompliance (see examples in Figures 1.1 and 1.2). Make certain that the student participates and also comprehends each of the items in the established protocol. Then, whenever a situation arises in which the student has behaved in an inappropriate way or broken a class rule, discuss his or her behavior with him

Rules for Appropriate Behavior	Possible Positive Consequences
Students must raise their hand whenever they wish to gain the teacher's attention or when they wish to answer a teacher's question.	The teacher will respond and will give them their fair share of opportunities to respond. The teacher will praise them for obeying.
Students must stay in their seats when doing quiet activities and obtain the teacher's permission to leave their seats or leave the room.	The teacher will give them opportunities to play with games and toys of their choice or to read a book or magazine that interests them.
Students must respect the property of the school, the teachers, and their fellow students.	The teacher will give them token reinforcements that they can later exchange for a tangible item of their choice.
Students must treat their classmates and the teachers and staff with respect.	The teacher will schedule special treats, such as showing them a video of a favorite or interesting movie.
Students must complete all assigned tasks within the established timelines, whenever possible.	The teacher will give them occasional "healthy" treats when they complete their assignments.
Students must sit in their seats in a proper manner.	The teacher will give them extra play periods so that they can have opportunities to use all their muscles in fun activities.
Students are responsible for keeping the area around the desks neat and clean and must return all materials to their proper storage areas.	The teacher will keep the classroom as attractive and uncluttered as possible and will post the names and photographs of students who keep their desks clean on the class bulletin board.

FIGURE 1.1. Classroom rules and possible positive consequences.

Rules for Appropriate Behavior	Negative Consequences
Students must raise their hand whenever they wish to gain the teacher's attention or when they wish to answer a teacher's question.	The teacher will either ignore or reprimand them when they fail to follow the rule, and will call on them only when they observe the rule.
Students must stay in their seats when doing quiet activities and obtain the teacher's permission to leave their seats or leave the room.	The teacher will take away their privilege of playing with games and toys of their choice.
Students must respect the property of the school, the teachers, and their fellow students.	The teacher will take away points or tokens earned.
Students must treat their classmates and the teachers and staff with respect.	The teacher will deny them the opportunity to join their classmates on field trips.
Students must complete all assigned tasks within the established timelines, whenever possible.	The teacher will not give them a special privilege (e.g., erasing the board) until they complete their assignments.
Students must sit in their seats in a proper manner.	The teacher will take away scheduled play periods.

FIGURE 1.2.   Classroom rules and possible consequences of inappropriate behavior.

or her. Explain that, because he or she chose to ignore the rule, he or she must accept the previously established consequences.

Secondary Level.   Involve the student in establishing class rules, as well as the rewards for compliance and the consequences of noncompliance. Make certain that the student participates and also comprehends each of the items in the established protocol. Remember that *both* winners and losers in athletic events should be praised for their *participation* and their *effort*. (The Special Olympics dramatically vivifies the power of this practice.)

Whenever a student loses in an athletic event or other competition, encourage him or her to try again, if it is within his or her capacity to perform at a higher level. Provide opportunities for the student to win or succeed in some activity, even if it means creating a special game or event to suit the student's abilities. Once the student has experienced "winning," he or she may be better able to cope with losing.

Family Interventions

Primary, Intermediate, and Secondary Levels.   Ask the parents to discuss good sportsmanship, contrasting it with poor sportsmanship. Encourage them to point out examples of each as depicted on television and as seen in community events (e.g., Little League games).

Ask them also to establish household rules (see example in Figure 1.3) and consequences. Remind them about consistency in applying both positive and negative consequences. Assist them, if needed, in establishing appropriate consequences.

Tell the parents that when they observe their youngster in an infraction of a household rule or a rule of society, they should directly confront their youngster with the infraction and encourage *not lying*, by asking their youngster questions, such as "Did you . . . ?" when they know that he or she broke the rule.

Hang up your clean clothing in your closet.

Put all clothing that needs to be cleaned in the laundry basket.

Make your bed as soon as possible after getting up in the morning.

Put away all grooming items after their use and clean the bathroom counter after you finish grooming yourself.

Close the bathroom door for privacy when you are using the commode.

Throw all garbage that cannot be recycled in the trash can and all items that can be recycled in the recycling container.

Complete all assigned household chores in a timely fashion.

Return cleaning supplies and equipment to safe storage areas.

Provide requested assistance to other members of the household.

FIGURE 1.3.   Sample household rules and regulations.

Specific Objective E

The student controls his or her temper when angry while expressing anger in an appropriate way.

Teacher Interventions

Infant and Toddler/Preschool Level. If the student expresses anger, tell him or her that you know that he or she is upset and angry. Encourage the student to talk about what made him or her angry, if possible.

Cut out pictures of faces from newspapers and magazines that show a variety of facial expressions, including happiness, sadness, and anger. Show the pictures to the student, and talk about the feelings being expressed and the possible reasons why a person might be feeling that way. Practice making different facial expressions that demonstrate these three basic emotions.

Primary and Intermediate Levels. Discuss situations that might arouse a person's anger and ways to express one's anger in a socially approved way. Then, role-play these situations with the student, demonstrating ways of controlling anger (e.g., counting silently to 10, thinking of something pleasant, leaving the situation, verbalizing one's feelings).

Secondary Level. Show the student excerpts from television programs and from videotapes or discs that depict people handling anger both appropriately and inappropriately. Ask the student to judge which ones are appropriate and which ones are not. For those that are not, discuss how else the scene should have been played and then role-play the preferred coping strategy.

Share newspaper stories of events that demonstrate what happens when someone loses his or her temper.

Family Interventions

Infant and Toddler/Preschool Level. Review with the parents the suggested activities described previously in Teacher Interventions, Infant and Toddler/Preschool Level, and encourage them to practice them in the home setting.

Remind the parents and other family members that they must demonstrate the healthy expression of anger in their interactions with each other, the youngster, and other people in general.

Discuss temper tantrums and the need to ignore rather than reinforce them.

Primary and Intermediate Levels. Tell the parents to encourage their child, whenever the situation arises, to verbalize his or her anger or to handle it in some other constructive way. Encourage them to discuss anger-provoking situations and the possible coping strategies for dealing with these situations. Remind them to respond to actual displays of anger by guiding the youngster to an appropriate response.

Ask the parents to share their own life experiences with their youngster and describe how they successfully handled anger.

Secondary Level.   Ask the parents to review with their youngster incidents reported in the media concerning how people were injured or became involved in the criminal justice system because they did not handle their anger responsibly.

Specific Objective F

The student responds positively to constructive criticism.

Teacher Interventions

Infant and Toddler/Preschool Level.   Provide the student with as many success experiences as possible, and develop any special skills or talents. Do so to develop the student's self-esteem as much as possible so that later corrections and constructive criticisms are accepted as challenges to be faced and met.

Primary Level.   Once the student has had a number of success experiences in the classroom and has developed some self-esteem, begin to make him or her aware that there are areas that need improvement. Explain that you are giving him or her "little" challenges that you know that he or she can successfully meet. (Make certain that these are realistic challenges that will lead to success if the student puts forth the effort.)

Whenever you correct or reprimand the student, explain that you are doing so in order to help him or her make progress. Be sure to reward all attempts as well as successes.

Intermediate Level.   During academic and special subject instruction and activities, correct the student if he or she is behaving unacceptably or doing a task incorrectly. Tell the student that what he or she is doing is unacceptable or incorrect, and assist him or her in modifying or correcting the behavior. Reward the student for responding positively to the correction and for changing his or her behavior.

If the student is upset by the correction, explain that *helpful* correction is one that will benefit him or her because it can help him or her lead a more successful life. Use positive responses to contribute to the student's self-esteem.

Secondary Level.   Assist the student in differentiating between criticism that is constructive, that is, *helpful,* and criticism that is *not helpful.* Role-play different situations in which criticism is helpful and in which it is not. Be sure to include simulated work, leisure, and diverse social situations with peers and adults.

Family Interventions

Infant and Toddler/Preschool Level.   Impress on the parents the need to develop as much self-esteem as possible in their child. Remind them that self-esteem grows out of success experiences and from positive reinforcement. Encourage and assist them to do so, especially when their child has very limited skills or talents.

Primary Level.   Ask the parents to explain to their child that there will be times when they will have to correct him or her. Tell them to communicate the concept that correction can be helpful, that is, by helping people to grow in their knowledge and skills.

Intermediate Level.   Encourage the parents to point out incidents that have occurred in their own lives when constructive criticism helped them.

Secondary Level.   Ask the parents to discuss with their youngster various work settings that are employment possibilities (depending on his or her level of functioning). Tell them to explain that on a job he or she will be responsible to a supervisor or boss and that there may be times when he or she might be criticized by that supervisor or boss. Ask the parents to help their youngster differentiate between constructive (i.e., helpful) criticism and correction and criticism that is not. Show the parents how to conduct productive role plays in which the two types of criticism are demonstrated and discussed.

Specific Objective G

The student copes with rejection and ignores or expresses his or her annoyance in constructive ways if belittled or ridiculed.

Teacher Interventions

Primary Level.   During recess or free play, listen to the students' conversations. If a peer calls the student a name or in some way rejects him or her as a playmate, take the student aside and ask him or her to explain his or her feelings. Then ask the student to enumerate his or her positive qualities as a possible antidote to the negative feelings he or she is experiencing. Explain that (a) ignoring rejection and ridicule, (b) doing something positive, and (c) thinking about his or her good qualities and achievements often will help to ease the pain of rejection and ridicule.

Role-play and reward the student for handling ridicule and rejection successfully. (Note: Remember that assisting the student in developing positive traits and making him- or herself more acceptable to the standards of others will increase the likelihood of his or her being accepted rather than rejected.)

Intermediate and Secondary Levels. Expand the suggested Primary Level activity to include situations that arise during the school day and on trips into the community. Review coping strategies whenever there is a need to do so. Use these actual occurrences as topics for class role plays and discussions. Reward the student for coping with rejection and ridicule not only in the role play but in the actual incidents that arise in the student's life.

At these levels, assist the student in clarifying when it is not possible or wise to ignore being ridiculed. Model how to express one's annoyance and resentment in a productive way, and provide the student with practice in role plays. Whenever possible, show the student teacher-made videotapes of the role plays of previous students.

Family Interventions

Primary Level. Ask the parents to help their child develop a realistic view of his or her assets and limitations. Ask them to explain that there are people who are uninformed, insensitive, and even cruel who ridicule other people.

Impress upon the parents that they need to assist their child in ignoring the rejection, ridicule, and taunts of others, and to assist the child in dressing, grooming, and behaving in ways that will lead to greater acceptance and to less rejection by others.

Intermediate and Secondary Levels. Ask the parents to take notice of those occasions when their youngster is rejected or ridiculed. Remind them to reward effective coping and to reenact in role plays the unsuccessful handling of these situations.

Encourage the parents to assist the youngster in discriminating between situations when ignoring is the appropriate strategy and when the youngster should voice his or her annoyance and resentment.

Specific Objective H

The student dresses and grooms him- or herself according to the social situation.

Teacher Interventions

Infant and Toddler/Preschool Level. Show the student photographs of people (if possible, people with whom he or she is familiar) who are wearing different clothing, depending on the situation. Comment on the connection (e.g., explain that a person is wearing work clothes in one picture because that person is working in the garden, whereas the same person is dressed more formally in another picture because the person is having dinner in a restaurant).

Primary Level. Show the student pictures from newspapers and magazines, videotapes, and filmstrips of people in different situations (e.g., on a job requiring uniforms, at a religious service, at a formal dance, in a parade, mountain climbing, on the beach). Comment on the clothing being worn, and discuss the reason for the particular choice of clothing. Follow up by naming articles of clothing and asking the student to identify a situation in which it might be worn (e.g., a bathing suit—the beach; an apron—while cooking; a police officer's uniform—when the person is working as a police officer; and a baseball uniform—when the person is playing baseball in Little League or a major league).

Intermediate and Secondary Levels. Plan and go on various trips in the community (e.g., to a fancy restaurant to eat unfamiliar ethnic food, to the local swimming pool, to a neighborhood bowling alley) and school-based activities (e.g., a cooking class, a school dance, and a student-developed vegetable garden) in which the student must decide on the appropriate clothing to be worn.

As part of planning for the activity, confer with the parents to determine the student's available clothing choices. Also, as part of the planning, ask the student to identify his or her choice of clothing for the particular occasion. Compliment the student for making a suitable choice.

Family Interventions

Infant and Toddler/Preschool Level. Ask the parents to comment on their own choice of clothing, based on the specific situation, whenever they take the child for trips into the community. Tell them to comment also on why they are dressing the child in particular clothing. Encourage them to explain that they are dressing him or her, for example, in play clothes because he or she is going out to play and in dress-up clothes when he or she is going to visit a relative for a holiday celebration or going to a religious institution.

Primary Level. Ask the parents to review their child's wardrobe with him or her and to comment on whether various items of apparel are for sports, play, work, or dress-up.

Encourage the parents to take their child on shopping trips for the child's clothing. Tell them to make comments before starting out on the trip and before entering the store, such as "We are going shopping for a bathing suit because you are going to visit relatives in Ocean City."

Intermediate and Secondary Levels. Share with the parents the suggested activity described previously in Teacher Interventions, Intermediate and Secondary Levels. Ask them to engage in similar activities. Urge them to expand the activity so that the youngster is increasingly expected to select appropriate garment(s) for the occasions in which he or she will be involved *and* shop for the appropriate article of clothing for occasions when a new clothing item or accessory is needed. See Figure 1.4 for examples of situations and their appropriate clothing.

Situation	Appropriate Clothing
Outdoor play	Casual clothes: Warm clothing for winter play, light clothing (including shorts) for summer play, and beachwear for swimming
Household work	Old clothing
Employment	Any required uniform or accessories (including safety equipment)
Religious institution	Formal dress clothing
Funeral	Black or other clothing with muted colors and little frills or decorative touches
Formal occasion	Formal wear (black tie) and gowns or evening dresses

FIGURE 1.4. Social and other situations and appropriate clothing.

Specific Objective 1

The student works cooperatively with others in group projects and work situations in a supportive and facilitative manner.

Teacher Interventions

Infant and Toddler/Preschool Level. Engage the student in play situations in which he or she must cooperate with others (e.g., holding one end of a rope while a classmate holds the other end so that a third student may jump rope, dancing and moving to "Ring-Around-the-Rosy," similar group dancing/moving and chanting/singing games).

Primary Level. Involve the student in cooperative academically oriented games. For example, after you have given the student flash cards with warning signs printed on them and given a classmate photographs of the situations to which these warnings apply, the student must work cooperatively with his or her classmate to make the matches (e.g., "Keep Off the Grass"— photograph of a grassy knoll in a public park, "Beware of Dog"—a photograph of a dog behind a closed gate).

Intermediate and Secondary Levels. Whenever possible, provide the student with experiences in which he or she must cooperate with others in a group activity. For example, putting on a play or making a videotape requires the cooperation of several students working with you in a cooperative and facilitative way.

Setting up a bulletin board, making a mural, preparing for a class party, planting a vegetable garden, participating in a community cleanup campaign, and holding a class flea market and arts and crafts sale are only a few of the myriad possibilities available to meet this objective. See Figure 1.5 for examples of class group activities.

Family Interventions

Infant and Toddler/Preschool Level. Ask the parents to communicate to the student, as early as possible, the need for cooperation. For example, while helping to dress their child, they should say such things as, "Help me by pushing your arms through the sleeve," and while reading a picture book, "Please turn the page so we can look at the next picture."

Primary Level. Tell the parents that, as early as possible, they should involve the child in household tasks, for example, helping as they set the table

Putting on a production: Play, puppet show, arts and crafts exhibit, and dance or musical recital

Creating a class mural, bulletin board, or exhibit

Preparing a luncheon or celebration with invited guests

Planting and tending a class vegetable and/or flower garden

Engaging in a community beautification and cleanup campaign

Working on a class fund or charity drive

FIGURE 1.5. Possible classroom group activities.

Preparing snacks, parts of meals, and meals

Doing fall and spring cleaning and general cleaning

Taking care of household pets and the lawn and garden areas

Planning and holding parties, celebrations, entertaining, and cookouts

Purchasing household furniture, furnishings, and decorations

Painting, general household maintenance, and household repairs

Planning shopping lists, food shopping, and food storage

Cleaning, maintenance, and repairs of clothing and household linens

FIGURE 1.6. Sample household cooperative activities.

together, assisting in separating the laundry into piles of dark and light clothing, and beating the eggs for the omelet.

Intermediate and Secondary Levels. Ask the parents to take the youngster on shopping and other trips in the community. Encourage them to involve their youngster as much as possible in these trips, such as in finding some of the food items in a supermarket, locating the section of a store where children's clothing are found, buying a cold drink at a movie theater, and putting coins in a parking meter.

Ask the parents to take the youngster to their workplaces as a demonstration of how coworkers cooperate with each other to get the job done. See examples of possible cooperative household activities in Figure 1.6.

Specific Objective J

The student completes assigned tasks and otherwise fulfills assigned duties and obligations.

Teacher Interventions

Infant and Toddler/Preschool Level. Give the student simple tasks that he or she is able to complete without assistance and with minimal effort and in a short period of time (e.g., building a small tower with building blocks, removing the empty milk cartons after a mid-morning snack, watering the plants, getting the play equipment for the storage area/closet). Praise the student for completing the task successfully.

Primary Level. Give the student classroom tasks that he or she is capable of doing without assistance and that require a substantial commitment of time (e.g., placing drawings and paintings done by him or her and peers on a classroom bulletin board, folding and placing invitations to a class play in envelopes for distribution to invited guests, preparing a simple meal for him- or herself and classmates). Praise the student for completing the task successfully.

Intermediate and Secondary Levels. Involve the student in as many tasks as possible that he or she can complete without assistance. Whenever possible relate these tasks to real work situations, for example, sorting nuts and bolts by size and then packaging them for sale, conducting an inventory of classroom books and supplies, and making an arts and crafts project that can be sold at a school fair.

Also, engage the student in a community cleanup campaign, and urge him or her to complete his or her assignment as part of being a responsible citizen. See Figure 1.7 for examples of classroom tasks.

Family Interventions

Infant and Toddler/Preschool Level. Ask the parents to give the child simple household tasks that he or she can complete without assistance and in a short period of time (e.g., putting away his or her toys, picking up and putting dirty laundry in the laundry basket, dusting some of the furniture in his or her room).

Primary Level. Ask the parents to involve the child in household tasks that require some expenditure of time in which the child works independently of adult

Erase and wash chalkboards

Collect trash and empty wastebaskets

Pass out class supplies and snacks

Collect and return class supplies to storage area

Take care of classroom pets and animals

Water and take care of plants

Help put up and take down bulletin boards and other exhibits

Help decorate and keep the room clean

FIGURE 1.7.   Sample classroom tasks.

supervision (e.g., cleaning his or her bedroom, preparing a simple snack item or part of a meal requiring minimal cooking, emptying the waste baskets and generally picking up household trash).

Intermediate and Secondary Levels.   Ask the parents to assign their youngster tasks, when feasible, that the youngster can do in the community (e.g., shopping for food and other items from a prepared pictorial or written shopping list, returning a defective item that has been purchased to a department store, taking and supervising a younger sibling on a trip to a nearby playground or park).

(Note: Remind the parents of safety factors and the need to provide supervision and guidance as necessary to prevent exploitation and danger to the youngster.)

Specific Objective K

The student arrives on time to scheduled appointments/meetings and attends regularly when attendance is required or expected.

Teacher Interventions

Primary Level.   Discuss with the student the time he or she needs to wake up to arrive at school on time. Include in the calculations time needed for toileting, washing, dressing, grooming, preparing and eating breakfast, cleanup, preparing lunch (if needed), collecting needed school materials, transportation time, and leeway time. Check with the parents to arrive at a realistic time. Once the wake-up time has been determined, practice with the student setting the wake-up time on an alarm clock and an alarm radio.

When the student returns to school after being absent, discuss the work missed and emphasize that, if he or she were working on a job, he or she could lose a day's pay or even the job if there were too many absences.

Role-play situations in which the student might be late because of external unpredictable factors (e.g., an ice storm or a highway shut down because of an accident). Demonstrate calling an employer to let him or her know of an anticipated unavoidable delay. (See Figure 1.8 for acceptable and unacceptable reasons for being late and Figure 1.9 for acceptable and unacceptable reasons for being absent.)

Intermediate and Secondary Levels. Involve the student in establishing a daily class schedule or in reviewing the assigned class schedule. Make time an important element in classroom practices; that is, for each activity within a class period, establish a time in which the student must complete the assigned task.

Reinforce the importance of time by referring to the time periodically as the task is under way. Remind the student of the *time left* and that he or she needs to try to complete the task *in time* so that he or she will be *on time* for the next scheduled task or period.

If the student's schedule involves moving from class to class, reward him or her for getting to the next class on time. If the student partici-

Acceptable Reasons	Unacceptable Reasons
Poor Traveling Conditions—"The busses are running late because of the icy roads."	"I was out late, and I was so tired that I slept a little longer."
Personal Situation—"I will be late because I cut my finger and waited until the bleeding stopped!"	"I left my watch home on my bureau, and I didn't know what time it was."
Family Situation—"My mother is sick, and I had to make breakfast for the rest of the family."	"I was playing a game with my friend and was having a good time. When I checked the clock, I realized I was going to be late."
Equipment Problems—"The electricity went out during the night in my community, and my electric alarm clock didn't go off on time."	"I am at the record store. I was on my way to meet you, but since it was on my way, I stopped to pick up the record I've been wanting to buy."

FIGURE 1.8. Acceptable and unacceptable reasons for being late.

Acceptable Reasons	Unacceptable Reasons
Personal Illness—"My bad back is so painful that I can hardly walk, so I won't be in today."	"I don't feel very well today. I guess I stayed out too late last night."
Family Illness—"My father is being operated on Friday, and I am taking him to the hospital. I'll have to be out on Friday."	My friends are going to the beach today, and I decided to go too."
Death—"My Aunt Susie's funeral service is Wednesday morning. I won't be in school on Wednesday."	"Tomorrow is the first day of the baseball season, and I'd like to be there for the opening game, so I won't come to school tomorrow."
Civic Duty—"I have been called for jury duty so I will be absent tomorrow."	"The tickets for the rock concert will go on sale tomorrow, and I'm going to stand in line to get tickets, so I probably won't come to work tomorrow."
Personal Situation—"I am a witness in a trial so I will be absent from work tomorrow."	"I have an ugly pimple on my chin, so I guess I'll stay out a couple of days."

FIGURE 1.9.   Acceptable and unacceptable reasons for being absent.

pates in a work–study program, communicate with the employer to make certain that he or she is present and on time to work sites.

Family Interventions

Primary Level.   Ask the parents to set specific times of the day to engage in identified tasks and activities. Tell them to urge the child to be on time for these events (e.g., dinner time, homework time, story time).

Encourage the parents to make time an integral part of family life. They can say things such as, "Grandma is coming to visit us tonight at 7:00, after dinner, so we must finish dinner and clean up by 7:00 so that we will be ready to spend some time with her as soon as she arrives," and "Your bedtime is 8:00 so that you can get enough sleep to keep you healthy and strong."

Intermediate and Secondary Levels.   Ask the parents to demonstrate to their child how they handle their latenesses and absences in terms of their job. Encourage them to have the youngster present to listen to telephone conversations in which they indicate expected lateness and necessary absences. Urge them to discuss the need for the telephone call prior to the call and to discuss the message after the youngster has listened to the call.

Remind the parents to refer to the time factor for the host of family activities and events (e.g., "We must be ready by 10:30 if we are going to be in time for services," and "We need to be dressed by 5:30 if we are going to be at the restaurant in time for our 6:00 reservations").

Specific Objective L

The student returns borrowed materials, equipment, money, and other items.

Teacher Interventions

Infant and Toddler/Preschool Level. Develop the concept that things need to be returned to their proper places. Start, at this level, by involving the student in returning objects (toys, crayons, pencils, books) to their storage areas after their use.

Primary Level. Start to develop the concept of ownership in which the student is expected to identify his or her property and the property of others (classmates, teacher). The development of this concept can begin with reference to clothing items, lunch boxes, and school supplies. Continue by scheduling activities in which the student must borrow equipment (e.g., scissors, stapler, hole puncher) from you to complete a task.

When giving the student the requested item, remind him or her to return the item when finished. Praise him or her for returning the object when he or she is through with it.

Intermediate and Secondary Levels. Role-play diverse situations in which the student needs to borrow items from a classmate, a neighbor, or a coworker. Reward the student for returning the item immediately after the object has been used. Include situations in which the object is consumed and has to be replaced (e.g., borrowing sugar and eggs from a neighbor for a recipe, or business envelopes and stamps).

Pay particular attention to the many problems associated with borrowing money, making certain to explain how friendships are lost when money is borrowed and not returned. Explain that borrowing without returning or replacing can be viewed as a kind of "stealing."

Family Interventions

Infant and Toddler/Preschool Level. Ask the parents to introduce the concept that things need to be returned to their rightful places. Tell them, for example, to point out when they return unused ingredients to their storage areas (e.g., ice cream containers to the freezer, milk containers to the refrigerator, spice cans to the pantry).

Urge them, for example, to require the child to return grooming items (e.g., toothbrush, comb) and toys to their storage areas after play.

Primary Level. Ask the parents to develop the concept of ownership as it applies to household items. Tell them to explain to a child what items in the house belong to him or her and which ones belong to other members of the family (e.g., "This is your coat, but this coat belongs to your brother").

Remind the parents to clarify which household items are owned by the entire family and therefore are shared by everyone in the home (e.g., "These are the family's dishes and eating utensils and, therefore, can be used by everyone").

Intermediate and Secondary Levels. Encourage the parents to model the borrow–return concept in the ebb and flow of household events. For example, they may say to the youngster, "Our radio is broken. May we borrow yours while it is being repaired?" or "We would like to take pictures of the family party. May we borrow your camera?" Remind parents to return the borrowed item promptly after its use.

Urge the parents to involve the youngster in three borrowing situations that may occur: (a) when they borrow from and then promptly return items to neighbors, friends, and relatives; (b) when neighbors, friends, and relatives borrow and then promptly return items; and (c) when neighbors, friends, and relatives borrow and fail to return items and have to be asked to return them. Explain to parents that they need to emphasize that failure to return borrowed items can have an adverse affect on relationships and on future requests to borrow materials.

Specific Objective M

The student reciprocates for the kindnesses and generosity of others.

Teacher Interventions

Primary Level. Invite the student to play a game with you. After you finish playing, say to the student, "I enjoyed playing with you. I invited you to play with me this time. Remember to invite me some time to play with you."

Engage in a variety of reciprocating situations (e.g., sharing a snack brought from home, offering help, inviting someone to join a recreation activity). Reward the student for reciprocating.

Intermediate and Secondary Levels. Engage the student in a discussion of how one acquires and keeps friends and how one maintains friendly relations with family members. In your discussion, be certain to develop the concept of reciprocity.

Ask the students to give examples of times and ways people in their lives have reciprocated and ways they have reciprocated with others. Make sure they understand that reciprocity is one way to maintain friendly relations with people.

Family Interventions

Primary Level. Ask the parents to introduce the concept of reciprocity in their interactions with family members (providing help, sharing, extending various invitations for recreational activities). Explain that this behavior will help their child in acquiring and maintaining friendships.

Intermediate and Secondary Levels. Urge the parents to assist their youngster in establishing ways and providing the needed resources (time, place, money) for him or her to reciprocate (e.g., arranging for the youngster to have a birthday party so that he or she can reciprocate for similar invitations, inviting a friend to accompany the youngster to a special community event such as a parade or fair).

Specific Objective N

The student behaves in an acceptable manner with people of all ages, of both sexes, and from different cultural groups.

Teacher Interventions

Infant and Toddler/Preschool Level. Read the student stories or show him or her picture books in which one of the characters is an infant or small child. (You may use a book that deals with animals and their young because of the abundance of books of this nature for young children.) As you read the story and look at the illustrations, comment on how carefully and gently the older children and adults handled and took care of the very young.

Talk about the special care needed by the very young. Play games and sing songs to the student that he or she may use later when dealing with his or her peers and with younger children.

Primary Level.   Contact the Red Cross, a hospital center, or other community group that offers instruction in child care. Invite a person from the agency as a class guest to demonstrate handling, holding, and caring for infants and young children.

Play dress-up games in which *both* "Daddies" and "Mommies" take care of their "babies." (A trunk or other storage area with adult clothing and a variety of dolls of different racial groups and both sexes would be of great assistance in meeting this objective.)

Introduce the idea that people of different ages have different activities and interests. Show the student videotapes/discs of adults of various age groups and children engaging in different activities. Include individuals with various medically related disabilities and people of advanced age who show evidence of physical infirmities or limitations.

Intermediate and Secondary Levels.   Make certain that you treat all your students and colleagues of both sexes equally since you are an important model of behavior in the student's life. Introduce the idea of cultural diversity by identifying different ethnic and racial groups present in the class and among the school staff while commenting favorably on the diversity.

Read stories and show films and videotapes that depict different cultural groups in a favorable light. Be sure to discuss not only the different customs and traditions but also the similarities among all people.

Invite a speaker from the community or from an ethnic organization (e.g., Americans of Italian Descent, the National Association for the Advancement of Colored People, and B'nai B'rith) to talk to the student and classmates.

Take trips to ethnic museums, exhibits, restaurants, and fairs. If possible, arrange for a trip to a senior citizen center or a nursing home or arrange for a senior citizen to read stories to the class.

Family Interventions

Infant and Toddler/Preschool Level.   Ask the parents to show the child photographs of younger siblings or other relatives and any infants or younger children he or she knows. Tell them to comment on the fact that the people in the pictures are younger and smaller than he or she is and need special care and handling.

Encourage the parents to follow up by demonstrating how they handle and take care of the infants and younger children whose pictures he or she has been shown.

Primary Level.   Ask the parents to show the child photographs of older members of the family and friends who are no longer robust. Tell them to point out that some people who get old may be weaker and more susceptible to illness than younger adults and that they may need special attention or care.

Encourage them to show movies and videotapes/discs that depict the special care requirements of very young children, people with medically related disabilities, and older people who have physical limitations.

Intermediate and Secondary Levels. Ask the parents to acquaint their youngster with his or her ethnic background and heritage (as appropriate to his or her level of understanding) as a starting point to informing the child about different cultural groups.

Whenever it is feasible, ask the parents to take the youngster to ethnic museums, exhibits, restaurants, and fairs. Remind the parents not only to discuss the differences but also to emphasize the similarities among people.

Encourage the parents, if possible, to discuss with their youngster the changing and more enlightened perceptions of the roles of males and females and perceptions about differences in relating to a person of the same and opposite sex.

Specific Objective O

The student respects the property, privacy, and civil rights of others. (See also Goal III, Specific Objective E, of this chapter.)

Teacher Interventions

Infant and Toddler/Preschool Level. Take games, toys, and books that belong to you personally into the classroom. Show them to the student and explain that, although these items are your property, you would like to share them with him or her. Explain that he or she must treat your property, as well as the property of others, with care.

Relate the concept of property to the concept of ownership established in Specific Objective L.

Also, introduce the idea of privacy as it relates to peers who are using the bathroom and as it relates to items stored in desks, school bags, and lunch boxes.

Primary Level. Ask the student and his or her classmates to bring favorite games, toys, books, or hobby collections to class. Before these items are shared, explain that everyone's property must be carefully handled because they are of monetary and emotional value to the owner and might not be easily replaced for various reasons, including cost and availability.

Also, discuss the concept of privacy as it relates to modesty (toileting and various grooming and dressing activities) and information the person does not wish to share (private letters and diaries).

Intermediate and Secondary Levels. Discuss vandalism and read newspaper and magazine articles that tell about incidents of vandalism and destruction of personal and community property. Talk about its economic impact on individuals (replacement of destroyed items) and the community (e.g., repair of school windows).

Also, point out the damaging impact of vandalism on the beauty of the environment (e.g., the dumping of garbage, the ugliness of graffiti on buildings and monuments).

Take trips into the community to witness examples of the desecration and destruction of the community. Introduce the topic of civil rights and review the ways the student needs to behave so as not to infringe upon the civil rights of others.

Family Interventions

Infant and Toddler/Preschool and Primary Levels. Ask the parents to model respecting the privacy of other family members, by knocking when someone is in the bathroom and before entering a bedroom whose door is shut. If the child is too young to understand and depends greatly on adult care, ask the parents to close the door if other people are in the house when assisting the child with toileting or when the child is being dressed.

Ask them to relate privacy, when feasible, to private bodily functions such as toileting and private parts. Remind the parents to reward the child when he or she respects the privacy and property of others.

Intermediate and Secondary Levels. Ask the parents to extend the concept of privacy (beyond privacy and bodily functions) to situations in which a person's personal effects or personal business may be invaded or compromised (e.g., eavesdropping on a person's telephone conversation, going into someone's drawers without permission, and reading someone's mail). Remind the parents to reward the youngster for respecting the privacy of household members.

Encourage the parents to take the youngster for trips into the community to view examples of the destruction and pollution of the environment. Tell them to talk about the cost of these desecrations, economically and aesthetically, and their impact on health and safety.

Specific Objective P

The student participates in projects of benefit to the community.

Teacher Interventions

Primary Level. Involve the student in projects that maintain and improve the school building, school playground, and other school areas. Take the student for walks around the school and the school property. Try to develop a sense that the school belongs to him or her, all the students, the teachers and other staff, their parents, and the members of the community.

Develop the concept that the care of the school and school property is a special responsibility of students and teachers. Involve the student in such projects as decorating the classroom and picking up papers on the playground.

Intermediate and Secondary Levels. Expand the concept of serving the school community to the larger community. Take trips to the neighborhood around the school and point out things that need repair and ways to improve the community in terms of reducing pollution and beautifying the environment.

Determine whether there are any community organizations involved in improving the physical environment, and explore the possibility of involving the student in a community improvement project.

Family Interventions

Primary Level. Ask the parents to involve the child in household projects designed to improve the home, for example, shopping trips to buy furniture and furnishings. Tell the parents, before going on these shopping trips, to say such things as, "We are going shopping to buy some pretty dish towels and placemats for the kitchen" or "Let's pick out a beautiful plant for the living room."

Intermediate and Secondary Levels. Encourage the parents to extend the idea of improving and beautifying the home to improving the community. Tell them to investigate with the youngster any community organizations that are concerned with community improvement.

Encourage the parents to introduce the concept of volunteering and to join the youngster in such service to the general community.

Specific Objective Q

The student obeys all pertinent rules, regulations, and laws.

Teacher Interventions

Infant and Toddler/Preschool Level.   Establish a daily schedule of activities as a start in the development of the concept that there are rules and regulations to be observed, that is, that our actions are ruled or governed, in part, by time and sequence.

Establish any other rules and regulations that the young student is able to comprehend.

Primary Level.   Join the students in establishing classroom rules and regulations, as well as the positive consequences of obeying them and the negative consequences of disobeying them. In establishing these rules, be certain to explain why they are necessary (e.g., "We do not play ball in the classroom because the balls could damage or break something and perhaps hurt someone," "We do not put our feet in the aisle because someone could be tripped and hurt him- or herself"). Whenever a student breaks a rule, sit down and discuss it with him or her. Review the rule and its underlying purpose or reason. Remember to be consistent in applying the consequences and to reward the student for obeying the rules.

Intermediate Level.   Ask a police officer or other law enforcement officer to speak to the student and his or her classmates. Help the student make the association between class and household rules and the rules of living in the general community.

Explain that some rules are called *laws*. Read stories or show videotapes/discs of people who break the law and are held responsible for their actions.

Take trips into the community, and point out any laws that should govern one's behavior. For example, when crossing streets, discuss laws concerning jaywalking, and when passing fences and sides of buildings, discuss laws concerning defacing property.

When using public transportation on trips into the community, point out signs that refer to laws, such as "Smoking is Prohibited," and rebuses that communicate this information.

Secondary Level.   Discuss job safety with the student, and explain that work sites, such as at the home, school, and community, have rules and regulations. Explain that most of the rules have to do with protecting him or her and coworkers. Tell the student that, as a worker or employee, it is part of the job to be aware of and obey the rules of the job.

Discuss the laws established by the government and briefly explore the criminal justice system. If possible take the student to a courtroom to help him or her see the relationship of rules and regulations to laws and to possible punishment.

Family Interventions

Infant and Toddler/Preschool Level. Ask the parent to establish a daily schedule of activities as a way to develop the concept that there are rules and regulations that determine much of our behavior. Tell them to establish any other rules and regulations that their young child can comprehend.

Primary Level. Encourage the parents to establish household rules and regulations, along with the consequences of compliance and noncompliance. Remind them that consistency is critical in shaping appropriate behavior.

Intermediate and Secondary Levels. Explain to the parents that they need to assist the youngster in making the association between household rules and regulations and laws. Encourage them to take frequent trips into the community so that they can discuss laws that apply to living and traveling in the community. For example, ask them to discuss shoplifting when on a trip to a supermarket or department store, remind them to discuss "No Trespassing" signs, and tell them to point out stray dogs when the community has a leash law.

Urge them to comment on television and print media stories that depict the breaking of laws while being sure to explain the rationale for the laws and the possible punishments for disobeying them.

GOAL II.

The student will function as optimally as possible in diverse interpersonal and social situations that depend on effective oral communication skills.

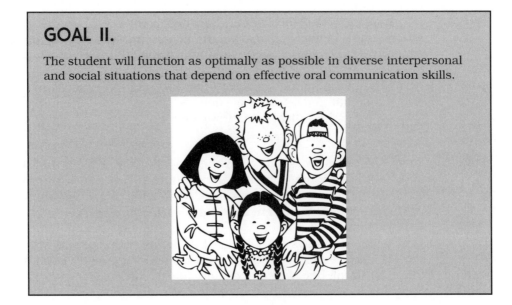

SPECIFIC OBJECTIVES

The student:

❐ A. Greets and bids farewell to others in a socially acceptable manner.

❐ B. Introduces him- or herself at appropriate times and in acceptable ways.

❐ C. Uses language courtesies.

❐ D. Asks for help in an appropriate way and only when needed.

❐ E. Compromises when necessary and "irons out" problems that occur in interpersonal and social situations.

❐ F. Praises and is generally reinforcing of others, when appropriate.

❐ G. Communicates successfully with others during play and work situations.

❐ H. Engages in simple conversations (small talk) while observing the implicit rules of polite conversation.

❐ I. Expresses his or her feelings, thoughts, beliefs, and opinions in socially acceptable ways and in a nonthreatening and constructive manner.

❐ J. Identifies and communicates with family members and successfully participates as a member of a family unit.

❐ K. Communicates successfully in acquiring and maintaining friendships.

❐ L. Communicates and interacts differently with significant individuals in his or her life and with persons who are acquaintances or strangers.

❐ M. Behaves and communicates with others in a mutually supportive and facilitative way.

❐ N. Provides assistance to others, when appropriate, in emergency situations.

❐ O. Visits and communicates via the telephone with relatives, friends, and neighbors at appropriate times, including when they are ill and experiencing problems.

❐ P. Invites and joins others in social activities.

❐ Q. Identifies and communicates effectively with human service professionals, community helpers, and other service personnel.

SUGGESTED ACTIVITIES

Specific Objective A

The student greets and bids farewell to others in a socially acceptable manner.

Teacher Interventions

Infant and Toddler/Preschool Level. Be sure to greet the student as he or she arrives in the classroom or when you arrive in the classroom and the student is waiting for you. Use a variety of greetings, for example, "Good morning Valerie," "Hello Tony," and "Hi, Audrey, how are you?" Encourage the student to respond in some way, even if only with a smile or nod. If the student is able to, expect an oral response, either a return greeting or a response to the question.

Work with the farewell bid in a similar fashion, making certain that the student differentiates between when one is leaving the area temporarily (e.g., to go to another room and then return) and when one is going away for a longer time, thus necessitating a farewell greeting.

Primary Level. Work with the student on associating different greetings with different times of the day. Model greeting and bidding farewell to visitors to the classroom.

Discuss the different ways one may greet relatives and close friends versus acquaintances or people to whom one is being introduced for the first time.

Role-play greeting and bidding farewell at different times of the day and with different people. Emphasize avoiding touching others excessively for routine greetings and avoiding handshaking unless appropriate to the situation (e.g., when the other person has extended his or her hand or on meeting someone for the first time).

Intermediate and Secondary Levels. Practice the suggested activity identified for the Primary Level, and add the dimension of casual greetings (e.g., with peers) versus more formal greetings, using titles such as "Mr.," "Ms.," "Mrs.," and "Dr." with adults.

Family Interventions

Infant and Toddler/Preschool Level.   Review with the parents the Teacher Intervention activity for the Infant and Toddler/Preschool Level. Ask them to practice the activity in the home and on trips into the community.

Primary Level.   Ask the parents to use the greeting and bidding farewell activity to introduce and teach family relationships with the child (e.g., "Good morning, Aunt Rose"; "Good afternoon, Uncle George"; "Good evening, Cousin Helen").

Intermediate and Secondary Levels.   Encourage the parents to provide the youngster with opportunities to observe them as they greet different people at different times of the day and to *explain* the difference in terms of the time of day and the difference in the nature and status of the person greeted. For example, if it is a family pattern to hug another family member when greeting that individual, tell the parents to say something like, "You saw that I hugged Cousin Grace when I saw her. In our family, we hug each other when we meet a family member, but we don't hug people who are not family members."

Specific Objective B

The student introduces him- or herself at appropriate times and in acceptable ways.

Teacher Interventions

Infant and Toddler/Preschool Level.   On the first day of school or when a new student enters the learning area, model introducing yourself. Explain that when meeting someone for the first time, if no one else introduces you, it is always good manners to introduce oneself.

When visitors enter the room, be sure to introduce the student, for example, "Mrs. McMillan, I'd like to introduce Marvin Fischer." Encourage the student to say in turn, "Hello, my name is Marvin; I am pleased to meet you," or some other response appropriate to his or her level of functioning.

Primary Level.   Arrange for the student to introduce him- or herself in role plays. Introduce the idea that there are occasions when he or she should not introduce him- or herself to others. Make a list of these times. Emphasize that he or she should not introduce him- or herself to strangers unless it is appropriate, for example, when meeting a stranger in the company of a parent or the teacher.

Also, point out that there are people he or she will meet while moving about the community (e.g., salespeople) to whom it is not appropriate to introduce him- or herself. Emphasize also that it is unnecessary to introduce oneself to someone one already knows.

Intermediate and Secondary Levels. At interschool functions (e.g., Special Olympics, sporting events, dances), encourage the student to meet new people and to introduce him- or herself to participants who are new to him or her.

Also, explain to the student that if he or she is ever lost and needs help, he or she should introduce him- or herself to a police officer and ask for help (e.g., "Hello, my name is _____, and I am lost. Could you please help me?").

Discuss a variety of situations that might require seeking help: being lost, losing bus fare, and being separated from an adult at a shopping center. Practice this skill in various role plays. Role-play going on job interviews in which the student is expected to introduce him- or herself to prospective employers.

Family Interventions

Infant and Toddler/Preschool Level. Ask the parents to introduce their child to friends and neighbors who visit their home and whom they meet while in the community. Tell them to encourage the child to introduce him- or herself in some way, even if it is merely to repeat or to attempt to vocalize his or her name.

Primary Level. Ask the parents to assist you in practicing when and when not to introduce oneself and to emphasize the potential danger of introducing oneself to strangers *unless* one has been introduced to the unfamiliar person by a responsible adult, such as a family member or teacher.

Intermediate and Secondary Levels. Encourage the parents to provide the youngster with a variety of leisure-time activities in which he or she must introduce him- or herself to other participants with whom he or she is not familiar. Encourage the parents to also role-play interviewing for a job.

Specific Objective C

The student uses language courtesies.

Teacher Interventions

Infant and Toddler/Preschool Level. During everyday activities and conversations, model saying "Please," "Thank you," and "You're welcome" at appropriate times. Explain that people use these words when speaking and working with others.

Practice with the student various everyday interactions in which these language courtesies should be used. Reward the student for attempts as well as successes.

Primary Level. Discuss why good manners are important to maintaining good relations with others. Explain, for example, that when requesting someone's help, the person is more likely to help then and in the future if one says "Please" at the time of the request and "Thank you" when the help has been provided.

If the student is able to acquire additional language courtesies, include "Excuse me" when requesting a pathway in a crowded space and when one has inadvertently belched, as well as "Bless you" when someone has sneezed.

Ask the student how he or she feels when someone uses language courtesies and how he or she feels when someone fails to do so.

Intermediate and Secondary Levels. Introduce more advanced language courtesies such as "Pardon me," "I beg your pardon," and "I'm sorry." Take the student for trips in the community to model and practice a variety of situations in which language courtesies are appropriate (e.g., saying "Excuse me" when trying to negotiate passage through a crowded aisle in a department store or when pushing a shopping cart through a supermarket).

Family Interventions

Infant and Toddler/Preschool Level. Explain to the parents that, if they model language courtesies, their child will be more likely to do so as part of his or her language development and will continue the practice if it is reinforced by them and other family members.

Primary Level. Ask the parents to expect their child to behave courteously in various home situations. Tell them to include ways of behaving courteously at mealtimes (e.g., when wishing someone to pass a plate of food) and when wishing to use the same facilities (e.g., the bathroom) or materials (e.g., a pair of scissors that is being used).

Intermediate and Secondary Levels. Remind the parents to praise their youngster for using language courtesies in different situations. Ask them to provide various experiences (especially in leisure-time pursuits) for the youngster to practice using language courtesies to both peers and adults. Ask them to take the youngster to one of their job sites, if possible, to demonstrate how coworkers are courteous with each other.

Specific Objective D

The student asks for help in an appropriate way and only when needed.

Teacher Interventions

Infant and Toddler/Preschool Level.   Observe the student carefully to determine what behaviors he or she can perform successfully without help. If the student requests help or seeks help in some way for a behavior that he or she can successfully perform, refuse to give help by saying, for instance, "You can remove your socks by yourself and do not need anyone's help!" If, on the other hand, the student cannot perform the task independently, demonstrate how one asks for help in performing classroom tasks that are typically required at this level. Reward the student for doing tasks independently and for requesting help, when needed, in courteous ways.

Primary Level.   Set up a buddy system, explaining that good buddies help each other when needed. Monitor to make certain that unnecessary help is not being provided.

Introduce the topic of community helpers. Show the student pictures of police officers, firefighters, sanitation workers, and other community helpers, and discuss what help they provide and the circumstances in which they provide assistance. Make certain that the student further develops the concept that help should be sought only when needed.

Also, discuss and demonstrate, on an unconnected telephone, *when* and *how* to dial 911 in emergency situations (involving threatening situations or serious injuries and illness in the home). Spend sufficient time, because of the complexity of the concept, to clarify when to call 911 for help and when to seek the help of others such as physicians, neighbors, and family members. See Figures 1.10 and 1.11 for examples of individuals who might be considered community helpers and other people in the community who provide assistance.

Intermediate and Secondary Levels.   Take the student on a trip and demonstrate how one differentiates a salesperson from a fellow shopper (e.g., a name tag, standing behind a cash register, not wearing outdoor clothing during inclement or cold weather). Demonstrate how to ask a salesperson for help in a courteous and explicit way.

Police officers

Firefighters

Letter carriers

Sanitation workers

Street and highway repair persons and snow and ice removers

Traffic light installers and repairers

FIGURE 1.10. Community helpers.

Bank tellers

Servers in restaurants

Salespersons

Receptionists

Ticket sellers

Ushers

Doorpersons

Porters and baggage handlers

FIGURE 1.11. Other people in the community who provide help.

Review the use of the 911 number, and discuss and role-play a variety of emergency situations that do not involve calling 911 (e.g., clogged plumbing, electric power outage, suspected gas leak) (see Figure 1.12). Practice seeking help by telephoning the appropriate service representative.

Family Interventions

Infant and Toddler/Preschool Level. Ask the parents to help their child to differentiate between when he or she can do a self-care activity without assistance and when help is needed. Tell them to refuse to provide unneeded help by saying such things as, "You can put on your shoes by yourself, so you don't need my or anybody else's help."

Primary Level. Ask the parents to point out to their child when they need help and how they should ask for it. Encourage them, also, to take the child for walks in the community for the express purpose of pointing

Serious Emergencies	Nonemergency— Outside Help Needed	Nonemergency— No Help Needed
Someone has bleeding that will not stop	Commode keeps running—call a skilled neighbor or plumber	Electricity has gone off in house only—check fuse box
Someone is unconscious	Television set won't work—call repair shop	Someone has a small cut—get first aid kit
Someone is suddenly unable to move or walk	New toaster doesn't work—call store where purchased	Baby is crying—diaper needs changing
Fire cannot be controlled even with the home fire extinguisher	Mistake made by supermarket cashier—call manager	Milk container has dropped—clean up mess
Someone is attacking the home or its occupants	Need new bookcases built—call carpenter	Jar won't open—use jar opener

FIGURE 1.12.   Emergency and nonemergency situations.

out community helpers. Tell them, if it is feasible, to introduce the child to the worker (first, explaining the situation to the person) and to explain what that person does to help people in the community.

Remind the parents to explain to the child when and how to use the 911 number and how to seek help from specific others during emergencies.

Intermediate and Secondary Levels.   Ask the parents to take the youngster for a variety of trips in the community for the express purpose of obtaining help from people other than the generally identified community helpers, such as salespersons ("Can you tell me where men's suits are located?"), bank tellers ("May I have two twenties, one ten, and five ones. Thank you."), and servers in restaurants ("May I please have another fork? I dropped mine on the floor!").

Specific Objective E

The student compromises when necessary and "irons out" problems that occur in interpersonal and social situations.

Teacher Interventions

Primary Level.   Ask the student what he or she would like to do during free times. If the activity is acceptable, give him or her permission to do so.

Set up a situation in which another student is using desired equipment or materials. Explain that the student will have to wait or select another activity. Follow this up by setting up a situation in which the student and a peer want to use the same equipment or materials at the same time.

Demonstrate how to compromise by taking turns using the materials or equipment for shorter periods of time. Explain that a compromise means each person gives up something to arrive at something to which they both can agree.

Also, prepare a list of classroom jobs. Ask the students to select a preferred assignment for the day or week. If two or more students want the same job, help them establish a compromise by alternating jobs or by sharing them. Reward the student and his or her peers for compromising in other situations that arise in the classroom.

Intermediate and Secondary Levels.   Read stories from the newspapers and discuss instances when people have compromised as reported over the radio and television.

Talk about worker and management disputes, the passage of widely discussed legislation, and other compromises that are prominently reported in the media.

Present everyday problems that people face on a personal and social level (e.g., persons on a date want to engage in different leisure activities, family members want to eat at different restaurants, people want to do something at different times and days). Role-play these different situations to demonstrate the need to compromise to avoid arguments and to contribute to satisfactory relationships and to an eventual good time.

Family Interventions

Primary Level.   Ask the parents to help the child differentiate between things that are negotiable (e.g., a choice of activities) and things that are not (e.g., cleaning his or her room). For negotiable items, ask them to demonstrate how to "iron out" the problem through a compromise. Ask them to explain that a compromise means each person gives up something to arrive at something to which they both can agree.

Encourage them to explain to the child any compromises that occur between and among family members, pointing out what each party gave up and what the solution was.

Intermediate and Secondary Levels.   Ask the parents to help the youngster negotiate compromises that arise both in family matters and in his or her friendships. Remind them to impress on the youngster that, if he or she wishes to maintain friendships and good relations with family members and neighbors and if he or she wants to be successful on a job, he or she needs to compromise.

Specific Objective F

The student praises and is generally reinforcing of others, when appropriate.

Teacher Interventions

Infant and Toddler/Preschool Level.   Reward the student for listening to, sharing with, taking turns with, and being kind to his or her peers and to you and other adults in the school setting.

Primary Level.   Discuss the student's good qualities with him or her. Follow up this discussion by pointing out, with the student's participation, the qualities of his or her peers that deserve to be praised. Praise the identified students for these qualities, and encourage the student to do so as well. Reward the student for praising and reinforcing others.

Intermediate and Secondary Levels.   Explain to the student that he or she will be more successful with friendships and family relations and on dates and on the job, if he or she praises and is kind to others. Give examples from your own life that demonstrate that, when you reinforced others, you were more successful in meeting your own objectives.

Ask the student (if it is not an invasion of his or her privacy) to give examples of instances when reinforcing others proved beneficial and instances when failure to do so resulted in negative consequences.

Role-play work, dating and courtship, and leisure experiences in which the participants demonstrate positive reinforcement of each other.

Family Interventions

Infant and Toddler/Preschool Level.   Review with the parents ways that they can reinforce their child.

Primary Level.   Tell the parents that, for their child to be reinforcing to others, they ought to have had many years of being positively reinforced by family members. Describe the nature of the different types of reinforcers (tangible and social) and reinforcement schedules (fixed and intermittent), and help them plan to move from tangible to combined tangible and social reinforcements and, finally, to predominantly social reinforcers.

Intermediate and Secondary Levels. Ask the parents to observe their youngster in his or her various interactions. Encourage them to praise their youngster when he or she is reinforcing others and to point out situations in which the youngster should have been reinforcing and failed to do so.

Urge the parents to role-play the failure situation, turning it into a successful interaction so that the youngster can see how the scene might have played out differently, if the person or persons had been reinforcing of others.

Specific Objective G

The student communicates successfully with others during play and work situations.

Teacher Interventions

Infant and Toddler/Preschool Level. Arrange for play situations that require participants to communicate in some way, including speech, with one or more players. Playing pretend games, such as playing house, tea time, and school, are especially effective in developing oral communication skills.

Also, give the student a simple task (e.g., erasing the chalkboard) in which he or she must follow the directions, complete the task, and then tell someone else about what has occurred.

Primary Level. Play board and table games in which the student must communicate processes (e.g., "It's your turn!") and game-specific information (e.g., "Have you any 10s?" as in the card game "Go Fish").

Assign the student and a peer or peers a cooperative task in which they must work out the plan of action and then communicate orally as these plans are carried out.

Intermediate Level. Involve the student in physical and sports activities that take place outside the home and that require active communication (e.g., playing a game of baseball in which instructions are given relative to where fielders should stand and how to pitch to a hitter).

Also, provide the student with several simulated work-related tasks that require communication and cooperation with peers relative to planning and implementing a desired course of action (e.g., conducting an inventory of materials, preparing a meal, planting a vegetable or flower garden).

Secondary Level. If possible, provide the student with a work–study program in which he or she must communicate successfully with coworkers and supervisors.

Family Interventions

Infant and Toddler/Preschool Level. Ask the parents to play various pretend games with toys and other props (e.g., playing house with a doll house, dolls, and a doll carriage; playing cook and cleaner with toy pots, pans, utensils, and cleaning materials; playing grown-ups with large-size "dress-up" clothes).

Primary Level. Ask the parents to assign their child various household chores in which the child must follow directions, carry out the task, and then communicate the results and his or her experience.

Ask the parents to also play various table and card games that require players to communicate with each other as an integral part of the game.

Intermediate Level. Encourage the parents to involve the youngster in organized recreational activities in the community, whether as a spectator communicating with fellow spectators or as an active participant sharing directions and information with coaches and fellow players.

Secondary Level. Encourage the parents to take the youngster to their job sites to witness how people employed there communicate with each other.

Also, ask them to set up a group family task in which family members must work together on a project (e.g., wrapping holiday gifts, preparing a party, planning a family trip).

Specific Objective H

The student engages in simple conversations (small talk) while observing the implicit rules of polite conversation.

Teacher Interventions

Infant and Toddler/Preschool Level. Engage the student in simple conversations about storybooks, preferred toys, and favorite people and foods. Do so even if the student is not able to comprehend everything being said. (By doing so, you are practicing listening skills, demonstrating vocal patterns, reinforcing gestural and body language, and establishing a model of interpersonal communication, even if the student does not completely comprehend the message.)

Primary Level. Engage the student in simple conversations during show-and-tell and sharing time activities. Talk about items of interest to the student (e.g., a hobby; a preferred toy or game; a favorite entertainer, musical selection, athlete, or athletic team).

Intermediate and Secondary Levels. Role-play various social gatherings (e.g., a party or picnic) and practice simple conversations, such as talking about the weather, a recent video and music recording, a current popular movie, a new dance, and other topics that are of high interest but are not controversial in nature, although various opinions are likely to be expressed.

Family Interventions

Infant and Toddler/Preschool Level. Encourage the parents to engage the child in simple conversations during caregiving activities (e.g., "Doesn't the applesauce taste real good? Daddy made it just for you. Mmmm, I bet it tastes real good. You look like you are really enjoying it. If you are, show me or tell me how you like your applesauce.") and during play activities (e.g., "You be the Mommy and I will be the little baby, and you show me the pictures you cut from the magazine and tell me what they are pictures of".).

Primary Level. Encourage the parents to set aside a time of day when the family members engage in simple conversations, whether these concern specific family matters (e.g., chores, family trips) or deal with general topics (e.g., weather, the new amusement park that is being built nearby).

Intermediate and Secondary Levels. Ask the parents to share interesting experiences they have had as a means of stimulating and maintaining conversations. Advise the parents, if feasible, to engage their youngster in conversations that explore his or her opinions, feelings, and attitudes.

Ask the parents to help the youngster differentiate situations in which certain topics are appropriate or not. For example, sexuality is likely to be a more appropriate topic with a close family member, whereas the weather might be an appropriate topic for conversing with a new acquaintance.

Specific Objective 1

The student expresses his or her feelings, thoughts, beliefs, and opinions in socially acceptable ways and in a nonthreatening and constructive manner.

Teacher Interventions

Primary Level. Model the appropriate way one expresses basic emotions, including happiness, sadness, anger, and fear. Pay particular attention to anger.

Also, discuss problems and issues related to class rules, responsibilities, and routines. Encourage the student's active participation and, if the student does not express a divergent opinion, state that there are different ways people might view the problems and issues and demonstrate some of the various ways of viewing topics of particular interest to the student.

Model ways of expressing one's thoughts, feelings, and beliefs in an acceptable way without being confrontational or obnoxious. If a situation arises in the classroom in which feelings run high, encourage their expression in a controlled class discussion.

Intermediate Level. Read the student stories from newspapers and magazines that deal with persons who have been subjected to emotional experiences (e.g., the death of a loved one), and review the reactions of these people as well as the student's response to both the incident and the emotional reactions of the people.

Secondary Level. Explain that people have different opinions about all sorts of things. Topics can range from being generally *unemotional* (e.g., the quality of one consumer product vs. another, the television station with the preferred weather report) to *highly emotional* (e.g., political candidates, the passage of controversial legislation, executive actions designed to solve community problems).

Discuss current community and national issues, delineating the positions people are taking and encouraging the student to express his or her feelings and opinions.

Family Interventions

Infant and Toddler/Preschool Level. Ask the parents to model appropriate ways of expressing their emotions as these emotional responses occur in their lives.

Encourage them to verbalize their feelings, for example, "I am so happy now that Grandma is coming home from the hospital. I guess you can tell I'm happy from the smile on my face and the fact that I have been singing a happy song as I work in the kitchen."

Primary Level. Encourage the parents to engage the child in discussions of his or her likes and dislikes pertinent to foods, toys, games, clothing, and activities. Urge them to develop the concept that one's likes or preferences and one's dislikes are expressions of one's thoughts, feelings, and opinions.

Intermediate Level. Ask the parents also to point out examples of the expression of feelings as depicted in television programs. Tell them to comment on whether the characters involved expressed themselves in appropriate ways.

Secondary Level. Ask the parents to hold family discussions relevant to problems and issues that affect the household and family relations. Urge them to encourage the youngster's participation in the conversation, even if it is simply to express his or her support of someone else's position.

Also, ask the parents to share the ways they have expressed their feelings, thoughts, and opinions when they held divergent views from others in family, social, and work contexts.

Specific Objective J

The student identifies and communicates with family members and successfully participates as a member of a family unit.

Teacher Interventions

Infant and Toddler/Preschool Level. Show the student photographs of his or her family members (borrowed from the family). Place them face down on a desk. Turn each one over and ask the student to identify the family member by relationship ("Mommy" and "Daddy") or by relationship and name ("My brother, Angelo" and "Cousin Gertrude"). Continue by adding photographs of yourself and others. Ask the student to separate the photographs into two piles: "My Family" and "Not My Family." After the student has separated out all of his or her family members, tell him or her to name each of them.

Primary Level. Read books about family life and point out how the characters interact, share responsibilities and experiences, and care for each other.

Role-play various family situations, assigning the student the part of each family member in successive role plays. If feasible, encourage the student to make a bulletin board display or collage titled "My Family." Give the student photographs that fall into four separate categories: family members, friends, neighbors, and strangers.

Model placing at least one example of each category in a separate pile before asking the student to pick up each photograph, name its category, and then place it in the appropriate pile.

Intermediate and Secondary Levels. Explain to the student that being a class member is like being a family member in that the class is his or her "school family." Continue by explaining that members of a class share school and other learning experiences and have responsibilities and care for each other just as members of a family do.

Encourage the student's group identification and communication with his or her classmates by initiating a variety of class assignments. Praise the student for communicating effectively with his or her school family.

Family Interventions

Infant and Toddler/Preschool and Primary Levels. Ask the parents to begin a photograph album and to take videos of the family and to use these pictures to identify the various family members.

Encourage the parents to set up a "Family Bulletin Board" in the child's bedroom. Encourage the parents to impress upon their child those behaviors and activities that are suitably engaged in with family members, friends, and neighbors (and any limitations such as "Only when I am present!") and those that are not appropriate or safe to do with casual acquaintances or strangers.

Intermediate and Secondary Levels. Ask the parents to include their youngster in diverse family activities, including household chores and family social and recreational events. Encourage them to involve the youngster in planning and in meeting assigned roles and responsibilities. Remind them to praise the youngster for being a contributing family member.

Specific Objective K

The student communicates successfully in acquiring and maintaining friendships.

Teacher Interventions

Primary Level. Assist the student in distinguishing among the different categories of people: family members, friends, neighbors, casual acquaintances, and strangers. Begin by discussing ways to turn classmates into friends by being kind to them, playing games with them in school, sharing with them, and helping them. Explain that, to turn these classmates into special friends, they must take an additional step by extending the relationship outside the school to such things as visiting each other's homes and arranging with parents to get the classmates together in outside-of-school recreation activities. Emphasize not only that it is important to develop friendships but that it is equally important to maintain them by continuing to behave in friendly ways with friends.

Intermediate and Secondary Levels. Expand the activity suggested at the Primary Level to include other settings in which one can acquire friends (e.g., religious events, sports teams, community recreation centers, after-school clubs, work places). Emphasize that friendships will last only if individuals continue to behave in friendly ways after becoming friends. (See Figures 1.13 and 1.14.)

Meet in neighborhood play areas.

Belong to the same group (e.g., Boy and Girl Scouts) or club.

Go to the same church or temple or meet at a social function held there.

Attend the same school or religious school.

Meet at a community leisure site, such as a bowling alley, shopping mall, movie theater, or skating rink.

Meet at a party or other social gathering at a friend's, neighbor's, or relative's home.

Be introduced by a friend or family member.

Go to the same gym or physical fitness center.

Take private lessons from the same teacher or at the same center.

Belong to the same sports team.

Meet because parents are friends of each other.

Meet at a rehabilitation agency, hospital, clinic, or other service agency.

FIGURE 1.13.   Some ways to meet and acquire friends.

Invite friends to your home to play, for meals, and for parties.

Invite friends to join you in community-based recreation activities (e.g., going shopping).

Share experiences, tell anecdotes, and otherwise engage in small talk and serious conversations.

Engage together in hobbies and projects.

Remember their special occasions (e.g., birthdays) and join them in celebrating and remember to send greeting cards and give gifts.

Comfort them when they are sad, upset, or grieving.

Communicate with them on a regular basis face-to-face, by telephone, and in writing.

Assist them when they need help.

Provide them with advice and counseling when appropriate.

Avoid exploiting them, acting immature, being selfish, and other behaviors that often result in quarrels and friction and may end the friendship.

FIGURE 1.14. Some ways to maintain friendships.

Family Interventions

Primary Level. Ask the parents to help the child in the acquisition and maintenance of friendships by encouraging the child to invite a preferred classmate to join their child in home and community leisure-time activities. Encourage the parents to monitor the developing friendship to make certain that the child and his or her friend are behaving in friendly ways with each other.

Intermediate and Secondary Levels. Ask the parents to share with their youngster how they have acquired and maintained friendships throughout their lives. Ask them to share problems experienced in friendships and how these problems were worked out so that these friendships could continue.

Urge them to enumerate the various ways communication is kept open, such as writing letters, making telephone calls, providing help, reinforcing friends, being loyal and supportive, and not taking advantage of or being exploitive of friends.

Specific Objective L

The student communicates and interacts differently with significant individuals in his or her life and with persons who are casual acquaintances or strangers.

Teacher Interventions

Primary Level. Clarify with the student the difference among people who play a major role in his or life, those who play a minor role (i.e., acquaintances), and those who are strangers. Once the student is able to make this differentiation, engage in role plays in which he or she is expected to interact and communicate differently with significant persons in his or her life (e.g., family members, friends, educators, other human service personnel providing direct services) and people who are casual acquaintances and strangers. Be sure to emphasize the difference between friends and acquaintances and to conduct role plays for each of the subgroups.

Explain that, under certain conditions, strangers can become friends (i.e., friendships can develop from being acquainted with people for a period of time, such as after being introduced to someone by a family member or having met a new person at a social function or work situation).

Intermediate and Secondary Levels. Review television and radio news reports and television dramas that report or depict people who have been exploited, molested, or hurt by strangers or casual acquaintances. (Be certain not to unduly frighten or alarm the student, but stress caution.)

Make sure you also point out that people are sometimes hurt, molested, and exploited by family members, neighbors, and friends and that they need to be cautious of anyone who is touching him or her in private places, is abusive, and is being unfair. Do not make the student frightened of all strangers because most strangers one meets as one moves through life are not dangerous. In your summary, be certain to pay attention to what should be done when being exploited, molested, or abused in some way. See Figure 1.15 for examples of behaviors to be avoided when dealing with strangers.

Never let a stranger in the house unless asked to do so by a responsible family member or member of the household.

Never give a stranger on the telephone information of a personal nature or about family members.

Never accept a car ride from a stranger.

Never give a stranger your telephone number.

Never accept pills, candy, or money from a stranger.

Never go with a stranger to that person's home or room in a hotel or motel.

FIGURE 1.15. Behaviors to avoid with strangers.

Family Interventions

Primary, Intermediate, and Secondary Levels. Ask the parents to review who the important people are in the life of each member of the household. Encourage the parents to periodically ask the child to identify the people in his or her life by their relationships (e.g., "That is Mr. Salpino; I know him well—he is my physical therapist" and "This is Mrs. Pine, our neighbor").

Encourage the parents to verbalize the reason for their behavior when dealing with different categories of people. For example, tell them to say such things as, "Mary is a good friend who is especially responsible and good with young people, so I have asked her to baby-sit" and "The person on the telephone is a stranger who claimed I won a prize and asked me for my credit card number. I refused to give him the number because one should never give a credit card number to a person over the telephone unless one knows the company or business one is dealing with."

Ask the parents to establish a list of procedures to follow regarding strangers (e.g., never let a stranger in the house, never give a stranger on the telephone important information about the family, never accept a car ride from a stranger).

Specific Objective M

The student behaves and communicates with others in a mutually supportive and facilitative way.

Teacher Interventions

Primary Level. Spend a substantial amount of class time on cooperative activities. Throughout these endeavors, make certain that all participants are contributing in some way to the final product. Encourage each student participating in the activity to praise the others' efforts and achievements.

Intermediate and Secondary Levels. Ask the student to analyze his or her skills and problem areas to determine when he or she requires assistance from others. Once the student has done so, help him or her to identify the skills and the needs of his or her classmates. For example, say to the student, "Your classmate, Sabine, does wonderful drawings and makes beautiful arts and crafts projects. We must remember to praise her when she does these and other things well. She often needs help, however, in following directions, but you are very good at doing so. Therefore, if you notice that she doesn't understand, please explain the directions to her."

Family Interventions

Infant and Toddler/Preschool and Primary Levels. Ask the parents to establish a house-hold atmosphere in which the members of the household reinforce and assist each other in the many individual and collaborative household and personal tasks.

Intermediate Level. Ask the parents to share anecdotes with the youngster of how they were reinforcing and supportive of each other and how these incidents strengthened their relationship and contributed to the welfare of the family.

   Tell the parents to share other anecdotes with the youngster, if possible, about incidents when family members were *not* reinforcing or supportive and how this caused problems for the individual or friction or disharmony in the family.

Secondary Level. Review the Intermediate Level activity with the parents. Additionally, ask them to share anecdotes about work situations, leisure-time pursuits, and avocational activities in which cooperation and support helped get the work accomplished and contributed to the welfare of both the individual and the group.

Specific Objective N

The student provides assistance to others, when appropriate, in emergency situations.

Teacher Interventions

Primary Level. Explain what an emergency is, making sure to differentiate it from other difficult situations. Emphasize that an emergency situation usually requires help as quickly as possible from a person or persons with special skill and/or equipment.

   If an emergency situation arises—for example, a student is hurt on the playground and has to be rushed to a hospital—explain why that is an emergency situation. Explain that a fire drill is a way the school practices in case there were a real fire emergency in which firefighters would have to be called to get to the school as quickly as possible with their fire-fighting and other emergency equipment.

Intermediate and Secondary Levels. Ask the student and his or her classmates to recount incidents when they were witnesses to emergencies and to describe how they handled the situation.

Role-play experiencing and handling emergency situations, such as calling for an ambulance or emergency squad when someone has stopped breathing, is unconscious, or bleeding severely; calling the police when someone has been assaulted; and helping a crying child who has been separated from his or her parents. Involve the student and his or her classmates in role plays about problems that are not emergency situations, such as a student has been injured but requires only first aid and a child is lost in a department store and a security guard is nearby.

Arrange for class visits from police officers and firefighters. If possible, schedule a class trip to a firehouse and a police station.

Family Interventions

Infant and Toddler/Preschool and Primary Levels. Ask the parents to describe emergencies that could happen in the home (e.g., a grease fire, an injury, a burglary) and to prepare the child to handle them. Encourage them to practice home fire drills and to compare them to the school's fire drills.

Intermediate and Secondary Levels. Ask the parents to tell the student about emergencies they and other family members have experienced. Remind them to relate incidents that were handled successfully and emergencies that were not handled properly.

Encourage, if possible, to arrange for a visit to a local hospital to see such things as the ambulance entrance and the emergency room. Urge them to visit a local fire station to view the fire-fighting and other emergency equipment located there.

Specific Objective O

The student visits and communicates via the telephone with relatives, friends, and neighbors at appropriate times, including when they are ill and experiencing problems.

Teacher Interventions

Infant and Toddler/Preschool Level. Play various pretend games (with dress-up clothes and props) in which people visit each other (e.g., to join others for a snack, to return a borrowed item, to share good news).

Primary Level. Engage the student in role plays in which relatives, friends, or neighbors are visited. Role-play different situations when people visit each other.

Talk about the pleasure people have sharing time with each other during casual and planned visits (parties and other celebrations). Explain how the telephone can be used to "visit" with people when a real visit is not practical (e.g., inclement weather) or not possible (distance constraints).

Intermediate and Secondary Levels. Discuss and then role-play situations in which the purpose is to comfort relatives and significant others at times of illness and sorrow.

Ask the students to share their experiences and to talk about the good times they have had and how they have benefitted emotionally from the visits of others during times of need.

Family Interventions

Infant and Toddler/Preschool and Primary Levels. Ask the parents to take their child, whenever feasible, on visits to relatives, friends, and neighbors. Encourage them to share the reason for the visit and to point out the feelings engendered, such as "We are going to visit Aunt Anna because I need some advice, and she is a wise woman who has always helped me with good advice before" and "We are going to visit our neighbor, Mrs. Chin, because she is a great baker and promised to give me her recipe for whole wheat bread."

Intermediate and Secondary Levels. Ask the parents to include their youngster, as much as possible, whenever they communicate with relatives, friends, and neighbors, whether in person or via the telephone. Remind them to share the reason for the visit or call before it is made and to discuss the benefits after the visit or call.

Specific Objective P

The student invites and joins others in social activities.

Teacher Interventions

Infant and Toddler/Preschool Level. At various times during the school day, give the student a break, and encourage him or her to visit with a peer or peers. It may be necessary to suggest a specific activity in which they may engage, until the student is able to set the social agenda without your assistance.

Primary Level.   Arrange visits to other classrooms. Introduce the students to each other, and encourage them to talk, play games, and otherwise visit with each other.

Plan a variety of social events, such as class parties and luncheons, and invite other classes to these events. Work cooperatively with one or more teachers so that the other teachers invite the student and his or her classmates to social events in their classrooms.

Intermediate and Secondary Levels.   Engage the student and his or her classmates in a discussion of the social and recreational activities available in the community.

When possible, arrange for trips in the community to sample and otherwise experience available social and recreational activities to which the student might invite others. Be sure to help the student identify the costs and time requirements of these activities.

Family Interventions

Infant and Toddler/Preschool and Primary Levels.   Ask the parents to set a pattern of joining significant others for recreational activities (e.g., picnics, sports events, holiday celebrations) and community activities (e.g., club meetings and socials, religious events, political or community action groups such as town meetings).

Intermediate and Secondary Levels.   Encourage the parents to make it possible for their youngster to join others in social events. Remind them that they may need to make arrangements (including being a family chauffeur) so that others may visit in their home and the youngster may visit others in their homes, as well as join others in various events.

Encourage the parents to make certain that the youngster develops the language and computational skills to participate successfully in these activities.

Specific Objective Q

The student identifies and communicates effectively with human service professionals, community helpers, and other service personnel.

Teacher Interventions

Infant and Toddler/Preschool Level.   For the younger student, make "community helper" costumes from brown paper grocery bags. Cut out arm and neck holes, and slit the bags down the front so the students can wear them. Paint the bag to simulate community helper uniforms (e.g., blue for police officer, white for a doctor or nurse, appropriate color for firefighters in the community). Assist the student as he or she adds details, such as brass buttons, badges, and name tags. Once the student has completed the costume, join him or her in a play situation. Tell the student to exchange costumes with his or peers and to play the parts of different community helpers.

Primary Level. Establish the fact that people are dependent on other people for tasks that they are unable to do for themselves. Review some of these tasks, and then role-play situations involving community helpers interacting with the student in representative situations (e.g., a lost student and a police officer, a student being tutored by a teacher, a student visiting a fire station, a student at a doctor's office being asked to describe his or her symptoms). Include situations the student is likely to experience. Repeat the activity to give the student the opportunity to play both the student and the helper.

Intermediate Level. Show the student photographs or magazine pictures of people at a barber shop, beauty parlor, physician's office, department store, bank, and any other place the student might have used in the past or might need to use in the future. Discuss what the people in the pictures are doing. Ask the student to identify the helper and describe how the helper is assisting the people who require services. Also, develop the concept that there are special helpers, called human service professionals, who provide medical and medically related services.

Secondary Level. Discuss with the student the role and scope of the various human service professionals, especially those with whom the student has come into or will likely come into contact in the future, including the traditional therapies (physical, occupational, and speech), creative therapies, and medical specialties. See Figure 1.16 for examples of medical specialties.

Family Interventions

Infant and Toddler/Preschool and Primary Levels. Ask the parents to point out various community helpers they encounter as they move about the community. Encourage them not only to name the helper but also to describe how the particular helper assists people in need of service. Remind parents that their child does not need to understand every word spoken to him or her.

Intermediate and Secondary Levels. Urge the parents to involve their youngster in any direct interactions they have with service people of any kind. Tell

Cardiologist—A physician who treats problems of the heart and circulatory system.

Dermatologist—A physician who treats problems of the skin.

Neurologist—A physician who treats diseases or problems of the nervous system.

Ophthalmologist—A physician who examines and treats diseases or problems of the eye or vision.

Orthopedist—A physician who treats problems and diseases of the bones, muscles, and joints.

Otologist—A physician who examines and treats diseases and problems of the ear or hearing.

Pediatrician—A physician who takes care of children and adolescents.

Psychiatrist—A physician who treats emotional and mental problems and conditions.

FIGURE 1.16. Medical specialties.

them to continue to assist the youngster in identifying tasks that he or she is or is not able to perform independently.

Encourage them to involve the youngster in interactions with human service providers, especially those whom they consult or who provide direct service to the youngster as part of his or her habilitative services. Tell them to make certain that the youngster understands the nature of each service provided.

GOAL III.

The student will refrain from engaging in disturbing, distracting, destructive, and self-destructive behavior

SPECIFIC OBJECTIVES

The student:

❑ A. Does not engage in distracting mannerisms and other disconcerting self-stimulatory behaviors.

❑ B. Does not engage in behaviors that are disturbing, distracting, or obnoxious to others.

❑ C. Does not engage in self-destructive behavior.

❑ D. Does not engage in behavior injurious of others.

❑ E. Does not engage in behavior destructive of the property and possessions of others.

❑ F. Does not engage in behavior exploitive of others.

SUGGESTED ACTIVITIES

Specific Objective A

The student does not engage in distracting mannerisms and other disconcerting self-stimulatory behaviors.

Teacher Interventions

Infant and Toddler/Preschool and Primary Levels. Observe the student to determine whether he or she engages in any distracting mannerisms or disconcerting self-stimulating behaviors. If so, try to substitute a behavior that is more acceptable. For example, if the student rocks in place, put him or her in a rocking chair and say, "Look at this special chair. It is made like this at the bottom so it can rock. Watch me as I rock the chair. Now you will sit (or I will put you) in this rocking chair so that you can enjoy rocking yourself." You may wish to start with a doll and a small-size rocking chair.

Another example is the student who makes repetitive movements with his or her hands. In such a case, explain, "A person's hands are for doing necessary things like brushing one's teeth or drawing a picture or playing ball or buttoning one's shirt. Let's hold hands and play 'Ring-Around-the-Rosy.' "

Intermediate and Secondary Levels. Observe the student to determine whether he or she engages in any distracting mannerisms or disconcerting self-stimulating behaviors. If so, point them out to the student using a mirror or a teacher-made movie (if viewing him- or herself is not too traumatic for the student), and explain why the specific mannerism might be annoying or disconcerting to others and, if the behavior continues, how it may interfere with his or her personal and social life. Depending on the student, you might include discussions dealing with dating and courtship.

Assist the student in becoming aware that a problem exists and the need to eliminate the unacceptable behavior. It may be necessary to deal with any problems that may occur with a student who is fondling, rubbing, or manipulating his or her genitals.

Family Interventions

Infant and Toddler/Preschool and Primary Levels. Ask the parents to observe the child to determine whether he or she engages in any distracting mannerisms or self-stimulating behaviors. If so, ask them to stop the behavior and to substitute a motor behavior that is more socially acceptable. For example, if the student rocks in place, tell the parents, as they physically stop their child, to say, "You shouldn't rock yourself unless you are sitting in a rocking chair or dancing a dance that includes rocking motions. Let's hold hands and rock to music on the stereo."

Intermediate and Secondary Levels. Ask the parents to observe their youngster and to correct any disconcerting mannerisms and self-stimulatory behaviors that occur. Encourage them not to be punitive about such behaviors, but rather to attempt, through reasoning, to stop the behavior because it may be interfering with the youngster's acceptance by others, especially as it relates to acquiring and maintaining friendships, gaining and keeping one's job, and dating and courtship.

Specific Objective B

The student does not engage in behaviors that are disturbing, distracting, or obnoxious to others.

Teacher Interventions

Infant and Toddler/Preschool and Primary Levels. Observe the student to determine whether he or she engages in any behaviors that are disturbing, distracting, or obnoxious to others. If so, stop the student, if possible, as soon as the behavior occurs. For example, if the student begins to pick his or her nose, stop him or her immediately and say, "Picking your nose is very unattractive. Let me help you use a tissue to clean your nose. When you use a tissue to clean your nose, you look better than if you pick your nose." Review some of the obnoxious behaviors in Figure 1.17.

Intermediate and Secondary Levels.   Observe the student to determine whether he or she engages in any behaviors that disturb, distract, or are obnoxious to others. If so, stop the student, if possible, as soon as the behavior occurs.

It is important to explain why a specific behavior is disturbing or obnoxious to others. For example, explain that when a person passes wind, it is embarrassing to others and the smell might also be annoying. Explain also that it is normal for people to pass wind, but that there is an appropriate place to do so, that is, a bathroom or some other private place if a bathroom is not readily available.

Family Interventions

Infant and Toddler/Preschool and Primary Levels.   Ask the parents to observe the child to determine whether he or she engages in any behaviors that disturb, distract, or are obnoxious to others. If so, tell them to stop the child as soon as the behavior occurs. For example, if the child repeats a profanity that he or she has heard, tell the parents not to be punitive but to say to the child, "That word is not a nice word. You shouldn't say words that are not nice. We love to hear you speak, but when you say words that are not nice, we do not like to hear them. So stop saying that word, and let's say some nice words like 'Mommy,' 'Daddy,' and 'cookie.'"

Belching or burping

Passing wind

Using profanity

Excessive touching, hugging, or kissing

Picking one's scalp or sores

Sniffing food, objects, or people

Fondling oneself in public

Staring at or standing too close to another person

FIGURE 1.17.   Obnoxious behaviors.

Intermediate and Secondary Levels. Ask the parents to observe the youngster to determine whether he or she engages in any behaviors that are disturbing, distracting, or obnoxious to others. If so, tell them to stop the youngster as soon as the behavior occurs.

Explain that at these levels, it is important to explain why a specific behavior is disturbing or obnoxious to others. For example, if the student fondles him- or herself, ask the parents to explain that while rubbing or touching him- or herself in the private areas of his or her body may feel good, it will disturb others if done in public. Tell them not to treat such a behavior as a terrible one, but to explain that, if one wants to fondle oneself, it should be done in a private place.

Specific Objective C

The student does not engage in self-destructive behavior.

Teacher Interventions

Infant and Toddler/Preschool and Primary Levels. Observe the student to determine whether he or she engages in self-destructive behaviors (biting, head banging, scratching, picking his or her skin, pulling out his or her hair, using sharp objects). If so, stop the student from injuring him- or herself as soon as possible, tell him or her that he or she is a good person and should *not* hurt him- or herself (while holding his or her hand), and then substitute a productive or creative activity. For example, give the student clay and show him or her how to use his or her hands to pound clay and to shape it into an interesting shape rather than using his or her hands to hurt him- or herself.

A further example is to give the student hard raw carrots or crisp celery to chew. As the student is chewing this nutritious snack, comment on the fact that his or her teeth not only make him or her look good but are needed to bite and chew food and not to hurt him- or herself or anyone else.

Intermediate and Secondary Levels. Observe the student to determine whether he or she engages in self-destructive behaviors. If so, stop the student from injuring him- or herself as soon as possible, tell him or her that he or she is a good person and should not hurt him- or herself (while holding his or her hand), and then substitute a constructive behavior. For example, encourage him or her to use his or her hands to do an arts and crafts activity that will lead to a gift for a favorite person or that he or she can use to decorate his or her room.

It may prove beneficial to discuss the topic of anger and frustration and how to deal with these feelings in acceptable ways. If feasible, help the student identify and subsequently avoid situations that are likely to precipitate self-destructive behavior.

Family Interventions

Infant and Toddler/Preschool and Primary Levels. Encourage the parents to observe the child to determine whether he or she engages in self-destructive behaviors (biting, head banging, scratching, picking his or her skin, pulling out his or her hair, using sharp objects). If so, tell them to (a) stop the child from injuring him- or herself as soon as possible, (b) tell him or her that he or she is a good person and should *not* hurt him- or herself, and (c) substitute a suitable behavior.

For example, encourage the parents to tell their child to use his or her hands to help roll the dough to make pizza or to help you fold the clean clothing. It may also be necessary for the parents to change elements in their child's environment (e.g., moving the child's bed from walls, removing sharp objects from the child's reach).

Intermediate and Secondary Levels. Tell the parents to observe their youngster to determine whether he or she engages in any self-destructive behaviors. If so, tell them to (a) stop the student from injuring him- or herself as soon as possible, (b) tell him or her that he or she is a good person and should *not* hurt him- or herself, and (c) substitute a constructive behavior.

For example, tell the parents to encourage the youngster to use his or her hands to do any enjoyable productive activity. If feasible, urge the parents to help their youngster identify and subsequently avoid situations that are likely to precipitate self-destructive behavior.

Specific Objective D

The student does not engage in behavior injurious of others.

Teacher Interventions

Infant and Toddler/Preschool Level. Engage the student in constructive play with dolls and stuffed animals. Model treating these toys in nice ways, such as hugging, petting, "feeding," and "dressing" them. If the student begins to be destructive with these toys, stop and reprimand him or her and then take away the toy while explaining why you are doing so.

Speak about the good qualities of the student's classmates, and plan activities that involve sharing, helping, and being nice to each other, such as playing tea time, in which they share milk or juice and a snack; helping each other complete arts and crafts projects while sharing one pot of paste and one box of crayons; and engaging them in a role play in which they take turns pretending to be a physician and a sick patient.

Primary Level. Begin by enumerating the good qualities of the student, and then proceed to enumerate the good qualities of his or her peers. Discuss the various ways one can treat people nicely (e.g., smiling at them; helping them when they are in need; sharing toys, snacks, and experiences).

Join the student in identifying the good qualities of his or her classmates and the important people in his or her life (e.g., in response to photographs of family members and friends). Ask the student to talk about the ways his or her family members and friends have treated him or her nicely and ways that others have been nice to the student. Continue by asking the student to identify the ways he or she can be nice to his or her classmates.

Schedule class times when each student is expected to say or do something nice to each peer. As in the previous Infant and Toddler/Preschool Level activity, if the student begins to be destructive of others, stop and reprimand him or her and require him or her to do something nice to the person involved either at the time if possible, and, if not possible, at a later time. It may be necessary to show the student ways of getting someone's attention, because destructive behaviors may be an attention-getting strategy.

Intermediate and Secondary Levels. Proceed in the same way as in the Primary Level activity in which the good qualities of others are enumerated, but do so at a more sophisticated level. At the earlier level, students are likely to concentrate on physical aspects and obvious behaviors such as *not* sharing. At these levels, however, try to deal with personality and temperament variables (e.g., "Richard is a good friend because he always listens to and comforts me when I am sad or upset," "Anna is a good person because she will join in a group activity that most of the other students want to do, even though she wanted to do something else").

Discuss stories heard on the radio and television and read from newspapers and magazines, emphasizing the effect on the *victims* of crimes that cause bodily harm. Include a review of the applicable laws and of crimes and punishments.

Family Interventions

Infant and Toddler/Preschool Level. Review with the parents the suggested activity under Teacher Interventions. Ask them to engage in the same activities, but instead to speak about the good qualities of all the members of the family and to plan household work and home-based and community-oriented leisure activities that involve sharing, helping, and being nice to and cooperating with others.

Remind parents that both positive and constructive behaviors and negative and destructive behaviors are contagious and that aggressive and hostile behaviors are imitated and perpetuated.

Primary Level. Review with the parents the suggested activities under Teacher Interventions. Ask them to join the child in identifying the good qualities of family members, friends, and neighbors. Encourage them to help develop the view that "I'm okay, and you're okay."

Intermediate and Secondary Levels. Review with the parents the suggested activities under Teacher Interventions. Ask them to assist their youngster in identifying the good qualities of others at a more sophisticated level. Also, expand the range, when feasible, to include, for example, political figures as an aid in making voting decisions.

Remember to caution the parents to stress positive attributes when they exist rather than emphasizing the negative.

Specific Objective E

The student does not engage in behavior destructive of the property and possessions of others.

Teacher Interventions

Infant and Toddler/Preschool Level. Place labels on the student's possessions (use a rebus or other nonword symbol, if necessary). Review with him or her the concept of ownership.

Place a different label (symbol) on possessions that you have brought to class. Pick up and handle carefully each of your possessions while saying, for example, "This is my favorite sweater, so I treat it very gently because I want it to last a long time" and "This is my family photograph album. It is very important to me. I have had it a very long time so I treat it with tender loving care." Ask the student to pick up and examine your possessions, and reward him or her for treating them with care.

Whenever students in the class (including the student him- or herself) treat someone's possessions roughly, stop them, reprimand them, and apply the designated negative consequence.

Primary Level. Ask the student and his or her classmates to bring a favorite game, toy, or book to class. Ask each one to show his or her item to the class and, if possible, to explain why it is cherished.

During a supervised play period, encourage the students to share their prized object with each other. Supervise closely, and reward proper handling. If students in the class (including the student him- or herself) treat a prized item roughly, stop them, reprimand them, and apply the designated negative consequence.

Intermediate and Secondary Levels. Take the students for walks in the community and identify the property of others. For example, point out that the public library "belongs" to all the citizens of a community, the department store "belongs to private citizens or owners," and the bicycle chained to the gate belongs to a private person.

Discuss the financial and emotional impact of the destruction of property on the community and individuals. Discuss stories heard on the radio and television and read from newspapers and magazines, emphasizing the effect on the *victims* of crimes against property. Include a review of the applicable laws and of crimes and punishments.

Family Interventions

Infant and Toddler/Preschool Level. Review with the parents the suggested activity under Teacher Interventions. Ask them to carry out this activity with their possessions and to include (one at a time) each of the other members of the household with their possessions, until all members have been involved.

Encourage the parents to praise and otherwise reward careful handling and, if any family member (including the child) treats a prized item roughly, to stop the individual, reprimand him or her, and apply the designated negative consequence.

Primary Level. Ask the parents to assist the child in differentiating collective property (dishes, furniture in the common areas, household appliances) from individual property (clothing, grooming items). Remind them to establish the need to treat all property gently and to review the impact of damaged property on the household budget and people's emotions.

Encourage the parents to praise and otherwise reward careful handling and, if any family member (including the child) treats a prized item roughly, to stop the individual, reprimand him or her, and apply the designated negative consequence. See Figure 1.18 for examples of collective and personal property.

Intermediate and Secondary Levels. Review with the parents the suggested activity under Teacher Interventions. Ask them to carry out this activity as a way of reinforcing your instruction and assisting in the carryover process.

Collective Property	Personal Property
Household appliances	Clothing
Eating and cooking utensils	Prescription medicines
Furniture in the common area	Bedroom furniture
Towels and linens	Personal grooming supplies
First aid supplies	Personal gifts

FIGURE 1.18.   Examples of collective and personal property.

Specific Objective F

The student does not engage in behavior exploitive of others.

Teacher Interventions

Primary and Intermediate Levels.   If you witness an occasion when a student has exploited or is exploiting another student (e.g., stealing money, eating the person's lunch, touching inappropriately), stop the behavior, reprimand the student, and explain why the behavior is inappropriate and not to be repeated. (As part of your behavior modification program, you may wish to increase the negative consequences for repeat offenders.) Work on developing empathy by sharing your reaction to times when you or others known to you have been exploited (keep it simple!), and then ask him or her to talk about how he or she felt or might feel under similar circumstances. Role plays in which the student plays the part of the victim might also assist in developing empathy.

Secondary Level.   If you witness an incident when a student is in the process of exploiting a classmate (e.g., stealing money, becoming sexually aggressive), stop the behavior, reprimand the student, and explain why the behavior is inappropriate and not to be repeated. (As part of your behavior modification program, you may wish to increase the negative consequences for repeat offenders.)

Discuss stories heard on the radio and television and read from newspapers and magazines, emphasizing the effect on the *victims* of exploitation by sex offenders and con artists. Include a review of the applicable laws and of crimes and punishments.

Family Interventions

Primary and Intermediate Levels. Review with the parents the suggested activity under Teacher Interventions. Ask them to carry out this activity as a way of reinforcing your instruction and assisting in the carryover process. Encourage them to concentrate especially on prevention of exploitation by others, as well as emphasizing the need to assist and help others and to refrain from exploiting other people.

Secondary Level. Ask the parents to discuss stories heard on the radio and television and read from newspapers and magazines, emphasizing the effect on the *victims* of exploitation by sex offenders and con artists. Include a review of the applicable laws and of crimes and punishments.

Remind parents that, if they witness the youngster exploiting someone (a friend, neighbor, or younger family member)—for example, stealing money or becoming sexually aggressive—they must stop the behavior, reprimand the youngster, and explain why the behavior is inappropriate and not to be repeated.

Sample Lesson Plan 1

Topic Area: Interpersonal Skills

Designed by: Marni Stratton

Time Recommended: 1 Hour 15 Minutes (May be done in two or more separate periods.)

Student Involved: Ralph (Secondary Special Class)

Background Information:

The student is generally cooperative and enjoys working with classmates in various work, play, and social situations. At times, however, he fails to modify his behavior, depending on the situation. For example, at a performance by a community theater group, he laughed too loudly and was generally boisterous. At times, he is careless about trash, either leaving it on his desk, stuffing it in his desk, or dropping it and failing to pick it up.

General Goal *(Interpersonal I):*

The student will function as optimally as possible in diverse interpersonal and social situations.

Specific Objective *(Interpersonal I-C):*

The student behaves in an acceptable manner when dealing with peers and adults in diverse interpersonal and social situations.

Lesson Objective:

While engaging in three role plays, the student will behave in an acceptable manner in markedly different interpersonal situations: a birthday party, a movie theater, and a hospital room.

Materials and Equipment:

- Picnic table, several table games, napkins, paper plates and cups, snack food items, cold drinks, and wastebasket(s)
- Simple birthday party decorations and accessories
- A movie screen, movie projector, several rows of chairs, ticket stubs, and popcorn
- A bed, two chairs, a television set, a telephone, and a meal tray and stand
- VCR, television set, and videotape or newspaper/magazine article

Motivating Activity:

Show the student a scene from a videotape that depicts Ralph's same-age peers in unacceptable behavior or read a report from a local newspaper or magazine that describes the inappropriate behavior of Ralph's same-age peers in a public setting. Engage another student in a discussion of the acceptable ways to behave in the situation depicted in the article.

Instructional Procedures:

Initiation—Discuss with Ralph the videotape or the newspaper or magazine article. Ask Ralph to share some of his recent interpersonal and social experiences with you and some of his classmates. For each experience shared, encourage Ralph to share how and why he behaved in a particular way. If possible, point out those behaviors that are acceptable and appropriate in one situation but are not appropriate in another.

Guided Practice—Select a happy or upbeat social event, such as a picnic, and role-play enjoying the food and table games without being boisterous or inconsiderate (e.g., putting the trash in a receptacle). Before the role play is initiated, ask the student if he has ever been on a picnic. Establish the appropriate behavior by playing a table game with a classmate, enjoying a snack and a drink, and cleaning up. Then ask the student to imitate your behavior by engaging in a picnic with a peer. Provide feedback and assistance, if and when needed.

Independent Practice—Proceed by describing the three different role plays (birthday party, movie theater, hospital room). After these situations have been fully described and the appropriate behavior explored, assign Ralph to a classmate who is highly skilled in this skill, and ask Ralph to proceed with each role play.

Closure—Hold a small celebration in recognition of the successful role plays, making sure to include the cooperating classmate(s) in the celebration.

Assessment Strategy:

Observe the student to determine whether he behaved in an acceptable manner in the three role plays and in the follow-up celebration.

Follow-Up Activity or Objective:

If the student achieves the lesson objective, proceed to a lesson on acceptable behavior when dealing with an infant or toddler in a social situation.

Sample Lesson Plan 2

Topic Area: Interpersonal Skills

Designed by: Eleana Blake

Time Recommended: 45 Minutes

Student Involved: Clara (Primary Special Class)

Background Information:

The student can be difficult when frustrated but will respond with appropriate reinforcements. She has a tendency to be impulsive both orally and with physical behaviors. At times, she will be careless about personal behaviors, being discourteous or rude.

General Goal *(Interpersonal II):*

The student will function as optimally as possible in diverse interpersonal and social situations that depend on effective oral communication skills.

Specific Objective *(Interpersonal II-A):*

The student greets and bids farewell to others in a socially acceptable manner.

Lesson Objective:

The student greets and bids farewell to others in a socially acceptable manner.

Materials and Equipment:

- Student Helper Chart
- Names of students, laminated
- Classroom, cafeteria, party room
- Videotape about social situations and varied behaviors of greeting
- VCR
- Tape recorder and blank tapes

Motivating Activity:

Show the student a scene from a videotape that depicts appropriate behaviors of greeting in varied settings. Discuss various social situations in which behaviors of greeting and bidding farewell are appropriate.

Instructional Procedures:

Initiation—Discuss the videotape. Ask Clara to share with you recent interpersonal and social experiences that required a greeting and a farewell. For each experience shared, ask Clara to share how she greeted the guest, whether in the classroom, at home, or during a party. If possible, point out those verbal and physical greetings and farewells that are acceptable and appropriate in each situation.

Guided Practice—Select the student as the classroom greeter for the week. Before the job assignment is initiated, ask the student to review appropriate greetings and farewells (e.g. handshake, wave, "Hello, how are you?"). Establish the appropriate behaviors by asking the student to greet guests and friends. Provide feedback and assistance, if and when needed.

Independent Practice—Proceed by describing the three social situations. After these situations have been fully described and the appropriate behavior explored, assign Clara to greet classmates who do well in this skill.

Closure—Have a discussion reviewing the successful greetings, making sure to include the classmate(s) in the discussion.

Assessment Strategy:

Observe the student to determine whether she behaved in an acceptable manner in a variety of unstructured situations that require social greetings or farewells.

Follow-Up Activity or Objective:

If the student achieves the lesson objective, proceed to a lesson on acceptable greeting with a classmate or adult who may be uncooperative or impolite.

Suggested Readings

Abramson, P. R., Parker, T., & Weisberg, S. R. (1988). Sexual expression of mentally retarded people: Educational and legal implications. *American Journal of Mental Retardation, 93,* 328–334.

Agran, M., Salzberg, C. L., & Stowitchek, J. (1987). An analysis of the effects of a social skills training program using self-instructions on the acquisition and generalization of two social behaviors in a work setting. *Journal of The Association for Persons with Severe Handicaps, 12,* 131–139.

Amish, P. L., Gesten, E. L., Smith, J. K., Clark, H. B., & Stark, C. (1988). Social problem-solving training for severely emotionally and behaviorally disturbed children. *Behavioral Disorders, 13,* 175–186.

Bash, M. A. S., & Camp, B. W. (1985). *Think aloud: Increasing social and cognitive skills—A problem-solving program for children. Classroom program grades 3–4.* Champaign, IL: Research Press.

Bash, M. A. S., & Camp, B. W. (1985). *Think aloud: Increasing social and cognitive skills—A problem-solving program for children. Classroom program grades 5–6.* Champaign, IL: Research Press.

Baum, D. D., Duffelmeyer, F., & Geelan, M. (1988). Resource teacher perceptions of the prevalence of social dysfunction among students with learning disabilities. *Journal of Learning Disabilities, 21,* 380–381.

Bender, W. N., & Smith, J. K. (1990). Classroom behavior of children and adolescents with learning disabilities: A meta-analysis. *Journal of Learning Disabilities, 23,* 298–305.

Berkell, D. E., & Brown, J. M. (Eds.). (1989). *Transition from school to work for persons with disabilities.* New York: Longman.

Bradley, L., & Meredith, R. (1991). Interpersonal development: A study with children classified as educable mentally retarded. *Education and Training in Mental Retardation, 26,* 130–141.

Brantlinger, E. A. (1988). Teachers' perceptions of the parenting abilities of their secondary students with mild mental retardation. *Remedial and Special Education, 9,* 31–43.

Brolin, D. E. (1991). *Life centered career education: A competency based approach* (3rd ed.). Reston, VA: The Council for Exceptional Children.

Bruininks, R., Thurlow, M., & Gilman, C. (1987). Adaptive behavior and mental retardation. *The Journal of Special Education, 21,* 69–88.

Bryan, T. (1991). Social problems and learning disabilities. In B. Wong (Ed.), *Learning about learning disabilities* (pp. 196–231). San Diego: Academic Press.

Camp, B. W., & Bash, M. A. S. (1985). *Think aloud: Increasing social and cognitive skills—A problem-solving program for children. Classroom program grades 1–2.* Champaign, IL: Research Press.

Carlson, C. I. (1987). Social interaction goals and strategies of children with learning disabilities. *Journal of Learning Disabilities, 20,* 306–311.

Chadsey-Rusch, J., Karlan, G. R., Riva, M., & Rusch, F. R. (1984). Competitive employment: Teaching conversation skills to adults who are mentally retarded. *Mental Retardation, 22,* 218–222.

Cheney, D., & Foss, G. (1984). An examination of the social behavior of mentally deficient workers. *Education and Training of the Mentally Retarded, 19,* 216–221.

Clark, G. M. (1979). *Career education for the handicapped child in the elementary classroom.* Denver: Love.

Clark, G. M., Carlson, B. C., Fisher, S., Cook, J. D., & D'Alonzo, B. J. (1991). Career development for students with disabilities in elementary schools: A position statement of the Division of Career Development. *Career Development in Exceptional Individuals, 14,* 109–120.

Clark, G. M., & Kolstoe, O. (1990). *Career development and transition education for adolescents with disabilities.* Boston: Allyn & Bacon.

Clement-Heist, K., Siegel, S., & Gaylord-Ross, R. (1992). Simulated and in-situ vocational social skills training for youths with learning disabilities. *Exceptional Children, 58,* 336–345.

Coleman, M., & Apts, S. (1991). Home-alone risk factors. *Teaching Exceptional Children, 23,* 36–39.

Cosden, M. A., & Haring, T. G. (1992). Cooperative learning in the classroom: Contingencies, group interactions, and students with special needs. *Journal of Behavior Education, 2,* 53–71.

Cronin, M. E., & Patton, J. R. (1993). *Life skills instruction for all students with special needs: A practical guide for integrating real-life content into the curriculum.* Austin, TX: PRO-ED.

Davis, D. E. (1977). *My friends and me. A program to promote the personal and social development of young children.* Circle Pines, MN: American Guidance Service.

Deshler, D. D., & Schumaker, J. B. (1983). Social skills of learning disabled adolescents: A review of characteristics and intervention. *Topics in Learning and Learning Disabilities, 3,* 15–23.

Dever, R.B. (1988). *A taxonomy of community living skills.* Washington, DC: American Association on Mental Retardation.

Dinkmeyer, D. (1973). *Developing Understanding of Self and Others–Revised (DUSO–R).* Circle Pines, MN: American Guidance Service.

Division on Career Development. (1987). *The transition of youth with disabilities to adult life: A position statement.* Reston, VA: The Council for Exceptional Children.

Dore, J. (1986). The development of conversational competence. In R. L. Schiefelbusch (Ed.), *Language competence, assessment and intervention* (pp. 85–96). Boston: Little, Brown.

Dupont, H., & Dupo, C. (1979). *Transition: A program to help students through the difficult passage from childhood through middle adolescence.* Circle Pines, MN: American Guidance Service.

Dupont, H., Gardner, S. O., & Brody, D. S. (1974). *Toward affective development (TAD)*. Circle Pines, MN: American Guidance Service.

Durand, V. M., & Carr, E. G. (1985). Self-injurious behavior: Motivating conditions and guidelines for treatment. *School Psychology Review, 14*, 171–176.

Fad, K. S. (1990). The fast track to success: Social-behavioral Skills. *Intervention in School and Clinic, 26*, 39–43.

Falvey, M. (1989). *Community-based curriculum: Instructional strategies for students with severe handicaps*. (2nd ed.). Baltimore: Brookes.

Ford, M. E. (1985). The concept of competence: Themes and variations. In H. A. Marlow & R. B. Weinberg (Eds.), *Competence development: Theory and practice in special populations* (pp. 3–38). Springfield, IL: Charles C Thomas.

Foxx, R. M., McMorrow, M. J., Storey, K., & Rogers, B. M. (1984). Teaching social/sexual skills to mentally retarded adults. *American Journal of Mental Deficiency, 89*, 9–15.

Gast, D. L., Collins, B. C., Wolery, M., & Jones, R. (1993). Teaching preschool children with disabilities to respond to the lures of strangers. *Exceptional Children, 59*, 301–311.

Gaylord-Ross, R., Haring, T. G., Breen, C., & Pitts-Conway, V. (1984). The training and generalization of social interaction skills with autistic youth. *Journal of Applied Behavior Analysis, 17*, 229–247.

Goldstein, A. P. (1988). *The prepare curriculum: Teaching prosocial competencies*. Champaign, IL: Research Press.

Goldstein, A. P., Sprafkin, R. P., Gershaw, N. J., & Klein, P. (1980). *Skillstreaming the adolescent*. Champaign, IL: Research Press.

Gollnick, D. M., & Chinn, P. C. (1994). *Multicultural education in a pluralistic society* (4th ed.). Columbus, OH: Macmillan.

Gray, B. J. (1990). *Problem solving for teens: An interactive approach to real-life problem solving*. East Moline, IL: Linguisystems.

Gresham, F. M. (1988). Social competence and motivational characteristics of learning disabled students. In M. Wang, M. Reynolds, & H. Walberg (Eds.), *The handbook of special education: Research and practice* (pp. 283–302). Oxford, England: Pergamon Press.

Gresham, F. M. (1988). Social skills: Conceptual and applied aspects of assessment, training, and social validation. In J. C. Witt, S. N. Elliott, & F. M. Gresham (Eds.), *Handbook of behavior therapy in education* (pp. 523–546). New York: Plenum Press.

Gresham, F. M., Elliott, S. N., & Black, F. L. (1987). Teacher-rated social skills of mainstreamed mildly handicapped and nonhandicapped children. *School Psychology Review, 16*, 78–88.

Gustafson, R. N., & Haring, N. G. (1992). Social competence issues in the integration of students with handicaps. In K. A. Haring, D. L. Lovett, & N. G. Haring (Eds.), *Integrated lifecycle services for persons with disabilities* (pp. 20–58). New York: Springer.

Hamre-Nietupski, S., Nietupski, I., & Strathe, M. (1992). Functional life skills, academic skills, and friendship/social relationship development: What do parents of students with moderate/severe/profound disabilities value? *Journal of The Association for Persons with Severe Handicaps, 17,* 53–58.

Hannon, K. E., & Thompson, M. A. (1992). *Life skills workshop: An active program for real-life problem solving.* East Moline, IL: Linguisystems.

Haring, T. G. (1992). The context of social competence: Relations, relationships, and generalization. In S. Odom, S. R. McConnell, & M. A. McEvoy (Eds.), *Social competence of young children with disabilities: Issues and strategies for intervention.* (pp. 307–320). Baltimore: Brookes.

Haring, T. G., Breen, C., Pitts-Conway, V., Lee, M., & Gaylord-Ross, R. (1987). Adolescent peer tutoring and special friend experiences. *Journal of The Association for Persons with Severe Handicaps, 12,* 280–286.

Haring, T. G., & Lovinger, L. (1989). Promoting social interaction through teaching generalized play initiation responses to children with autism. *Journal of The Association for Persons with Severe Handicaps, 14,* 58–67.

Haseltine, B., & Miltenberger, R. G. (1990). Teaching self-protection skills to persons with mental retardation. *American Journal on Mental Retardation, 95,* 188–197.

Hazel, J. S., Schumaker, J. B., Sherman, J. A., & Sheldon-Wildgen, J. B. (1981). *ASSET: A social skills program for adolescents.* Champaign, IL: Research Press.

Holland, A. L. (1980). *Communicative activities of daily living.* Baltimore: University Park Press.

Horner, R. H., Meyer, L., & Fredericks, H. D. (Eds.). (1986). *Educating learners with severe handicaps: Exemplary service strategies* (pp. 289–314). Baltimore: Brookes.

Hunt, P., Alwell, M., & Goetz, L. (1991). Establishing conversational exchanges with family and friends: Moving from training to meaningful communications. *Journal of Special Education, 25,* 305–319.

Jackson, N. F., Jackson, D. A., & Monroe, C. (1983). *Getting along with others: Teaching social effectiveness to children.* Champaign, IL: Research Press.

Johnson, D. W., Johnson, R., & Johnson-Holubnec, E. (1988). *Cooperation in the classroom* (Rev. ed.). Edina, MN: Interaction Books.

Lamkin, J. S. (1980). *Getting started: Career education activities for exceptional students (K–9).* Reston, VA: The Council for Exceptional Children.

Lapadat, J. C. (1991). Pragmatic language skills of students with language and/or learning disabilities: A quantitative synthesis. *Journal of Learning Disabilities, 24,* 147–158.

Larson, K. (1988). *Social Thinking Skills Program.* Santa Barbara: University of California.

Maheady, L., & Sainato, D. M. (1984). Social interaction patterns of high and low status behaviorally disordered students within self-contained classroom settings: A pilot investigation. *Behavioral Disorders, 10,* 20–26.

Matson, J., & Mulick, J. (Eds.). (1991). *Handbook of mental retardation* (2nd ed.). New York: Pergamon Press.

McCormick, L. (1987). Comparison of the effects of a microcomputer activity and toy play on social and communication behaviors of young children. *Journal of the Division of Early Childhood, 11,* 195–205.

McDonough, K. M. (1989). Analysis of the expressive language characteristics of emotionally handicapped students in social situations. *Behavioral Disorders, 14,* 127–139.

McEvoy, M. A., Twardosz, S., & Bishop, N. (1990). Affection activities: Procedures for encouraging young children with handicaps to interact with their peers. *Education and Treatment of Children, 13,* 159–167.

McGinnis, E., & Goldstein, A. P. (1984). *Skillstreaming the elementary school child.* Champaign, IL: Research Press.

McGinnis, E., & Goldstein, A. P., Sprafkin, R. P., & Gershawm, N. J. (1984). *Skillstreaming the elementary school child: A guide for teaching prosocial skills.* Champaign, IL: Research Press.

McGraw, D., & Turnbow, G. N. (1991). *On my own in the community.* East Moline, IL: Linguisystems.

McGraw, D., & Turnbow, G. N. (1992). *On my own at home.* East Moline, IL: Linguisystems.

McKinney, J. D. (1989). Longitudinal research on the behavioral characteristics of children with learning disabilities. *Journal of Learning Disabilities, 22,* 141–150.

Meyer, L. H., Peck, C. A., & Brown, L. (1991). *Critical issues in the lives of people with severe disabilities.* Baltimore: Brookes.

Miller, L. S., Glascoe, L. G., & Kokaska, C. J. (1989). *Life centered career education: Activity book one.* Reston, VA: The Council for Exceptional Children.

Morgan, D. P., & Jenson, W. R. (1988). *Teaching behaviorally disordered students: Preferred practices.* Columbus, OH: Merrill.

Morgan, R. L., Moore, S. C., McSweyn, C., & Salzberg, C. L. (1992). Transition from school to work: Views of secondary special education. *Education and Training in Mental Retardation, 27,* 315–323.

Nietupski, J. A., Hamre-Nietupski, S. M., Clancy, P., & Veerhusen, L. (1986). Guidelines for making simulation as effective adjunct to in vivo community instruction. *Journal of The Association for Persons with Severe Handicaps, 11,* 12–18.

Odom, S. L., McConnell, S. R., & McEvoy, M. A. (Eds.). (1992). *Social competence of young children with disabilities: Issues and strategies for intervention.* Baltimore: Brookes.

Park, H. S., & Gaylord-Ross, R. (1989). A problem-solving approach to social skills training in employment settings with mentally retarded youth. *Journal of Applied Behavior Analysis, 22,* 373–380.

Phillips, E. L. (1985). Social skills: History and prospect. In L. L'Abate & M. A. Milan (Eds.), *Handbook of social skills: Training and research.* New York: Wiley.

Polloway, E. A., & Patton, J. R. (1993). *Strategies for teaching learners with special needs* (5th ed.). New York: Merrill/Macmillan.

Prizant, B., & Bailey, D. B. (1992). Facilitating the acquisition and use of communication skills. In D. Bailey & M. Wolery (Eds.), *Teaching infants and preschoolers with disabilities* (2nd ed., pp. 299–361). New York: Merrill/Macmillan.

Ritter, J. (1993). *The world is a wild place: When you share life experiences.* North Billerica, MA: Curriculum Associates.

Schniedewind, N., & Davidson, E. (1983). *Open minds to equality: A sourcebook of learning activities to promote race, sex, class and age equity.* Englewood Cliffs, NJ: Prentice-Hall.

Schumaker, J. B., Hazel, J. S., & Pederson, C. S. (1989). *Social skills for daily living.* Circle Pines, MN: American Guidance Service.

Shure, M. B. (1992). *I can problem solve: An interpersonal cognitive problem-solving program—Intermediate elementary grades.* Champaign, IL: Research Press.

Shure, M. B. (1992). *I can problem solve: An interpersonal cognitive problem-solving program—Kindergarten and primary grades.* Champaign, IL: Research Press.

Shure, M. B. (1992). *I can problem solve: An interpersonal cognitive problem-solving program—Preschool.* Champaign, IL: Research Press.

Stiefel, B. (1987). *On my own with language.* East Moline, IL: Linguisystems.

Strain, P. S., & Odom, S. L. (1986). Peer social initiations: Effective interventions for social skills development of exceptional children. *Exceptional Children, 52,* 543–551.

Strully, J. L., & Strully, C. F. (1992). The struggle toward inclusion and the fulfillment of friendship. In J. Nisbet (Ed.), *Natural supports in school, at work, and in the community for people with severe disabilities* (pp. 165–177). Baltimore: Brookes.

Valletutti, P. J. (1987). Social problems. In K. A. Kavale, S. R. Forness, & M. Bender (Eds.), *Handbook of learning disabilities: I* (pp. 211–226). Boston: College Hill/Little, Brown.

Vaughan, S. (1991). Social skills enhancement in students with learning disabilities. In B. Wong (Ed.), *Learning about learning disabilities* (pp. 409–440). San Diego: Academic Press.

Vernon, A. (1989). *Thinking, feeling, behaving: An emotional education curriculum for children—Grades 1–6.* Champaign, IL: Research Press.

Vernon, A. (1989). *Thinking, feeling, behaving: An emotional education curriculum for adolescents—Grades 7-12.* Champaign, IL: Research Press.

Walker, H. M., McConnell, S., Holmes, D., Todis, B., Walker, J., & Golden, M. (1983). *The Walker social skills curriculum: The ACCEPTS program.* Austin, TX: PRO-ED.

Wehman, P., Renzaglia, A., & Bates, P. (1985). *Functional living skills for moderately and severely handicapped individuals.* Austin, TX: PRO-ED.

Zachman, L., Barrett, M., Huisingh, R., Orman, J., & Blagden, C. (1992). *Tasks of problem solving: A real life approach to thinking and reasoning—Adolescent.* East Moline, IL: Linguisystems.

Zaragoza, N., Vaughan, S., & McIntosh, R. (1991). Social skills interventions and children with behavior problems: A review. *Behavioral Disorders, 16,* 260–275.

Selected Materials/Resources

KITS/CURRICULAR MATERIALS

- *Back Off, Cool Down, Try Again: Teaching Students How To Control Aggressive Behavior*
  The Council for Exceptional Children
  1920 Association Drive
  Department K6092
  Reston, Virginia 20191-1589

- *Beyond School: "Keeping A Job's The Hard Part"*
  EBSCO Curriculum Materials
  Box 11521
  Birmingham, Alabama 35202-1521

- *The Equip Program—Teaching Youth To Think and Act Responsibly Through a Peer-Helping Approach*
  Research Press
  Department 961
  PO Box 9177
  Champaign, Illinois 61826

- *Getting Along with Others*
  Research Press
  Department 961
  PO Box 9177
  Champaign, Illinois 61826

- *Life Centered Career Education—The Complete Package*
  The Council for Exceptional Children
  1920 Association Drive
  Department K6092
  Reston, Virginia 20191-1589

- *Peer Mediation*
  Research Press
  Department 961
  PO Box 9177
  Champaign, Illinois 61826

- *The Prepare Curriculum—Teaching Prosocial Competencies*
  Research Press
  Department 961
  PO Box 9177
  Champaign, Illinois 61826

- *Reducing Undesirable Behaviors*
  The Council for Exceptional Children
  1920 Association Drive
  Department K6092
  Reston, Virginia 20191-1589

- *Social Skills in the School and Community*
  The Council for Exceptional Children
  1920 Association Drive
  Department K6092
  Reston, Virginia 20191-1589

- *Teaching Social Skills: A Practical Instructional Approach*
  The Council for Exceptional Children
  1920 Association Drive
  Department K6092
  Reston, Virginia 20191-1589

- *Viewpoints: A Guide to Conflict Resolution and Decision Making for Adolescents*
  Research Press
  Department 961
  PO Box 9177
  Champaign, Illinois 61826

- *The Walker Social Skills Curriculum: The ACCEPTS Program*
  PRO-ED, Inc.
  8700 Shoal Creek Boulevard
  Austin, Texas 78757-6897

- *Work Behavior Training Program*
  EBSCO Curriculum Materials
  Box 11521
  Birmingham, Alabama 35202-1521

VIDEOS

- *BeCool I, BeCool II, BeCool III*
  James Stanfield Publishing Company
  PO Box 41058
  Santa Barbara, California 93140

- *Being With People*
  James Stanfield Company
  PO Box 41058
  Santa Barbara, California 93140

- *A Collaborative Approach to Social Skills Instruction*
  The Council for Exceptional Children
  1920 Association Drive
  Department K6092
  Reston, Virginia 20191-1589

- *Community Man*
  James Stanfield Publishing Company
  PO Box 41058
  Santa Barbara, California 93140

- *Employability—Integrating People with Developmental Disabilities into the Workplace*
  Woolworth Corporation
  Northern Light Productions
  Boston, Massachusetts 02215

- *Dealing with Anger*
  Research Press
  Department 961
  PO Box 9177
  Champaign, Illinois 61826

- *First Impressions*
  James Stanfield Publishing Company
  PO Box 41058
  Santa Barbara, California 93140

- *Job Skills for Career Success Series*
  Cambridge Job Search
  PO Box 2153, Department JO3
  Charleston, West Virginia 25328-2153

- *Life After High School for Students with Moderate and Severe Disabilities: Great Expectations and Best Practices*
  Beach Center on Families and Disabilities
  University of Kansas, c/o Life Span Institute
  3111 Hawthorn Hall
  Lawrence, Kansas 66045

- *Mind Your Manners*
  James Stanfield Company
  PO Box 41058
  Santa Barbara, California 93140

- *The Peer Mediation Video Conflict Resolution in Schools*
  Research Press
  Dept. 961
  PO Box 9177
  Champaign, Illinois 61826

- *Social Skills and Self-Esteem*
  Attainment Company
  PO Box 930160
  Verona, Wisconsin 53593-0160

- *Working I—Help Your Students Get and Keep a Job*
  James Stanfield Company
  PO Box 41058
  Santa Barbara, California 93140

Competitive Job-Finding Skills

Monday	
Tuesday	
Wednesday	
Thursday	
Friday	

The transition from a school to a work environment for individuals with disabilities, under the best circumstances, is not an easy process. This is evidenced by the countless numbers of young adults with disabilities who are not successful in their jobs, are unemployed, or are underemployed (President's Committee on the Employment of People with Disabilities, 1990). Siegel and Gaylord-Ross (1991) reported that this situation is not always the result of lack of opportunity, lack of desire for success, or lack of perseverance, but rather of the failure of these individuals to meet the required job skills (Patton et al., 1996) and the demands of the workplace. Although success in employment does not necessarily mean success in life, it does influence many of the factors associated with it.

Transition plans only recently have acknowledged the need for inter-agency involvement. For example, individuals with learning disabilities have traditionally been viewed as having academic deficiencies (Dowdy, 1996), and little emphasis has been placed on their need for employment information and training. In addition, there has long existed a failure to recognize the *needs of the employer:* One tends to forget that employers hire individuals based on their potential to boost productivity and profits. Although many employers are sensitive to and understand the needs and concerns of individuals with disabilities, most would not be in operation if this were their primary business concern (Bender, 1994).

Many individuals with disabilities lead disadvantaged lives because they cannot obtain the economic and social benefits of employment (Muklewicz & Bender, 1988). In addition, finding and retaining employment have also proved difficult for this population. Until recently, few programs have addressed the need to teach job-finding skills and job readiness. Many programs continue to stress skills or tasks that no longer fit into today's changing job world with its continuing demand for high- and low-tech solutions to problems. Traditional school vocational programs for individuals with disabilities have grown outdated in terms of providing the necessary skills present-day employers are seeking. A further complication is that little consistency exists among the content of vocational-oriented programs in different areas of the country, or often within the same state. In essence, the same jobs are not always created equal (Blackorby & Wagner, 1996).

Vocational counselors, rehabilitation counselors, job placement interviewers, and employers continue to suggest that the best way of preparing an individual for a specific job is through some form of on-the-job training, supported by training in job readiness. Specifically, the individual needs to know:

- how to apply for work,

- how to get ready for work, and

- how to get to work.

In addition, the individual needs to

- be aware of following general and specific work rules and policies,

- demonstrate and practice appropriate interpersonal skills in the workplace, and

- understand his or her compensation for work as part of a bill-paying and savings plan.

The objectives of this chapter are based on the need to present the above information in a way that is both practical and responsive to the changing climate of the work environment. This is especially important in that it has become painfully clear that many individuals with disabilities do not possess adequate job-seeking skills. For example, although many students have reasonable work skills and abilities, they often fail to obtain employment because they experience difficulty with the interview process or have problems in completing job application forms. Problems that also require attention include the need to address an individual's poor self-concept, lack of communication skills, and resistance to change. The lack of these skills is especially critical whenever a small number of jobs are available in relation to the number of individuals seeking employment.

Although it is encouraging to see that more individuals with disabilities in the mainstream of work are depicted on television and in advertisements, this often does not reflect reality. Specifically, an increasing number of individuals with disabilities remain unemployed or underemployed. In fact, individuals with disabilities are less likely to be at work today than they were in the 1980s (President's Committee on Employment of the Handicapped, 1987). This is especially meaningful in light of Louis Harris and Associates' (1986) conclusion that being unemployed is the truest definition of what it means to be disabled. Louis Harris and Associates additionally reported that only 25% of persons with disabilities work full time and another 10% work part time. These statistics have not changed appreciably in the 1990s.

Today, individuals with disabilities must enter the world of work in much the same manner as other workers—through a competitive job process. The situations they encounter and the tasks they must successfully address form the basis for the general goals of this unit. It is important to note that the ability to search for employment, and to find and keep a job, often serves as a rite of passage into the mainstream of society. Successful completion of this transition is critical, as it determines eventual levels of personal and economic independence, as well as satisfaction and emotional growth.

A final note for those interested in teaching competitive job-finding skills: There is a critical need to start employment and transition programs at a much earlier age than previously suggested. Repetto and Correa (1996) have joined others in advocating that elementary and middle school personnel should start incorporating transition services early in their programs, when children are open to new ideas and thinking.

The References and Selected Readings provided at the end of this chapter contain numerous ideas for inclusion in a competitive job-finding program. The reader may also wish to review the Selected Materials/ Resources List for additional sources of information or suggestions.

General Goals of This Unit

I. The student will acquire those skills necessary to competitively apply for work.

II. The student will acquire those skills that allow him or her to get ready for work.

III. The student will acquire those skills that allow him or her to go to work.

IV. The student will follow work rules and policies.

V. The student will demonstrate appropriate interpersonal skills in the workplace.

VI. The student will understand his or her compensation for work and develop a bill-paying and savings plan.

GOAL I.

The student will acquire those skills necessary to competitively apply for work.

SPECIFIC OBJECTIVES

The student:

❑ A. Identifies the skills required in job descriptions and/or brochures.

❑ B. Locates the help wanted section of newspapers and identifies job offerings appropriate to his or her interests, needs, and skills.

❑ C. Identifies common abbreviations used in the help wanted section of newspapers and determines what they mean.

❑ D. Locates job announcements information found on business bulletin boards, in work pamphlets, at state and local job banks, and at employment agencies.

❑ E. Obtains a job application form and identifies key words that request personal data information, including name, address, telephone number, Social Security number, and birth date.

❑ F. Obtains and reviews all job-related brochures and forms, including health insurance, pension information, holiday schedules, and other components in an employee benefits package.

SUGGESTED ACTIVITIES

 ## Specific Objective A

The student identifies the skills required in job descriptions and/or brochures.

Teacher Interventions

Primary and Secondary Levels.   Obtain brochures and job descriptions from employment agencies, or from banks, federal and state office buildings, and private institutions. Point out to the student job information and other key facts described in this material.

In reviewing job descriptions, emphasize to the student the skills required in specific job clusters, such as construction, health occupations, graphics and communication media, food preparation, and manufacturing. Emphasize the essential prerequisites for the types of jobs that are parts of these clusters.

After reviewing general job-type descriptions, ask the student where he or she would go for additional information. Steer the student in the direction of the agencies and placement bureaus that concentrate in those specific areas of interest to the student.

Family Interventions

Primary and Secondary Levels.   Ask the parents to share with their youngster job information taken from brochures. Have them emphasize the skills needed for these jobs or, if they are not sure, have them call specific companies for clarification.

Ask the parents to collect a variety of brochures and job descriptions. Suggest they work with their youngster in grouping similar jobs and descriptions into clusters. Have them note in which types of job their youngster seems to show the most interest. This information will be used later as the student develops a job-seeking plan.

Specific Objective B

The student locates the help wanted section of newspapers and identifies job offerings appropriate to his or her interests, needs, and skills.

Teacher Interventions

Primary and Secondary Levels.   Show the student a newspaper that has all of its sections. Point out the contents or index box that lists the major sections of the newspaper. Ask the student to find this box on various newspapers you have brought in.

Using the contents box described above, ask the student to find the section or sections that list the help wanted or jobs available advertisements. See if the student can find the section. If the student has trouble, which often occurs with multiple classified advertisement sections of a Sunday paper, provide help or guidance. A sampling of job listings from a newspaper is provided in Figure 2.1.

Throughout the review of the help wanted section, emphasize the applicability of the job to the student's interests, needs, and skills. Also encourage discussion of other pertinent concerns, such as distance from home, availability of public transportation, and work hours.

(Note: It is important to state at this time that only 15% to 20% of jobs are found as a result of want ads. Tell this fact to the student up front so expectations remain realistic.)

Family Interventions

Primary and Secondary Levels.   Ask the parents to support their youngster in job-search activities by making newspapers readily available. Encourage

---

GENERAL
OFFICE CLERKS
KEYPUNCH OPERATOR
Part Time

Immediate openings in our general office and EDP department. Aptitude for figures required. Must be available and willing to work retail hours. Call for appointment.
363-1000

BEVITZ
FURNITURE CO.
9500 Deereco Rd.
Equal Opportunity Employer M/F

HELP WANTED
DOMESTIC (422)

BUTLER-HOUSEMAN Ref. Exp., Wages $110 week. Must have car. Call Mrs Johnson 547-5411 bet 9 am & 12 noon

---

COMPANION (live-in), retired, for elderly working widow (apt). Refs 844-1243 4-6 or aft 8 PM

COMPANION WANTED light housekeeping for man with broken hip. Call 425-5990

COMPANION to live-in, mature, rec refs. Minimum 1 yr exp. Gen duties, cooking, child care. 40 hr wk. $4.50/hr, free rm/board. Bring copy of ad to Md. State Employment, 1300 N Eutaw

---

POSITION WANTED
DOMESTIC (432)

COMPANION—elderly, Exp. Live-in 5-6 days, Drive. 564-0934.

LADY des. 5 days wk., refs. 548-9855.

NURSING AIDE wishes care of elderly, refs. 655-9685.

BABYSITTERS &
CHILD CARE (442)

BABYSITTER needed Rosedale, Ros Ridge Apts. days. Call 345-8756 aft 6

LICENSED DAY CARE MOTHER Will watch Pre school toddlers in my home. 564-9807.

WTD Depen. daycare for 8 yr old boy. Sparks are. 435-9876

FIGURE 2.1. Sample help wanted advertisements.

them to let their youngster do the activity of searching the want ads, rather than their choosing specific jobs for him or her.

Specific Objective C

The student identifies common abbreviations used in the help wanted section of newspapers and determines what they mean.

Teacher Interventions

Primary and Secondary Levels. As part of class activity, ask the students to review a section of the newspaper that has some specific want ads highlighted or circled. Ask them to identify some of the common abbreviations they find. Provide help if they appear not to understand the abbreviations.

Show the students a list of common abbreviations found in the help wanted section of the newspaper (see Figure 2.2). Ask them to determine

A.M.	= morning		sal.	= salary
P.M.	= afternoon and evening		exc.	= excellent
hrs.	= hours		comm.	= commission
Mon.	= Monday		w/	= with
Tues.	= Tuesday		w/sales	= with sales
Wed.	= Wednesday		w/stds.	= with standards
Thurs.	= Thursday		pd.	= paid
Fri.	= Friday		refs.	= references
wk.	= week		pos.	= position
wkly.	= weekly		mfr.	= manufacturer
mo.	= month		oppt.	= opportunity
eves.	= evenings		co.	= company
yr.	= year		mgr.	= manager
mgmt.	= management		exp.	= experience
ass't	= assistant		exp'd	= experienced
thru	= through		dept.	= department
pref.	= preferred		sts.	= streets
bldgs.	= buildings		equip.	= equipment
dntwn.	= downtown		lic.	= license
transp.	= transportation		appt.	= appointment
gen.	= general		nec.	= necessary
estab.	= established		perm.	= permanent
temp.	= temporary		avail.	= available

FIGURE 2.2. Common help wanted abbreviations.

what these abbreviations mean and how they relate to the job being advertised.

Make a matching game out of a list of abbreviations and their correct definitions. Have the students play the game.

Family Interventions

Primary and Secondary Levels. Ask the parents to share the Sunday newspaper with their youngster (the Sunday edition usually has more help wanted information) and to point out to them how to find the help wanted section. Once that section is found, have them identify several common abbreviations used in the ads.

Ask the parents to make a list with their youngster of all the abbreviations they find in the ads and the definitions or descriptions of these abbreviations.

 ## Specific Objective D

The student locates job announcements information found on business bulletin boards, in work pamphlets, at state and local job banks, and at employment agencies.

Teacher Interventions

Secondary Level. Collect a sampling of job announcement information typically found on business bulletin boards or at employment agencies. Show these announcements to the students and explain where they can be found.

Take the students on a trip into the community. Plan to stop by employment agencies, state office buildings, and places that advertise job openings. After arriving at these places, ask the students to find examples of job announcements. Provide help and guidance, especially in places where this information is not readily available.

Family Interventions

Secondary Level. Ask the parents to share with their youngster any job announcements they may find as they read newspapers or magazines.

When in the community, ask the parents to show their youngster places that may have job announcements. For example, a supermarket often has a bulletin board on which people post short-term jobs typically found in the neighborhood.

Specific Objective E

The student obtains a job application form and identifies key words that request personal data information, including name, address, telephone number, Social Security number, and birth date.

Teacher Interventions

Primary and Secondary Levels. Obtain a selection of job application forms from local businesses in the area. Have the students circle, underline, or list the key information each application is requesting.

Review all the types of key information requested on job application forms. Ask the students to respond to the request for this information by listing the required information. When the request on the application form is unclear, explain what is being requested and how the students can find this information. For example, a Social Security number can be found on one's Social Security card, which is usually in a wallet or a safe place at home.

Provide a good selection of job application forms in different prints and styles. Although most forms require the standard information of the applicant, some forms are worded differently or appear different in design.

Family Interventions

Primary and Secondary Levels. Ask the parents to bring home job application forms from where they work or from places the student may know. Have them work with their youngster in identifying key words found on the application forms.

Ask the parents to show their youngster a completed job application form. Ask them to point out the key information that was requested and the information they provided.

Specific Objective F

The student obtains and reviews all job-related brochures and forms, including health insurance, pension information, holiday schedules, and other components in an employee benefits package.

Teacher Interventions

Primary and Secondary Levels. Initially explain to the students what an employee benefits package is and why it is important to understand every component in it.

Collect examples of all types of benefit information, including health insurance, pension information, holiday schedules, and sick day policies. Ask the students to review each brochure or description and list questions they would like to ask. Answer their questions as best you can or direct them to someone who might have additional information.

Family Interventions

Primary and Secondary Levels. Ask the parents to show their youngster examples of job-related brochures, handouts, or forms they have received as part of working on their job. If they are currently unemployed, they can obtain this information at local job banks or employment agencies.

Ask the parents to demonstrate to their youngster how the information in benefit brochures relates to everyday work. For example, the parents can ask the youngster to identify the holidays or days off that a specific job allows; then the parents can show the youngster a calendar, and point out that the next holiday is a day that employees do not have to report to work.

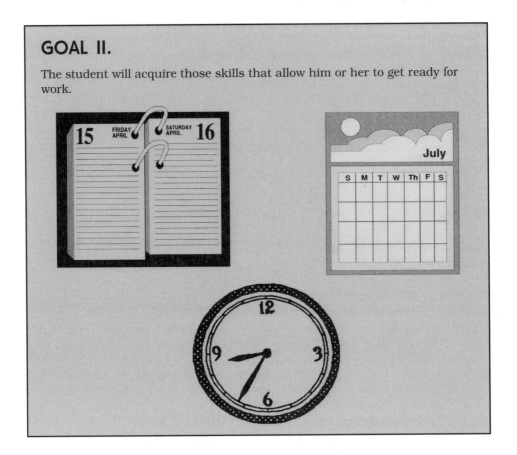

GOAL II.

The student will acquire those skills that allow him or her to get ready for work.

SPECIFIC OBJECTIVES

The student:

❑ A. Uses a calendar to identify work days and holidays when he or she does not have to go to work.

❑ B. Follows a daily wake-up schedule that makes it possible for him or her to wash, dress, and groom him- or herself and be ready for work.

❑ C. Identifies time by the hour, half hour, and other intervals, on clocks and watches, to be prepared to leave for work on time.

❑ D. Selects the type of clothing and accessories needed from a specially prepared work clothing list for specific jobs.

❏ E. Uses toiletries and grooming aids according to the directions appearing on them.

❏ F. Prepares a nutritious breakfast from recipes and other written sources.

SUGGESTED ACTIVITIES

 ## Specific Objective A

The student uses a calendar to identify work days and holidays when he or she does not have to go to work.

Teacher Interventions

Primary and Secondary Levels. Obtain a list of typical employee holidays that are provided in benefits packages. Use that list to chart the actual days on which the holidays fall on a calendar or appointment book page (see Figure 2.3). Review with the student where the holidays occur during specific months of the year.

Explain to the student the importance of working the days immediately before and after a holiday. Tell them that many companies are reluctant to grant vacation time for those specific days. Written medical excuses are often required.

After reviewing general job-type descriptions, ask the student where to go for additional information. Steer the student in the direction of the agencies and placement bureaus that concentrate in the student's preferred job areas.

Family Interventions

Primary and Secondary Levels. Ask the parents to share job information taken from brochures with their youngster. Have them emphasize the skills needed for these jobs or, if they are not sure, have them call specific companies for clarification.

Ask the parents to collect a variety of brochures and job descriptions. Suggest they work with their youngster in grouping similar jobs and descriptions into clusters. Have them make note of the type of job in which their youngster seems to show the most interest. This information will be used later as the student develops a job-seeking plan.

February 1997
S	M	T	W	T	F	S
						1
2	3	4	5	6	7	8
9	10	11	12	13	14	15
16	17	18	19	20	21	22
23	24	25	26	27	28	

March 1997
S	M	T	W	T	F	S
						1
2	3	4	5	6	7	8
9	10	11	12	13	14	15
16	17	18	19	20	21	22
23	24	25	26	27	28	29
30	31					

2 - 5 January

THURSDAY 2

8 _____ 1 _____

9 _____ 2 _____

10 _____ 3 _____

11 _____ 4 _____

12 _____ 5 _____

Evening

FRIDAY 3

8 _____ 1 _____

9 _____ 2 _____

10 _____ 3 _____

11 _____ 4 _____

12 _____ 5 _____

Evening

4 SATURDAY   **SUNDAY 5**

FIGURE 2.3. Sample appointment book page.

Specific Objective B

The student follows a daily wake-up schedule that makes it possible for him or her to wash, dress, and groom him- or herself and be ready for work.

Teacher Interventions

Primary and Secondary Levels. Discuss with the student the specific tasks he or she needs to do after waking up on a workday morning. Provide examples such as the need to wash or shower, dress, and groom oneself. Also include activities such as preparing and/or allowing time for breakfast, checking to make sure any needed materials for work are ready and available, and allowing time to hear weather reports. Make a checklist of the above tasks.

Stress to the student the importance of trying, whenever possible, to have certain tasks done or materials available the night before. Examples include prepacking a lunch, having transportation and emergency money available, and having inclement weather clothing or accessories available.

Family Interventions

Primary and Secondary Levels. Ask the parents to support your efforts to develop a wake-up schedule for their youngster. It is important that the parents allow the youngster independence and act as a monitor rather than a helper.

Suggest that the parents can help by doing such things as making sure bathrooms are available in the morning during the beginning days of using a wake-up schedule. They should try as much as possible to troubleshoot any problem areas that might create difficulties or frustrations for their youngster. Stress that the process needs to be as smooth and self-reinforcing as possible so the youngster can adapt to a routine.

Specific Objective C

The student identifies time by the hour, half hour, and other intervals, on clocks and watches, to be prepared to leave for work on time.

Teacher Interventions

Primary and Secondary Levels. Ask the students to bring to class a small clock with an alarm from home, preferably one they have in their bedroom. You may wish to bring in other alarm clocks for the students to see. Ask them to practice telling time with the clocks.

Demonstrate how to set the alarms of a variety of clocks. After the demonstration, ask each student to set his or her own alarm for a time he or she would typically want to be awakened in the morning. Emphasize the importance of including some extra time when determining an optimal wake-up time. This may be an appropriate opportunity to introduce the "snooze" alarm option on many clocks. Have the students practice setting various alarm times on their clocks.

Discuss with the students potential situations that may cause them to need to change the time or alarm setting on their clock. Examples to discuss include a change to or from daylight savings time, a power outage that affects a clock without a battery backup, and vacation time when the student may wish to sleep longer in the morning.

Family Interventions

Primary and Secondary Levels. Ask the parents to help their youngster purchase an alarm clock if he or she does not already have one. Suggest they purchase one with a large dial and large numbers so the time is easily read, and with few accessories and knobs and buttons to avoid confusion.

Ask the parents to show their youngster how to set the clock to wake up in the morning.

To check that the time is accurate on the clock, have parents call the "time" telephone number in their local area. This will give them the exact time. If this is not possible, have parents show their youngster where the exact time can be found (e.g., television channels that show running time, radio programs that have advertisements on the quarter hour).

Specific Objective D

The student selects the type of clothing and accessories needed from a specially prepared work clothing list for specific jobs.

Teacher Interventions

Secondary Level. Create a list of special clothing that is associated with special types of jobs. Show the student pictures of workers requiring special clothing (e.g., a construction worker, a hospital employee). Point out specific types of clothing or accessories that would be required for specific types of jobs (e.g., steel-toed shoes, heavy-duty gloves).

Take the students on a trip into the community. Plan to stop by job sites where workers are wearing special types of clothing. Point out this clothing to the students. Provide help and guidance in explaining why specific clothing is required for some jobs and not for others.

Family Interventions

Secondary Level. Ask the parents to share with their youngster any job announcements they may find, as they read newspapers or magazines. As they review the announcements, have them explain the types of clothing that may be necessary for specific jobs.

Ask the parents to save catalogs or magazines that advertise different types of work clothing and accessories. Suggest that they review these catalogs with their youngster, emphasizing why these specific types of clothing or accessories are needed.

Suggest that parents, when watching television, point out to their youngster workers in different types of jobs who are wearing appropriate work clothes.

 ## Specific Objective E

The student uses toiletries and grooming aids according to the directions appearing on them.

Teacher Interventions

Primary and Secondary Levels. Obtain a selection of toiletries and grooming aids. Ask the student to indicate the type of toiletries he or she uses (e.g., toothpaste, mouthwash, dental floss, deodorant). When appropriate, and in an appropriate place and time, ask the student to demonstrate the use of these toiletries. Make suggestions if the student is not correctly following the specific directions outlined on or in the package.

Review all the types of key information found on different types of bathroom and grooming aids. Ask the students to identify specific aids and explain why they need to use them. Provide guidance and information when needed.

Family Interventions

Primary and Secondary Levels. Ask the parents to take their youngster shopping with them to the supermarket or drugstore. Ask them to point out specific toiletries or grooming aids and explain their use.

Ask the parents to share with their youngster newspaper inserts that advertise toiletries and other grooming aids. Compare the sizes and prices of items as a way of adding consumer knowledge to the activity. Suggest that they point out to their youngster that buying a large amount of any toiletry might not be advisable until they know that they like it, they are not allergic to it, and it is reasonably priced.

 ## Specific Objective F

The student prepares a nutritious breakfast from recipes and other written sources.

Teacher Interventions

Primary and Secondary Levels. Initially explain to the students the importance of eating a nutritious breakfast before going to work. Provide examples of nutritious foods they might select.

Using simple recipes from a cookbook or other source, have them prepare and eat a nutritious breakfast. During this activity, ask them to make suggestions as to what foods they might substitute for future breakfasts.

Family Interventions

Primary and Secondary Levels. Ask the parents to model appropriate eating habits by preparing nutritious breakfasts for their youngster. Suggest that they permit the youngster to prepare a breakfast for the family or visitors using recipes that include nutritious food groups.

When eating breakfast in the community, stress that the parents emphasize nutritious foods when ordering.

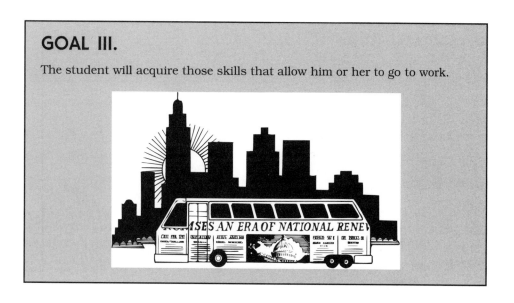

SPECIFIC OBJECTIVES

The student:

❑ A. Meets buses, car pools, and shuttle services after reviewing written departure schedules.

❑ B. Pays the correct fare on a taxi meter when using a taxi (in special instances) to go to work, and tips the driver appropriately.

❑ C. Takes the correct bus or other public transportation to work, using numeral and destination signs on public transportation vehicles.

❑ D. Selects alternate routes to get to work.

❑ E. Obeys traffic signs and signals and follows prescribed routes while driving to work.

❑ F. Locates the building or plant in which he or she works using street signs and address designations on buildings.

❑ G. Obeys signs on entrance doors leading to the workplace.

❑ H. Operates the buttons on self-service elevators and goes to the exact location of his or her job.

SUGGESTED ACTIVITIES

 ## Specific Objective A

The student meets buses, car pools, and shuttle services after reviewing written departure schedules.

Teacher Interventions

Secondary Level.   Obtain a list of bus schedules or shuttle services that operate in the student's general living area. Highlight those that will allow him or her to be dropped off at or close to work. Review the schedules with the student. (Figure 2.4 is an example of employee shuttle schedules.)

Practice meeting the bus or shuttle at the exact pickup spot at the appropriate time. Emphasize the importance of arriving early and allowing for extra time during inclement weather.

Discuss with the student the use of car pools. Emphasize the need to be prompt in meeting a car pool, especially because other riders depend on arriving to and leaving from work on time. Ask someone who is familiar with car pools to come in and discuss the advantages and disadvantages of using a car pool.

Whatever system of transportation is decided upon, plan backup systems in case public transportation or car pools are not operating on a specific day.

Family Interventions

Secondary Level.   Ask the parents to share transportation schedules and brochures with their youngster. Have them emphasize how to find information on these schedules. If the parents are not sure how to accurately read the schedules, have them call specific companies for clarification.

Ask the parents to follow in a car, with their youngster, the system of transportation they are considering using. Along the way, ask them to point out specific landmarks as a way of familiarizing their youngster with the daily route.

FAIRMOUNT SHUTTLE #1 REGULAR SHUTTLE

Departs 1750 E. Fairmount	Departs 707 N. Broadway
7:00	7:10
7:20	7:30
7:40	7:50
8:00	8:10
8:20	8:30
8:40	9:00
9:15	9:30
9:45	10:00
10:15	10:30
10:45	11:00
11:15	11:30
11:45	12:30
Drivers Lunch	1:00
12:45	1:30
1:15	2:00
1:45	2:30
2:15	3:00
2:45	3:30
3:15	4:00
3:45	4:20
4:10	4:40
4:30	5:00
4:50	5:20
5:10	

FAIRMOUNT SHUTTLE #2 PARKING LOT SHUTTLE

Departs 1750 E. Fairmount	Departs 707 N. Broadway
6:30	6:40
6:50	7:00
7:10	7:20
7:30	7:40
7:50	8:00
8:10	8:20
8:30	8:40
8:50	
4:20	4:10
4:40	4:30
5:00	4:50
5:20	5:10
5:40	5:30
6:00	5:50
6:20	6:10
	6:30

Scheduled mail pick ups are: 10:00 am and 2:00 pm at Broadway
10:15 am and 2:15 pm at Fairmount

PRESIDENT STREET PARKING LOT SHUTTLE

Departs President St.	Departs 707 N. Broadway
6:45	7:00
7:15	7:30
7:45	8:00
8:15	8:30
8:45	
4:30	4:15
5:00	4:45
5:30	5:15
	5:45
	6:15

BROADWAY - BIDDLE ST. SHUTTLE

Departs 2931 E. Biddle St.	Departs 707 N. Broadway
7:15	7:30
7:45	8:00
8:15	8:30
8:45	9:00
9:15	9:30
9:45	10:00
10:15	10:30
10:45	11:00
11:15	11:30
11:45	12:00
12:15	Drivers Lunch
Drivers Lunch	1:00
1:15	1:30
1:45	2:00
2:15	2:30
2:45	3:00
3:15	3:30
3:45	4:00
4:15	4:30
4:45	5:00
5:15	5:30

Scheduled mail pick ups are:
10:00 am and 2:00 pm at Broadway
10:15 am and 2:15 pm at Biddle St.

BROADWAY - TRIAD SHUTTLE

Departs 333 Cassell Drive	Departs 707 N. Broadway
	7:30
7:45	8:15
8:45	9:15
9:45	10:15
10:45	11:15
11:45	Drivers Lunch
Drivers Lunch	12:45
1:15	1:45
2:15	2:45
3:15	3:45
4:15	4:45
5:15	

This schedule subject to change without notice.

FIGURE 2.4. Sample employee shuttle schedules.

119

Specific Objective B

The student pays the correct fare on a taxi meter when using a taxi (in special instances) to go to work, and tips the driver appropriately.

Teacher Interventions

Secondary Level. Discuss with the student those special instances when he or she may need to take a taxi to work. This would include times when routine public transportation or car pools are not available. Discuss the need to have money available to pay the fare and a tip for the driver.

Show the student how to call for a taxi. Go on a taxi ride with the student. During the ride, point out the taxi meter and how it operates, and the location of the driver's identification. After the ride, suggest the amount of tip the driver should receive. Explain the purpose of the tip and what is considered a reasonable amount.

Family Interventions

Secondary Level. Ask the parents, when appropriate, to take their youngster with them when they take a taxi. Ask them to demonstrate how to tell the taxi driver the destination and how to pay the fare and tip. Have them model good passenger behavior while riding in the cab.

Ask the parents to show their youngster how to look up the telephone numbers of taxi services in the telephone book. Ask them to call a specific taxi service and ask for the approximate one-way cost of a trip to their work. Have them tell their youngster that this information will allow one to know in advance how much money one should take when planning to ride in a taxi to work.

Specific Objective C

The student takes the correct bus or other public transportation to work, using numeral and destination signs on public transportation vehicles.

Teacher Interventions

Secondary Level. Find out the location of the bus stop(s) within the general vicinity of where the student may obtain work. Visit the bus stop(s) and wait for a bus to appear. Point out to the student the numeral and destination signs on the bus. Explain the reason for the signs and the importance of locating them before traveling on a bus.

Explain to the student what he or she should do if uncertain of the bus destination signs due to defective letters, or if the signs are difficult to read because of inclement weather. Demonstrate how the student should ask the bus driver if this is the correct bus.

Family Interventions

Secondary Level. Ask the parents to use a bus as part of a family trip into the community or an outing. Have them point out the signs on the bus before they enter.

Ask the parents to show their youngster examples of bus schedules. Select at least one that has a picture of a bus on the front. Suggest that they show their youngster how to find the bus number and its destination in the tables and indicate where this information would be found on the bus pictured on the cover.

To check that the table is accurate, ask the parent to point out the sentence on the brochure that provides information concerning the dates for which the table is valid. If this cannot be found on the brochure, have them show their youngster how to call the bus company to verify that the schedule is current.

 Specific Objective D

The student selects alternate routes to get to work.

Teacher Interventions

Secondary Level. Suggest to the student that there may be times when the routine transportation he or she is taking to work will not be operating. Ask him or her to provide examples of when this might occur. Provide help when necessary by suggesting situations when this might occur (e.g., mechanical breakdown of transportation vehicles, road repaving requiring alternate routes, inclement weather).

Take the student on at least one alternate route to his or her work. If needed, select a different bus route. During the trip, point out landmarks or places that can be easily recognizable when this route is followed.

Family Interventions

Secondary Level. Ask the parents to share with their youngster other ways and routes to get to his or her work. For the youngster who is capable of understanding maps and directions, have the parents sketch or outline on a map these alternate routes.

Ask the parents to practice these alternate routes by taking their youngster on them. Stress the importance of pointing out landmarks and other places that their youngster would find easily recognizable, should he or she have to take these routes.

 Specific Objective E

The student obeys traffic signs and signals and follows prescribed routes while driving to work.

Teacher Interventions

Secondary Level. Review with the student who drives the routine signs and signals he or she will encounter on the way to work. Check to see if the student knows what to do when approaching these signs and signals and provide additional information or clarification as needed.

Ride along as the student drives to work. Monitor how he or she does when approaching signs and signals. Make notes of additional information you may wish to provide at a later time.

Find a section of the community that has a detour sign. Ask the student to drive that specific route and to follow the directions of the detour. Point out that at some time, his or her work route may have a detour due to an accident that closes the road, road repair, and so on, and he or she will have to know how to follow a similar type of detour to work.

Family Interventions

Secondary Level. Ask the parents to model for their youngster the appropriate behavior when they come to signs and signals. Suggest that they point out specific traffic rules and laws as they drive.

Ask the parents to review and share with their youngster specific traffic rules that pertain to areas near his or her work. For example, if the youngster is to pass a school zone, he or she needs to know about maximum speed, what to do when behind a school bus, and so on. Ask them to role-play with their youngster different situations that may occur during inclement weather, at road hazards, or during an emergency situation.

 ## Specific Objective F

The student locates the building or plant in which he or she works using street signs and address designations on buildings.

Teacher Interventions

Secondary Level.   Initially explain to the student where street signs can be found in the neighborhood where he or she works. Go with the student and point out these signs. Emphasize that in some instances a sign may not be readable or is so damaged it cannot be identified. Show the student how to find the next sign to confirm that he or she is still going in the correct direction.

Visit the student's working place. Chart or write down the different signs found on the building(s) and/or on marquees in front of the building. Review these signs and designations with the student.

Family Interventions

Secondary Level.   Before their youngster starts a job, ask the parents to take him or her to the place of work. While driving there, have the parents point out street signs and address designations on the buildings.

To reinforce their youngster's knowledge of the directions to his or her workplace, have the parents drive to the workplace on a nonworkday, such as Sunday. Ask them to allow the youngster to direct them to where he or she works without any cues or help from them. If the youngster has difficulty, the parents should stop and send the youngster into a gas station or grocery store for directions. Emphasize that parents should teach their youngster to be aware of safety, if he or she seeks additional directions or help.

Specific Objective G

The student obeys signs on entrance doors leading to the workplace.

Teacher Interventions

Secondary Level. Make a list or a videotape of the signs the student may encounter on entrance doors or partitions in an actual work site. Review these signs with the student and answer any questions he or she may have.

Monitor the student as he or she goes into the actual workplace. Check to see if the student obeys the appropriate signs on entrance doors. Explain door signs that have the word "caution," or that designate which personnel are allowed, and explain what to do at entrances that require a special identification card for entry.

Family Interventions

Secondary Level. Ask the parents to discuss with their youngster any questions he or she has about signs on doors at work that he or she might not understand.

During visits for medical checkups or other appointments, ask the parents to point out signs on entrance doors to their youngster. Ask them to see if their youngster knows what the signs mean. If not, have them provide the information.

Specific Objective H

The student operates the buttons on self-service elevators and goes to the exact location of his or her job.

Teacher Interventions

Secondary Level. List different stores or buildings with self-service elevators. Take the student on trips that require visiting these buildings and using the self-service elevators. While there, point out the different types of elevators and panels that have the floor buttons. Ask the student to go to a specific floor by using the elevator and pushing the correct button, and then to a specific location on the floor. If this is a practice exercise, make sure this activity is performed at a time when the elevator is not busy, so people using the elevator to get to work will not be late or inconvenienced.

When appropriate, practice with the student using an elevator to get to his or her exact job location. Try to use the elevator when it is least busy (i.e., before work, on weekends if the place is open, after work).

Family Interventions

Secondary Level. When in the community, ask the parents to take their youngster to a building with a self-service elevator and a place they need to visit. Suggest that they tell their youngster to be in charge of the elevator and help them to the correct floor.

Ask the parents to monitor how their youngster uses the self-service elevators. If their youngster is doing it incorrectly, or "playing" with the buttons, have them correct him or her and demonstrate how to do it properly.

GOAL IV.

The student will follow work rules and policies.

SPECIFIC OBJECTIVES

The student:

❑ A. Locates the number of his employer or employer representative in his or her personal telephone directory and calls that person if unable to report to work or when he or she is going to be late.

❑ B. Follows directions on the time clock and time card and verifies the time card after punching in and out to make sure it has been correctly stamped.

❑ C. Identifies work clothing, shop coats, and other personal items by name tags and labels.

❑ D. Obeys health rules pertinent to his or her job.

❑ E. Obeys safety rules pertinent to his or her job.

❑ F. Follows the directions and safety instructions on flammable and other dangerous substances with which he or she works.

❑ G. Follows posted directions and routing signs for fire escape procedures and uses them during a fire emergency and fire drill.

❑ H. Follows the operating and safety instructions for electric tools, appliances, and machinery used on the job.

❑ I. Locates signs leading to the supervisor, nurse, or other significant person's office and goes there when necessary.

SUGGESTED ACTIVITIES

Specific Objective A

The student locates the number of his employer or employer representative in his or her personal telephone directory and calls that person if unable to report to work or when he or she is going to be late.

Teacher Interventions

Secondary Level. Discuss with the student the need to have telephone numbers available in case he or she has to call a supervisor or other person to report an illness or other emergency that would make him or her late or absent from work. Have the student find and make a list of these numbers.

Go with the student to an office supply store and review the different types of pocket telephone directories available. Suggest the advantages and disadvantages of different types, and purchase one that seems appropriate. Ask the student to record important telephone numbers in the directory.

Advise the student to call the teacher using the information in his or her personal telephone directory when the student is ill or going to be late for school. If he or she is ill or will be late on a workday, advise the student to call his or her supervisor.

Family Interventions

Secondary Level. Ask the parents to provide telephone numbers of individuals their youngster might need to contact in case of illness or lateness for work. Suggest that they review this information and explain to their youngster the importance of contacting the employer in these special cases.

Ask the parents to note if their youngster calls his or her employer when ill or late. If he or she forgets to call, suggest that parents remind the youngster and review the importance of this task.

 ## Specific Objective B

The student follows directions on the time clock and time card and verifies the time card after punching in and out to make sure it has been correctly stamped.

Teacher Interventions

Secondary Level. Bring to class a variety of time cards with dates and times previously stamped on them. Show the student the cards and see if he or she can identify the dates and time notations. Initially, you may need to point out the date and time in terms of color, abbreviation, or location on the card.

Arrange to take the student to a company that uses a time clock and cards for its employees. Demonstrate how the time clock works and show the student the type of time card used. Have the student practice putting in a time card correctly and pushing the mechanism to stamp the card.

After stamping the time card, ask the student to check it for accuracy. Point out the time and compare it with the time on his or her watch or on a clock in the workplace. Also, have the student check the date by comparing it to a calendar or the date on that day's newspaper.

Family Interventions

Secondary Level.   Ask the parents to inquire if their youngster is using a time clock at work. Have them provide information or help if he or she is having trouble using it.

Suggest to the parents that they sit down with their youngster and compare the hours he or she has worked as listed on a paycheck stub with the hours he is arriving to and departing from work. If there is a significant discrepancy, they should suggest that their youngster review his or her time card for any possible errors.

Specific Objective C

The student identifies work clothing, shop coats, and other personal items by name tags and labels.

Teacher Interventions

Secondary Level.   Show the student various labels and name tags that are typically found on work clothing. Point out the way labels are used for identifying personal items.

Explain to the student that labels used for identification on work clothing or other materials usually require that workers write their names or initials on the label with a waterproof and/or indelible pencil or marker. Ask the student to explain why this is required. Provide assistance with answers (e.g., repeated washings will not remove the name or initials, identification might reduce clothing mix-ups or theft).

Family Interventions

Secondary Level.   Ask the parents to assist their youngster in placing labels or name tags on appropriate work clothing and other personal items. Have them go through closets at home or other places where work clothing might be stored to see how this has previously been done.

When shopping in the community, ask the parents to take their youngster to a store that sells work clothing. While there, have them demonstrate where labels are typically found on work clothing, or where a label might be sewn or attached at a later time.

For the youngster who has difficulty reading, suggest that the parents decide with the child what an age-appropriate symbol or rebus might be to place on a label. Have them use this symbol when appropriate on a variety of items.

Specific Objective D

The student obeys health rules pertinent to his or her job.

Teacher Interventions

Secondary Level. Review with the student the specific health rules that should be followed for jobs in which he or she has shown an interest. For example, jobs involving food handling or preparation require strict adherence to cleanliness through hand washing, appropriate dress, hair length, and so on.

Take the student on at least one trip to a work site that includes jobs similar to the ones in which he or she has shown interest. Point out the health rules that are being followed or that should be followed while observing the job.

Place the student on a temporary job assignment in the school that requires health rules to be followed. Evaluate the student on how well he or she follows the rules and make suggestions when improvement is needed.

Family Interventions

Secondary Level. If appropriate, ask the parents to review with their youngster different health rules and procedures they see others following while they are dining or shopping in the community.

Ask the parents to explain why health rules must be followed, for some youngsters need added information or clarification.

Specific Objective E

The student obeys safety rules pertinent to his or her job.

Teacher Interventions

Secondary Level. Show the student a variety of pictures of individuals in different jobs. Review with the student the different safety rules that might be required for these jobs. If possible, take a trip to visit some of these jobs in action.

Obtain a film or films from different agencies that promote job training. After viewing the film, ask the student to comment on the various safety rules he or she saw followed or not followed. Use that information as a basis for a discussion about obeying safety rules.

Family Interventions

Secondary Level. Ask the parents to model appropriate safety rule behavior when they are doing jobs with their youngster. Suggest that they point out specific rules as they work.

Suggest that the parents plan an activity that involves observing workers in the community. For example, they can drive through their neighborhood to find someone painting a house or doing roofing repair. While observing these workers and jobs, have them ask their youngster to note the safety rules they are following. After returning home, or at some later time, have them encourage their youngster to make a list of some of the safety rules they witnessed.

Specific Objective F

The student follows the directions and safety instructions on flammable and other dangerous substances with which he or she works.

Teacher Interventions

Secondary Level. Initially explain to the student why it is important to follow instructions on flammable and other dangerous substances. Point out or show pictures or a film of what can happen if directions are not followed (e.g., spray painting near an open flame).

Visit different workplaces within the school that use flammable or dangerous substances. In many instances the maintenance department of a school can help to set up this visit. Point out how the substances are handled and the safety procedures being used. Ask the student to chart or write down what he or she sees.

Family Interventions

Secondary Level. Ask the parents to identify specific products they use in their home that might be considered hazardous or flammable (e.g., cleaning products, paint removers, products under pressure in cans). Suggest that they explain to their youngster how these products are to be used, including their safe storage.

To reinforce knowledge of how to work with materials in a safe fashion, ask the parents to review with their youngster the directions found on a variety of items they have collected that require safety in their use and/or storage. Recommend to the parents that they preview the directions first, so they will be prepared to clarify any words or directions that might be confusing. Also ask them to emphasize that materials with dates should not be used beyond their expiration date as they might become volatile, dangerous, or ineffective.

Specific Objective G

The student follows posted directions and routing signs for fire escape procedures and uses them during a fire emergency and fire drill.

Teacher Interventions

Secondary Level. Read, review, and become familiar with the directions of the school's fire emergency plan. Check to make sure that signs are posted where they are supposed to be and walk through the plan. Once you are familiar with the plan and procedures, share this information with the student in a similar fashion.

Plan a fire drill after the student has indicated that he or she is aware of the fire plan and procedure. Conduct the drill, and evaluate with the student the effectiveness of the drill. Ask the student how the drill could be improved (i.e., getting out quicker).

Family Interventions

Secondary Level. Ask the parents to discuss with their youngster where they might find fire drill signs or procedures outside of their home. If appropriate, suggest that they take their youngster to the movie theater, where they can point out exit signs and arrows leading to a fire evacuation route.

Ask the parents to obtain information on fire emergencies and drills from their local fire department or the public library. Have them review with their youngster the different books, films, or brochures that are available on this subject.

Specific Objective H

The student follows the operating and safety instructions for electric tools, appliances, and machinery used on the job.

Teacher Interventions

Secondary Level. Make a list of different tools the student might encounter on a specific job. Take these tools and their operating instructions into class. Demonstrate appropriate and safe use of these tools.

When appropriate, practice with the student using a variety of tools, as he or she builds projects in class. Reinforce safe procedures the student is using and correct any unsafe ones. No student should be allowed to use a tool, appliance, or machinery in an unsafe fashion. (Note: It is of special importance to make sure tools and machinery are correctly working and in good condition before any activity is started.)

Family Interventions

Secondary Level. Ask the parents to review with their youngster the instructions on tools or appliances he or she uses at home. If the instructions are not available, send for them or find and copy similar ones in a store that sells the same or similar tools or appliances.

Ask the parents to monitor how their youngster uses tools and appliances (e.g., microwave ovens) that he or she uses both on the job and at home. Ask the parents to make suggestions and correct any habits that might be considered unsafe.

Specific Objective I

The student locates signs leading to the supervisor, nurse, or other significant person's office and goes there when necessary.

Teacher Interventions

Secondary Level. Tour the school with the student. As part of the tour, point out the signs that designate where the nurse, principal, or other significant persons' offices are located. After the tour, and at a later time, ask the student to take a note to one of those places visited on the tour, and monitor how well he or she performs this task.

When appropriate, and on trips to visit job settings, point out the different signs leading to offices or areas. With the student, follow some of the signs to see if the actual office is there. (In some cases, an office is moved without the signs being changed.)

Family Interventions

Secondary Level.   Ask the parents to encourage their youngster to read signs while in office buildings or other facilities. For example, when paying a bill in person, have them take their youngster with them and demonstrate how they follow signs to find the person or place where the bill is to be paid.

Ask the parents to monitor how their youngster independently locates and follows signs. Places to practice use of signs include office buildings, malls, airports, and parking garages. Ask the parents to help if the youngster appears to be having difficulty.

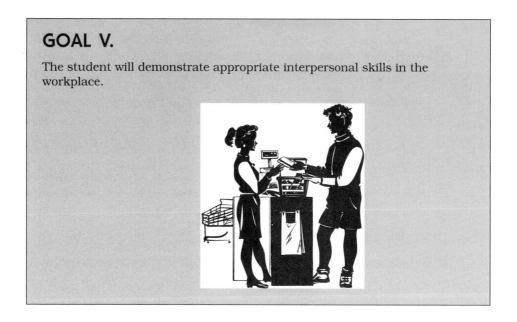

GOAL V.

The student will demonstrate appropriate interpersonal skills in the workplace.

SPECIFIC OBJECTIVES

The student:

❑ A.   Reviews work memos and, when appropriate, shares key information found on them with coworkers.

❑ B. Selects a personal label or rebus and puts it on his or her property.

❑ C. Leaves personal belongings, food, or special work articles in his or her locker or other assigned storage area.

❑ D. Follows the posted rules and/or procedures for returning tools, equipment, and unused materials to assigned areas, tool rooms, or sheds.

❑ E. On a voluntary basis, participates as an observer or participant in work sports activities.

❑ F. On a voluntary basis, takes his or her turn in treating coworkers to coffee and/or other beverages and snacks, as is the customary practice of the work group.

❑ G. Locates restrooms, telephones, exits and entrances, snack bars, and cafeterias by signs designating these areas, and uses them appropriately.

❑ H. Operates vending machines as desired during breaks and, when appropriate, shares contents with coworkers or friends.

❑ I. Shares company newspapers, bulletins, and magazines during leisure breaks.

❑ J. Functions in teams and works well with individuals from diverse backgrounds.

SUGGESTED ACTIVITIES

Specific Objective A

The student reviews work memos and, when appropriate, shares key information found on them with coworkers.

Teacher Interventions

Secondary Level. Provide the student with a variety of work memos from various work environments. Point out to him or her key information found on the memos, such as meeting times, dates, and places.

Review with the student work memos that describe company policies or regulations. Ask him or her to share this information with a fellow student and check on his or her accuracy in explaining and interpreting what he or she has read.

Provide the student with examples of work memos that describe safety procedures or safety drills. Review key information and clarify any questions he or she may have regarding the specifics of the memo.

Family Interventions

Secondary Level. Ask the parents to review with their youngster any correspondence received as part of his or her work experience. Suggest that they check on whether their youngster fully comprehends the content and provide assistance if clarification is needed.

Ask the parents to have their youngster share with them, when appropriate, work memos he or she has received. Suggest that they ask their youngster to point out the key information in these memos and provide assistance if he or she has difficulty doing this.

 ## Specific Objective B

The student selects a personal label or rebus and puts it on his or her property.

Teacher Interventions

Secondary Level. Take to class a variety of label makers and labels that are typically used to identify a worker's property. Ask the student to select a label he or she would like and to personalize it with his or her name or a rebus. Suggest that the student put these labels on his or her property and belongings.

Arrange to take the student to a company or manufacturing plant that requires employees to wear a variety of special clothing or uniforms. While there, point out the labels that are on specific clothing and ask the student to explain why he or she thinks they are necessary.

Family Interventions

Secondary Level. Ask the parents to reinforce the use of labels on property their youngster is taking to work or other places that might have similar property. Suggest that parents emphasize that labels should be short, clear, age appropriate, and whenever possible permanent or comprised of long-lasting material.

Specific Objective C

The student leaves personal belongings, food, or special work articles in his or her locker or other assigned storage area.

Teacher Interventions

Secondary Level. Visit work sites that have assigned areas for storage of personal property, such as lockers or store rooms. Point out and explain the need for these areas.

Visit work sites that require, for security and other reasons, that articles brought to work be "checked" at a specific place. These items may include bags, coats, radios, cameras, or other materials that are not allowed in the actual work environment.

Family Interventions

Secondary Level. If the company where the youngster is working has a refrigerator or cold storage for lunches, ask the parents, when appropriate, to assist their youngster in making a lunch he or she will take to work. Suggest that they make a lunch that requires refrigeration. Ask them to remind their youngster to store this lunch in the department or company refrigerator when he or she arrives at work.

When shopping in stores or malls in the community, ask the parents to point out to their youngster possible places where employees might store their personal belongings. Suggest that they emphasize that most of these places might be out of sight and in back rooms.

Specific Objective D

The student follows the posted rules and/or procedures for returning tools, equipment, and unused materials to assigned areas, tool rooms, or sheds.

Teacher Interventions

Secondary Level. Review with the student specific rules or procedures that exist at his or her workplace or a prospective workplace regarding the returning of tools, equipment, and materials to appropriate places. Alternatively, take the student on at least one trip to a work site that includes jobs similar to the ones in which he or she has shown an interest. Point out the rules being followed or that should be followed for returning tools, equipment, and materials.

Place the student on a temporary job assignment in the school that has procedures and rules for returning tools, equipment, and materials. Evaluate the student on how well he or she follows the rules and make suggestions when improvement is needed.

Family Interventions

Secondary Level. When appropriate, ask the parents to review with their youngster different work rules and procedures that he or she might not fully understand.

Ask the parents to review with their youngster specific work-related booklets, manuals, or guides given to them as part of their orientation to a new job. Suggest that they explain to their youngster why these rules must be followed. For example, the returning of tools to a tool room will allow a supervisor to see that he or she is a responsible individual and has respect for company property.

Specific Objective E

The student, on a voluntary basis, participates as an observer or participant in work sports activities.

Teacher Interventions

Secondary Level. Show the student a variety of pictures of individuals from different jobs participating in after-hours work sports activities. Point out the different logos or emblems on team uniforms, hats, or shirts.

Suggest to the student that he or she may wish to attend a work sports activity as an observer. Depending on the student's wishes, skills, and interest, this initial exposure may lead to a more participatory involvement.

Family Interventions

Secondary Level. Ask the parents to take their youngster to sports activities (e.g., softball, baseball, basketball games) that are sponsored by local businesses. While there, have them point out players they may know from work.

Ask the parents to watch for notices of company picnics or gatherings. For many of these activities, businesses invite the entire family and include sports activities. Suggest that these events might offer ideal opportunities for their youngster to observe or, when appropriate, participate in these activities.

Specific Objective F

The student, on a voluntary basis, takes his or her turn in treating coworkers to coffee and/or other beverages and snacks, as is the customary practice of the work group.

Teacher Interventions

Secondary Level. Explain to the student why it is important to treat coworkers to coffee or other beverages or snacks, especially if coworkers have previously treated the student. Also explain that many coworkers do not like to share with or treat other workers, and that is also an acceptable situation.

Visit working places within the neighborhood that have different facilities for purchasing drinks and snacks (e.g., a school with vending machines, a construction site that has a food wagon visiting on a regular basis, a local store that has an honor-system coffee or drink system in which individuals pay for each drink by placing money in a container). Point out how one might treat coworkers in each situation. Ask the student to chart or write down what he or she sees.

Family Interventions

Secondary Level. Ask the parent to identify to their youngster places or situations in which individuals might be expected to share in the treating of others to beverages or snacks (e.g., car pool participants who regularly stop for doughnuts and coffee before work).

Suggest that the parents may wish to take their youngster to a sporting event, such as a professional ball game. While there, parents can point out to their youngster the way people often take turns buying each other drinks or snacks during the game.

Specific Objective G

The student locates restrooms, telephones, exits and entrances, snack bars, and cafeterias by signs designating these areas, and uses them appropriately.

Teacher Interventions

Secondary Level. Ask the student to locate signs that designate different places around the school environment, such as the cafeteria, restrooms, exits, and entrances. Point out signs he or she may not have noticed.

Ask the student to do several errands for you that require him or her to find places around the school by using signs. Afterward, discuss with the student how he or she found the specific location, emphasizing the use of signs.

Family Interventions

Secondary Level. Ask the parents to monitor how well their youngster is able to use signs in the community. Suggest that they provide help when needed.

During visits to such places as libraries, museums, or restaurants, suggest that the parents ask their youngster for help in finding a restroom. They might need to tell their youngster to ask someone for directions, if no signs are obvious.

Specific Objective H

The student operates vending machines as desired during breaks and, when appropriate, shares contents with coworkers or friends.

Teacher Interventions

Secondary Level. During an ongoing activity, plan for the student to have a break. Suggest that he or she purchase a drink or snack from a vending machine. Provide the opportunity for the student to share this time and snack, if desired, with a fellow student.

Practice with the student using a variety of vending machines. Demonstrate how to carefully make a selection and the procedure to follow. When the machine is not working correctly, or if specific change is not returned, point out how to contact the vending machine company or the person in charge of the machines in the building.

Demonstrate to the student the money changing function that exists on most current vending machines. Show him or her how to use this function to change paper money into coins for use in the machine. Explain that it might be necessary to insert a paper bill into the money changer several times before it registers and converts the bill into coins.

Family Interventions

Secondary Level.   Encourage the parents to use vending machines when out in the community. Suggest that they have their youngster operate the machines, monitoring how accurately he or she makes selections and checks the returned change.

When traveling, encourage the parents to make at least one stop at a roadside service area. Most of these stops have a vast array of vending machines. Ask the parents to give their youngster several coins and a paper bill and request him or her to purchase selected items from the machines.

Specific Objective I

The student shares company newspapers, bulletins, and magazines during leisure breaks.

Teacher Interventions

Secondary Level.   Tour the school with the student and find where the school's copies of newspapers or magazines are available. Suggest that the student borrow some and take them back to the classroom. During breaks or leisure time, suggest that the student read or look through the materials and share them with classmates.

Ask the student to bring to school some company magazines or advertising materials obtained from work or another local manufacturer or business. As part of a class project, have him or her share the information in these materials or use them during leisure breaks.

Family Interventions

Secondary Level. Ask the parents to encourage their youngster to read a variety of company bulletins and magazines as a way of knowing more about a specific company. Suggest that they have their youngster call the public relations or information departments of major companies to request these materials.

Ask the parents to visit several companies with their youngster. Many have an office where outsiders can obtain company reading material. Have the student share the information found in some of these materials with you.

Specific Objective J

The student functions in teams and works well with individuals from diverse backgrounds.

Teacher Interventions

Secondary Level. Take the student to tour different companies or local industries that employ teams of workers as part of the production process. While touring, point out to the student the importance of teamwork in producing a product. When appropriate, try to arrange a meeting for the student to talk with a team member regarding the specifics of his or her job.

Obtain a film or films showing the different facets of industry. This might include a film on manufacturing, distribution, or other areas that involve employment. While viewing the film, indicate to the student the way people of diverse backgrounds are working together. Ask whether the student can provide other examples of situations where he or she has viewed teamwork and diverse populations working together.

Develop a project in class that requires the students to work in teams. As part of this process, emphasize the importance of everyone doing his or her job and how to seek help if someone has questions or concerns. Monitor the process and reinforce appropriate positive behaviors.

Family Interventions

Secondary Level. Ask the parents to support their youngster when he or she is working as part of a team. Stress the importance of allowing their youngster to take some risks that might lead to some failures. Provide them with suggestions on what they should say to their child should failures occur.

Ask the parents to model appropriate behavior when interacting and working with diverse populations. Emphasize that children are highly influenced by their parents' actions and will often imitate them.

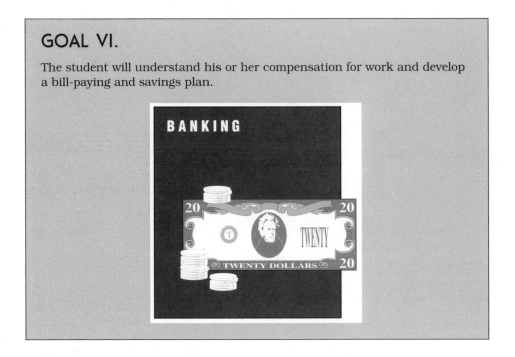

GOAL VI.

The student will understand his or her compensation for work and develop a bill-paying and savings plan.

SPECIFIC OBJECTIVES

The student:

- ❑ A. Checks the gross amount of his or her paycheck and compares it to time worked and pay rate.
- ❑ B. Locates on the pay stub and verifies correctness of deduction information and net pay.
- ❑ C. Opens a savings account in a financial institution.
- ❑ D. Opens a checking account and uses it for depositing a portion of his or her salary for paying bills.

SUGGESTED ACTIVITIES

 ## Specific Objective A

The student checks the gross amount of his or her paycheck and compares it to time worked and pay rate.

Teacher Interventions

Secondary Level. Provide the student with several examples of paychecks and stubs and point out specific information including gross amount of pay, time worked, and rate of pay. Once the student can identify these categories and designations, if applicable, have him or her repeat the activity with his or her own paycheck and stub.

Ask the student to chart on a separate piece of paper the daily hours worked during a specific pay period. When the student is paid, ask him or her to compare the hours worked on the pay stub with those charted. If there is a difference, ask him or her to verify the figures with the appropriate person at work.

Family Interventions

Secondary Level. Ask the parents to review with their youngster one of his or her paycheck stubs. Ask them to discuss the information related to hours or time worked and rate of pay. If their youngster works irregular hours each pay period, have the parents explain how the amount of time worked directly affects the amount of pay received.

Ask the parents to have their youngster share with them any question(s) he or she has concerning the paycheck. When answering these questions, parents should be specific and clear with their answers. If they are unsure about specific facts or details, suggest they have their youngster call the payroll office at work.

 ## Specific Objective B

The student locates on the pay stub and verifies correctness of deduction information and net pay.

Teacher Interventions

Secondary Level. Prepare a list, with abbreviations, of all possible deductions that might appear on a pay stub (e.g., FICA, medical insurance, federal taxes, state and/or local taxes, and credit union). (See example in Figure 2.5.) Review this list with the students and explain the reasons for these deductions.

Ask the student to identify from his or her pay stub, or a facsimile, the specific categories of gross pay, deductions, and net pay. Develop a master sheet that itemizes the exact amount of these deductions and pay facts. Review this master sheet with the student and have him or her verify what is on this sheet with what is on the paycheck.

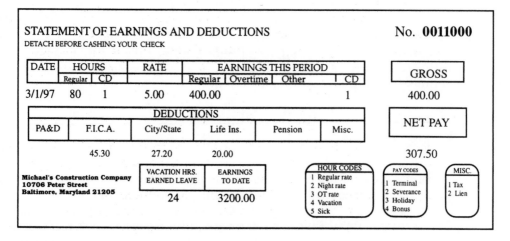

FIGURE 2.5. Pay check and stub information.

Family Interventions

Secondary Level. Ask the parents to review with their youngster the amounts and categories listed on their pay stub or a facsimile. Suggest that they take their youngster through the process of verifying the information found on the stub.

Suggest that the parents explain that pay stubs might look different for jobs that pay by the hour and for salaried jobs. For example, when hours are irregular, deductions and gross and net pays may differ for each pay period. Have parents provide examples of how different hours worked result in different totals and pay.

 ## Specific Objective C

The student opens a savings account in a financial institution.

Teacher Interventions

Secondary Level. Take the student to visit different banks and a credit union (if the student is eligible) and collect information on the various savings accounts offered. Review the rules that accompany each account, paying special attention to minimum balance requirements, current interest rate and long-term rates, and penalties for withdrawals.

Before opening a savings account, have the student make a list of questions to have answered by the bank or credit union staff. If the questions are answered in a favorable fashion, assist the student in opening a savings account. Caution the student that a savings account is for savings and should be used for withdrawals only during an emergency.

Family Interventions

Secondary Level. Suggest that the parents discuss with their youngster the benefits of opening and maintaining a savings account. They may wish to show the youngster their savings account records and explain why they have tried to save money over a long period of time.

On occasions, a person might need to close a savings account and open a new one. Reasons include increased minimum balance requirements, significantly better interest rates in another institution, or a move to a different location that is not readily serviced by the current bank or credit union. When this occurs, suggest that the parents assist their youngster in opening another savings account, following the information described previously.

Specific Objective D

The student opens a checking account and uses it for depositing a portion of his or her salary for paying bills.

Teacher Interventions

Secondary Level. Have the student open a checking account using the procedure described in Specific Objective C for opening a savings account. Explain the need to deposit money into this account on a regular basis from his or her income so he or she can use a portion to pay bills.

Explain to the student the caution he or she must take to accurately write and record checks in his or her register and to record deposits into the account. Develop lessons or exercises that teach how to balance a checking account.

Practice writing checks with copies of an existing check that has been voided. Correct any errors the student makes and point out the reason for the correction.

Demonstrate to the student how and when to reorder checks. Emphasize the importance of not waiting until the last check is written before ordering, as it may take several weeks before new checks arrive.

Family Interventions

Secondary Level. Suggest to the parents that they provide opportunities for their youngster to write a check (e.g., to reimburse the parents for something the youngster did not previously have sufficient funds to pay for). Have them monitor the accuracy of his or her check writing.

Ask the parents to review with their youngster the need to be aware of how to safely handle and store his or her checkbook and statement information. Ask them to stress that the information in these materials is confidential and should be shared only with select people.

Sample Lesson Plans

Sample Lesson Plan 1

Topic Area: Competitive Job-Finding Skills

Designed by: Madelyn Sydney

Time Recommended: 30 Minutes

Student Involved: Andy (Secondary Special Class)

Background Information:

Andy has erratic reading and comprehension skills at the third- to fourth-grade level. He has difficulty with abbreviations, and does not appear to make use of context cues while reading. He is easily reinforced with praise and positive acknowledgments. He does not like loud noises or being touched.

General Goal *(Competitive Job-Finding Skills I)*:

The student will acquire those skills necessary to competitively apply for work.

Specific Objective *(Competitive Job-Finding Skills I-B)*:

The student locates the help wanted section of newspapers and identifies job offerings appropriate to his or her interests, needs, and skills.

Lesson Objective:

When Andy is asked to locate a description of a job in which he is interested, using the help wanted section of the newspaper, he finds one and marks it with a marker, highlighter, or pen.

Materials and Equipment:

- Help wanted section of a daily or Sunday newspaper
- Highlighter, marker, or pen

Motivating Activity:

Make a transparency of a newspaper help wanted page that describes some potential jobs. Point out the requirements for these jobs, as well as their benefits and drawbacks. For example, although an outdoor wilderness guide might sound exciting, it requires specific skills and a willingness to work outdoors in all types of weather.

Instructional Procedures:

Initiation—Tell the student to bring to class the help wanted section of the Sunday or daily newspaper. If he does not have access to newspapers or this proves difficult, have a number of papers available for his use.

Guided Practice—Use the basic words and abbreviations found in the help wanted section of the newspaper to develop flash cards. On one side of the card, write one word or abbreviation found in the ads. On the other side, write the definition or nonabbreviated word. Play a game with the student in which he is asked to identify and define as many words or abbreviations as he can in a certain amount of time. Provide clarification when the student has difficulty.

Independent Practice—Ask the student to circle jobs in the help wanted section of the newspaper that he finds interesting, might wish to know more about, or might consider as potential employment.

Closure—Ask the student to fold up and put away the help wanted section of the newspaper he has been using. When he is asked, have him show other students where to find this section in the newspaper and to demonstrate how to use it to find descriptions of potential job openings.

Assessment Strategy:

Observe the student to determine whether he is using the help wanted section of the newspaper in an appropriate fashion.

Follow-Up Activity or Objective:

If the student achieves the lesson objective, proceed to a lesson involving the use of this information. For example, the student may wish to arrange for an interview for one of the jobs.

Sample Lesson Plan 2

Topic Area: Competitive Job-Finding Skills

Designed by: Stephen Andrew

Time Recommended: 30 Minutes

Student Involved: Missie (Secondary Special Class)

Background Information:

Missie has the ability to read schedules and identify signs consistently. Her difficulty is being on time for activities and knowing what to do after an activity is over. She works well with simple praise and is eager to please people.

She is used to riding public transportation with a friend or family member, but does not do so on a regular basis. She also needs to be reminded of safety rules as she does not always appear as alert in this area as she should be.

General Goal (*Competitive Job-Finding Skills III*):

The student will acquire those skills that allow him or her to go to work.

Specific Objective (*Competitive Job-Finding Skills III-A*):

The student meets buses, car pools, and shuttle services after reviewing written departure schedules.

Lesson Objective:

When the student is asked to meet a bus, shuttle, or car pool after reviewing the schedules, she meets them at the appropriate time and place.

Materials and Equipment:

- Bus, car pool, and shuttle service schedules
- Notebook and pencil or pen
- Phone numbers of bus company, car pool contact, and shuttle service company

Motivating Activity:

At an appropriate time, take Missie to the place where the bus, car pool, or shuttle service departs. Point out the geography of the location and indicate how the passengers wait for the transportation to arrive. If possible, videotape this activity and show it in the class. This will allow specifics of the location and activity to be highlighted.

Instructional Procedures:

Initiation—Tell the student to bring to class bus, car pool, or shuttle service schedules. If she does not have access to these schedules, have a number of them available for her to use.

Guided Practice—Work with the student to correctly and accurately read transportation schedules. Have her choose the specific mode of transportation with which she feels most comfortable and develop a plan for following this specific schedule. Go with the student and take the bus, car pool, or shuttle service to her place of work. While riding with her, point out specifics about the ride. For example, the destination signs on the bus should match the place she is going. She must always practice being safety conscious in terms of selecting where to sit and whom to sit beside, and entering and exiting the vehicle. Provide assistance when the student appears to be having difficulty.

Independent Practice—Ask the student to meet and take the appropriate bus, car pool, or shuttle service that will allow her to be at work on time. Ask her to take this vehicle and go to work. If possible, follow her in a separate vehicle to make sure she has selected the correct route and time.

Closure—Ask the student to save the transportation schedules in a convenient and safe place for future use. When she is asked, have her show other students how to use the schedule. She may also wish to show them the videotape made previously so they understand the many facets involved in using the bus, car pool, or shuttle service.

Assessment Strategy:

Observe the student to determine whether she is using transportation schedules appropriately to meet bus, car pool, or shuttle services that can take her to work.

Follow-Up Activity or Objective:

If the student achieves the lesson objective, proceed to a lesson involving the use of this information. For example, the student may wish to select alternate routes and systems to work that may be shorter or more enjoyable.

References

Bender, M. (1994). Learning disabilities: Beyond the school years. In A. J. Capute, P. J. Accardo, & B. K. Shapiro (Eds.), *Learning disabilities spectrum: ADD, ADHD, and LD.* (pp. 241–254). Baltimore: York Press.

Blackorby, J., & Wagner, M. (1996). Longitudinal postschool outcomes of youth with disabilities: Findings from the National Longitudinal Transition Study. *Exceptional Children, 62,* 399–413.

Dowdy, C. A. (1996). Vocational rehabilitation and special education: Partners in transition for individuals with learning disabilities. *Journal of Learning Disabilities, 29,* 137–147.

Louis Harris and Associates. (1986). *The ICD survey of disabled Americans: Bringing disabled Americans into the mainstream.* New York: International Center for the Disabled.

Muklewicz, C., & Bender, M. (1988). *Competitive job-finding guide for persons with handicaps.* Austin, TX: PRO-ED.

Patton, J., Polloway, E., Smith, T., Edgar, E., Clark, G., & Lee, S. (1996). Individuals with mild mental retardation: Postsecondary outcomes and implications for educational policy. *Education and Training in Mental Retardation and Developmental Disabilities 31,*(2), 75–85.

President's Committee on Employment of the Handicapped. (1987). *Out of the job market: A national crisis.* Washington DC: Author.

President's Committee on the Employment of People with Disabilities. (1990). *From paternalism to productivity—Whatever it takes.* Washington DC: Author.

Repetto, J. B., & Correa, V. I. (1996). Expanding views on transition. *Exceptional Children, 62,* 551–563.

Siegel, S., & Gaylord-Ross, R. (1991). Factors associated with employment success among youths with learning disabilities. *Journal of Learning Disabilities 23,* 213–19.

Suggested Readings

Bender, M., & Valletutti, P. (1982). *Teaching functional academics: A curriculum guide for adolescents and adults with learning problems.* Austin, TX: PRO-ED.

Brolin, D. E. (1993). *Life centered career education: A competency-based approach.* Reston, VA: Council for Exceptional Children.

Cohen, S. B., Joyce, C. M., Rhodes, K. W., & Welks, D. M. (1985). Educational and vocational rehabilitation. In M. Ylvisaker (Ed.), *Head injury rehabilitation: Children and adolescents.* (pp. 383–410) Austin, TX: PRO-ED.

Dowdy, C. A., Carter, J. K., & Smith, T. E. C. (1990). Differences in transitional needs of high school students with and without learning disabilities. *Journal of Learning Disabilities, 23* (6), 343–348.

Gerber, P. J., Ginsberg, R., & Reiff, H. B. (1992). Identifying alterable patterns in employment success for highly successful adults with learning disabilities. *Journal of Learning Disabilities, 25* (8), 475–487.

Gilbert, P., & Rajewski, J. (1993). Applying continuous quality improvement principles in secondary school vocational education with emphasis on special populations. *The Journal for Vocational Special Needs Education, 15* (3), 19–24.

Gobble, E. M. R., Dunson, C., Szekeres, S., & Cornwall, J. (1987). Avocational programming for the severely impaired head injured individual. In M. Ylvisaker & E. M. R. Gobble (Eds.), *Community re-entry for head injured adults.* (pp. 349–379) Austin, TX: PRO-ED.

Kennedy, J. L., & Laramore, D. (1993). *Joyce Lain Kennedy's career book* (2nd ed.). Lincolnwood, IL: NTC Publishing Group.

Lamendella, D. (1987). *Pathways: A job search curriculum.* Northridge, CA: Milt Wright and Associates.

Latham, P. S., & Latham, P. H. (Eds.). (1994). *Succeeding in the workplace.* Washington, DC: JKL Communications.

Muklewicz, C., & Bender, M. (1988). *Competitive job-finding guide for persons with handicaps.* Austin, TX: PRO-ED.

Murphy, S. T., & Rogan, P. M. (1994). *Developing natural supports in the workplace: A practitioner's guide.* St. Augustine, FL: Training Resource Network.

National Association of State Directors of Special Education (NASDSE). (1992). Job skills of '90s require new educational model for all students. *Liaison Bulletin, 18*(5), 2–17.

Patton, J., Polloway, E., Smith, T., Edgar, E., Clark, G., & Lee, S. (1996). Individuals with mild mental retardation: Post secondary outcomes and implication for educational policy. *Education and Training in Mental Retardation and Developmental Disabilities, 31*(2), 75–85.

President's Committee on the Employment of People with Disabilities. (1990). *From paternalism to productivity—Whatever it takes.* Washington, DC: Author.

Repetto, J. B., & Correa, V. I. (1996). Expanding views on transition. *Exceptional Children, 62,* 551–563.

Rusch, F. R., DeStefano, J., Chadsey-Rusch, J., Phelps, L. A., & Szymanski, E. (1992). *Transition from school to adult life: Models, linkages and policy.* Sycamore, IL: Sycamore.

Siegel, S., & Gaylord-Ross, R. (1991). Factors associated with employment success among youths with learning disabilities. *Journal of Learning Disabilities, 23,* 213–219.

Siegel, S., Robert, M., Greener, K., Meyer, G., Halloran, W., & Gaylord-Ross, R. (1993). *Career ladders for challenged youths in transition from school to adult life.* Austin, TX: PRO-ED.

Smith, M. D., Belcher, R. G., & Juhrs, P. D. (1995). *A guide to successful employment for individuals with autism.* Baltimore: Brookes.

Supported Employment Parent Training Technical Assistance Project. (1992). *A bibliography of supported employment and transition resources.* Minneapolis: PACER Center.

Supported Employment Parent Training Technical Assistance Project. (1992). *A reference manual for parent training about supported employment.* Minneapolis: PACER Center.

Tindall, L. (1991). *Still puzzled about educating students with disabilities? Vocational preparation of students with disabilities.* Madison: University of Wisconsin Vocational Studies Center.

Wehman, P. (1992). *Life beyond the classroom: transition strategies for young people with disabilities.* Baltimore: Brookes.

Wehman, P., Kregel, J., Sherron, P., Nguyen, S., Kreutzer, J., Fryer, R., & Zasler, N. (1993). Critical factors associated with the successful supported employment placement of patients with severe traumatic brain injury. *Brain Injury, 7,* 31–34.

Wehmeyer, M. (1992). Self-determination: Critical skills for outcome-oriented transition services. *Journal for Vocational Special Needs Education, 15,* 3–7.

West, L. L., Corbey, S., Boyer-Stephens, A., Jones, B., Miller, R. J., & Sarkees-Wircenski, M. (1992). *Integrating transition planning into the IEP process.* Reston, VA: Council for Exceptional Children.

KITS/CURRICULAR MATERIALS

- *The Beta Program*
  Boulder Valley Technical Education Center
  6600 Arapahoe Road
  Boulder, Colorado 80303

- *Beyond School: "Keeping a Job's the Hard Part"*
  EBSCO Curriculum Materials
  Box 11521
  Birmingham, Alabama 35202-1521

- *Career/Transition Development Plan*
  Piney Mountain Press, Inc.
  PO Box 86
  Cleveland, Georgia 30528

- *The Complete Job Finder's Guide for the 90's*
  Cambridge Job Search
  PO Box 2153, Department JO3
  Charleston, West Virginia 25328-2153

- *Curriculum Materials: A Review for Workplace Education Programs*
  Center on Education and Work
  University of Wisconsin
  964 Educational Sciences Building
  1025 West Johnson Street
  Madison, Wisconsin 53706-1796

- *Dakota Training Modules: Supported Employment*
  Dakota Inc.
  680 O'Neill Drive
  Eagan, Minnesota 55121

- *A Dictionary of Holland Occupational Codes Computer Search Program*
  Psychological Assessment Resources, Inc.
  PO Box 998
  Odessa, Florida 33556

- *Dictionary of Occupational Titles*
  Cambridge Job Search
  PO Box 2153, Department JO3
  Charleston, West Virginia 25328-2153

- *A Guide to Successful Employment for Individuals with Autism*
  Paul H. Brookes Publishing Co.
  PO Box 10624
  Baltimore, Maryland 21285 -0624

- *How To Get a Job—Practical Advice for Job Interviews*
  EBSCO Curriculum Materials
  Box 11521
  Birmingham, Alabama 35202-1521

- *How To Get Interviews from Classified Job Ads*
  Cambridge Job Search
  PO Box 2153, Department JO3
  Charleston, West Virginia 25328-2153

- *Integrating Academic and Vocational Education*
  Center on Education and Work
  University of Wisconsin
  964 Educational Sciences Building
  1025 West Johnson Street
  Madison, Wisconsin 53706-1796

- *LCCE: Occupational Guidance and Preparation*
  The Council for Exceptional Children
  1920 Association Drive
  Department K6092
  Reston, Virginia 20191-1589

- *Life Centered Career Education—The Complete Package*
  The Council for Exceptional Children
  1920 Association Drive
  Department K6092
  Reston, Virginia 20191-1589

- *Practical Issues in Employment Testing*
  Psychological Assessment Resources, Inc.
  PO Box 998
  Odessa, Florida 33556

- *SAM—Skills Assessment Model*
  Piney Mountain Press, Inc.
  PO Box 86
  Cleveland, Georgia 30528

- *Self-Directed Search*
  Psychological Assessment Resources, Inc.
  PO Box 998
  Odessa, Florida 33556

- *Standards of Work Performance*
  Paul H. Brookes Publishing Co.
  PO Box 10624
  Baltimore, Maryland 21285-0624

- *Teaching the Possibilities: Resource Guides for Transition Planning*
  Minnesota Educational Services
  70 County Road B2
  Little Canada, Minnesota 55117-1402

- *Tools of the Trade: A Hands-On Training Program for Supported Employment Personnel*
  Rise, Inc.
  8406 Sunset Rd.
  Minneapolis, Minnesota 55432

- *Using the Newspaper To Teach Basic Living Skills*
  EBSCO Curriculum Materials
  Box 11521
  Birmingham, Alabama 35202-1521

- *Vocational Program Evaluation Profile (VPEP)*
  EBSCO Curriculum Materials
  Box 11521
  Birmingham, Alabama 35202-1521

- *The Walker Social Skills Curriculum: The ACCEPTS Program*
  PRO-ED, Inc.
  8700 Shoal Creek Boulevard
  Austin, Texas 78757-6897

- *Work Behavior Training Program*
  EBSCO Curriculum Materials
  Box 11521
  Birmingham, Alabama 35202-1521

- *Working Together: A Minnesota Guide to Excellent Practices*
  Transition Technical Assistance Project
  Institute on Community Integration
  University of Minnesota
  109 Pattee Hall
  150 Pillsbury Drive SE
  Minneapolis, Minnesota 55455

- *Workplace Education Design*
  Center on Education and Work
  University of Wisconsin
  964 Educational Sciences Building
  1025 West Johnson Street
  Madison, Wisconsin 53706-1796

- *Workplace Education Evaluation*
  Center on Education and Work
  University of Wisconsin
  964 Educational Sciences Building
  1025 West Johnson Street
  Madison, Wisconsin 53706-1796

- *Workplace Journal*
  EBSCO Curriculum Materials
  Box 11521
  Birmingham, Alabama 35202-1521

- *Workplace Simulation–Revised*
  EBSCO Curriculum Materials
  Box 11521
  Birmingham, Alabama 35202-1521

- *The World of Work*
  EBSCO Curriculum Materials
  Box 11521
  Birmingham, Alabama 35202-1521

- *Your Paperchase to Employment*
  EBSCO Curriculum Materials
  Box 11521
  Birmingham, Alabama 35202-1521

VIDEOS

- *Beta Employer Video Presentation*
  Boulder Valley Technical Education Center
  6600 Arapahoe Road
  Boulder, Colorado 80303

- *Career Connections*
  Cambridge Job Search
  PO Box 2153, Department JO3
  Charleston, West Virginia 25328-2153

- *Employability—Integrating People with Developmental Disabilities into the Workplace*
  Woolworth Corporation
  Northern Light Productions
  Boston, Massachusetts 02215

- *Finding the Perfect Job*
  Cambridge Job Search
  PO Box 2153, Department JO3
  Charleston, West Virginia 25328-2153

- *It's All Part of the Job*
  Attainment Company, Inc.
  PO Box 930160
  Verona, Wisconsin 53593-0160

- *Job Development: Coaching Winners*
  Attainment Company, Inc.
  PO Box 930160
  Verona, Wisconsin 53593-0160

- *Job Search Skills For Teens*
  EBSCO Curriculum Materials
  Box 11521
  Birmingham, Alabama 35202-1521

- *Job Skills for Career Success Series*
  Cambridge Job Search
  PO Box 2153, Department JO3
  Charleston, West Virginia 25328-2153

- *Life After High School for Students with Moderate and Severe Disabilities: Great Expectations and Best Practices*
  Beach Center on Families and Disabilities
  University of Kansas, c/o Life Span Institute
  3111 Hawthorn Hall
  Lawrence, Kansas 66045

- *Life Centered Career Education Training Package*
  The Council for Exceptional Children
  1920 Association Drive
  Department K6092
  Reston, Virginia 20191-1589

- *Making It On Your First Job*
  Cambridge Job Search
  PO Box 2153, Department JO3
  Charleston, West Virginia 25328-2153

- *Skills for First-Time Job Seekers*
  Cambridge Job Search
  PO Box 2153, Department JO3
  Charleston, West Virginia 25328-2153

- *Take This Job and Love It*
  Cambridge Job Search
  PO Box 2153, Department JO3
  Charleston, West Virginia 25328-2153

- *Tough Times Job Strategies*
  Cambridge Job Search
  PO Box 2153, Department JO3
  Charleston, West Virginia 25328-2153

- *The Very Quick Job Search Video*
  Cambridge Job Search
  PO Box 2153, Department JO3
  Charleston, West Virginia 25328-2153

- *Winning the Job You Really Want*
  Cambridge Job Search
  PO Box 2153, Department JO3
  Charleston, West Virginia 25328-2153

- *Working I—Help Your Students Get and Keep a Job*
  James Stanfield Company
  PO Box 41058
  Santa Barbara, California 93140

- *Workplace Learning Video Packages*
  EBSCO Curriculum Materials
  Box 11521
  Birmingham, Alabama 35202-1521

Leisure-Time Skills

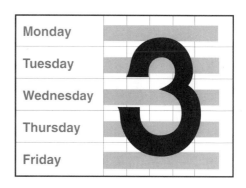

Monday	
Tuesday	
Wednesday	
Thursday	
Friday	

Traditionally, leisure experiences have been viewed as sports-related, competitive activities that are secondary to more basic curricular areas. For many individuals with disabilities, recreational activities and their related experiences have been nonexistent or difficult to access. When programs have emphasized leisure education, they typically have been provided by parks and recreation agencies or by specialists working in the areas of recreation, therapeutic recreation, and physical education. There has been no strategic planning for the inclusion of leisure and recreational experiences in the everyday lives of individuals with disabilities. However, participation in fully integrated leisure activities has been demonstrated to play a significant role in the inclusion of individuals with disabilities with their nondisabled peers. Leisure activities enhance the development of socialization, mobility, independence, and community integration. Furthermore, recreation and leisure experiences can play an expanding role in developing and promoting skills required to access and maintain employment.

Methodology and approaches to teaching the area of leisure have been either narrowly defined or absent altogether from educational programs. In part, this phenomenon can be attributed to the attitude held by many professionals and parents that leisure activities are of secondary importance in planning programs of instruction. More recently, leisure is becoming more broadly defined through activities that facilitate relaxation, fun, amusement (Moon, 1994), and adventures (Havens, 1992). Bedeni, Bullock, and Driscoll (1993) presented the need for school programs to teach leisure education so individuals with disabilities will know how to "enjoy and use their leisure" (p. 72).

Typically, adapted physical education programs provide a developmental sequence of motor activities that recognize individual styles of learning for students with disabilities. Adapted physical education incorporates movement education, skill development, and physical fitness activities. It may include leisure activities, including sports, dance, and aquatics (Winnick, 1995).

Leisure experiences are a positive and valuable resource to people as they function on a daily basis in society (Bender, 1994; Wehman & Schleien, 1980). Leisure experiences facilitate learning, adapting, and adjusting during nonwork hours; combat negative stress (Compton & Iso-Ahola, 1994); develop physical fitness; enhance the work experience (McCarron, Kern, & Wolf, 1979); and foster relaxation. The findings of a survey by Louis Harris and Associates (1986) indicated some critical information regarding the recreation and leisure lifestyles of individuals with disabilities. Fifty-six percent of those responding indicated that their disabilities limit their mobility and prevent them from attending cultural or sporting events or from socializing with friends outside of their homes. The figure rose to 79% among individuals with severe disabilities. This type of information highlights the need for leisure education programs to address these barriers.

Leisure, in a comprehensive educational context, offers an innovative channel that

1. Allows an individual to know him- or herself in relation to others.

2. Enhances the quality of his or her life.

3. Addresses the individual's specific needs, capabilities, and values through the self-selection of meaningful experiences.

4. Enables an individual to evaluate his or her use of time and behaviors in situations ranging from the simple to complex.

5. Teaches critical social and interpersonal skills (Mathews, 1977).

The student with disabilities has increased leisure time, especially the student who is no longer eligible for educational programs. Lack of adequate facilities, age limits, eligibility restrictions, and limited summer and after-school programs have added to the need for leisure-time programming. With increasing emphasis on inclusion activities for all persons with disabilities, students are exposed to a wide range of recreational and leisure experiences. Without adequate planning for opportunities, community members are provided minimal interactions with individuals with disabilities, and rarely get to observe the benefits and strengths of individuals with disabilities. As a result of these limited exposures, many individuals in the community continue to foster negative attitudes concerning the disabled (Sparrow & Mayne, 1990).

This section of *A Functional Curriculum* has been developed to provide objectives and activities to help meet an individual's leisure needs. It is important to underscore that this chapter does not specifically stress skill development because we believe that leisure-time activities should be primarily for enjoyment (Voeltz, Wuerch, & Wilcox, 1982), fitness (Beasley, 1982), and social experiences (Adkins & Matson, 1980). Although skills may be incidentally learned while these primary objectives are being attained, they should be utilized to enhance the program. The activities may require modification in materials, positioning, and mobility (York & Rainforth, 1995) for some students. The activities presented in this chapter will enable the student with disabilities to participate in a variety of leisure experiences at home (Hanley, 1979) and in the community (Brannan, 1979) and will afford the student the opportunities to learn the rules of games, participate as a player and as a spectator in a variety of sports and games (Marchant, 1979), meet people with whom he or she may make friends (Kingsley, Viggiano, & Tout, 1981), actively engage in hobbies (Giangreco, 1983) and arts and crafts experiences (Frith & Mitchell, 1983), and use community facilities in his or her leisure time.

Providing a student with disabilities with ways of using leisure time in a satisfying manner is also a way of enhancing the student's self-esteem and emotional well-being (Allen, 1980). The student who is able to initiate or join in activities during his or her leisure time may become more self-confident than the student who has much leisure time and few ideas about how to use it. Because leisure time is a major component of the daily routine of students with disabilities, parents, teachers, and other significant persons must encourage them to seek a variety of interesting leisure-time activities (Joswiak, 1979) and discourage non-productive activities such as watching television without regard to program content.

The growing number of older students with disabilities who have completed their formal school programming represents a large population that requires leisure education (Salzberg & Langford, 1981). The integration of persons with disabilities into the mainstream of community life is greatly facilitated by the development of leisure and leisure-related skills.

For many people, social encounters are largely a direct result of participating in leisure experiences (Nietupski & Svoboda, 1982). Because of this, the integration of leisure experiences is a *sine qua non* of functional educational programming. An organized instructional program designed to develop a repertoire of leisure-time interests and skills is essential for preparing students with disabilities for a life that is as satisfying, pleasurable, stimulating, and enriching as possible (Sternlight & Hurwitz, 1981). Leisure offers all individuals the opportunity to experience new and creative avenues for fulfilling their lives.

The selected readings and references provided at the end of this chapter represent a review of some current as well as past leisure skills information, techniques, and programs. The reader may also wish to review the Selected Materials/Resources list at the end of this chapter for additional information on specific resources in this area.

General Goals of This Unit

I. The student will participate in play activities and choose from a variety of games of leisure.

II. The student will engage in sports and activities of physical fitness.

III. The student will participate in camping and diverse outdoor activities.

IV. The student will use information from the study of nature to engage in relevant leisure activities.

V. The student will identify activities and opportunities to use as hobbies.

VI. The student will select craft activities to engage in leisure and hobby activities.

VII. The student will engage in performing and visual arts.

VIII. The student will seek a variety of entertainment and cultural opportunities.

GOAL I.

The student will participate in play activities and choose from a variety of games of leisure.

Leisure activities are associated with the use of free time and are an important function of life. To participate in leisure, individuals must be prepared to use their knowledge to exercise decision making. Efforts should be made to educate individuals with disabilities to make more independent efforts to improve the quality of their lives through leisure pursuits. The unique needs of these individuals require leisure education to facilitate their participation in a wide range of recreation and leisure activities. Adaptation of games of leisure requires that individualization strategies are utilized, from the implementation of early intervention through adaptations to curriculum in the classroom and recreational activities.

SPECIFIC OBJECTIVES

The student:

- ❏ A. Participates in games of make-believe and role playing.
- ❏ B. Selects durable and safe toys and games.
- ❏ C. Engages in water play.
- ❏ D. Plays low-activity games.
- ❏ E. Plays high-activity games.
- ❏ F. Plays target games.
- ❏ G. Plays balance games.
- ❏ H. Plays table games.
- ❏ I.   Plays card games.
- ❏ J. Plays games of chance.
- ❏ K. Plays strategy games.
- ❏ L. Plays real-life games.
- ❏ M. Plays knowledge and word games.
- ❏ N. Chooses a variety of toys and games.
- ❏ O. Plays multiple types of video games.

SUGGESTED ACTIVITIES

Specific Objective A

The student participates in games of make-believe and role playing.

Teacher Interventions

Infant and Toddler/Preschool Level. Using an animal- or clown-shaped rattle, shake it in front of the infant, encouraging the infant to reach for the rattle. Repeat the activity using hand puppets and imitating the sounds of the animals. Use a handkerchief to play peek-a-boo with the infant, repeating "peek-a-boo" each time you look out.

Read Dr. Seuss books in a circle, having the student repeat the rhyming verses and acting out the actions of the stories when possible. Discuss the stories, asking the student to add additional details, the sillier the better.

Primary Level. Read the student a story with a simple but interesting plot. As you read the story, add additional details. When you have completed the story, discuss the characters and assign each student a part as a character in the story. Reread the story slowly, encouraging each student to act out the story, adding his or her own details. Repeat the activity using a variety of stories or rhymes. Use verbal praise and animated facial expressions to reinforce each detail.

Create a "home" station in the classroom. Purchase or create wooden or cardboard appliances and add additional items such as clothing and household articles. Discuss common activities of the household, such as meals, bedtime, family parties, holiday celebrations, and cleaning routines. Discuss family roles, encouraging the student to select roles and act out family situations. Have the student switch roles to provide the opportunity for him or her to pretend to be a variety of family members.

Intermediate Level. During recess provide the student with a variety of options to engage in fantasy play, through games, videotape opportunities, or art supplies, using these things as opportunities to explore themes for creative dramatics.

Secondary Level. Encourage the students to role-play a variety of adult situations, including dating activities, social encounters in malls, community workers, and home-related situations. Use these role plays as an opportunity for the students to examine their feelings and attitudes.

Family Interventions

Infant and Toddler/Preschool Level. Ask the parents of an infant to use an animal or doll puppet on the hand, wiggling it back and forth and pairing the movement with appropriate sounds. The goal is to catch the infant's attention and have his or her eyes follow the puppet. They can also hide the puppet and pull it out, repeating the activity.

Recommend books for the parents to read that provide rhyming words or short nursery rhymes. Explain to the parents how important it is to be animated as they pantomime the words and engage their child in the actions. "Itsy Bitsy Spider" and "This Little Piggy Went to Market" can be converted to easily remembered words and actions.

Ask the parents to arrange play dates for their preschooler and encourage the children to play school, doctor, or grocery shopping.

Primary Level. Encourage the parents to suggest that their children create plays around favorite cartoon characters, creating scenery, drawing characters, and using straws to operate the figures through slits in the scenery. Many children enjoy being videotaped as a family activity and will watch the tape afterward, describing the activity.

If appropriate, ask the parents to purchase figures based on characters from popular television programs and movies, dolls, and animals to encourage fantasy play and role playing.

Intermediate and Secondary Levels. Ask the parents to encourage their youngster to participate in dramatic productions in school to increase his or her exploration of the dramatic arts. When watching movies or television, encourage the parents to discuss the themes with their youngster, encouraging him or her to express feelings and attitudes.

Specific Objective B

The student selects durable and safe toys and games.

Teacher Interventions

Infant and Toddler/Preschool Level. Provide a selection of toys and games that are appropriate for preschool children. Demonstrate each toy, use a sentence to comment on each toy or game, and say the name aloud. If the child has language, encourage the child to imitate the name. Place each toy within reach on a shelf. Tell the children the attributes that make the toy or game durable (e.g., "This toy is a wooden truck," "This toy is unbreakable and has no sharp parts"). Remind the child to place the toys on the shelf. Labeling the shelf with pictures or using baskets that are color coded can assist young children in replacing toys on shelves.

Primary Level.   Provide the student with a variety of games that are appropriate to his or her functional level. Ask the student about special interests that may assist the student in selection of games of interest. Demonstrate the components of the games (markers, dice, cards) and explain that these are part of the game and should be used only with the game. Explain to the student that game parts should never be placed in the mouth, nose, or ears. Remind the student to keep the small parts away from young children who could choke on them.

Family Interventions

Infant and Toddler/Preschool and Primary Levels.   Provide parents with information on the selection of toys and games. Assist them in understanding the functioning level of their child and the need for appropriate toys and games. Regardless of the child's age, caution the parents that if their child puts objects in his or her mouth, they should not purchase toys or games with small or removable parts.

Intermediate and Secondary Levels.   Ask the parents to take their youngster to a toy store and encourage him or her to select toys and games of interest. Remind the parents to monitor the selection to ensure that the youngster selects safe and durable games and toys. Parents need to be aware of the violent themes of certain games and toys aimed at adolescents. Even adolescents often need to be provided with incentives to put away games after their use (e.g., additional game time, inviting a friend to play).

Specific Objective C
The student engages in water play.

Teacher Interventions

Infant and Toddler/Preschool Level.   Provide a water play table or use a classroom sink, if available, for water play opportunities. Give the child a variety of containers, sieves, colanders, and pourers, assisting the child with transferring water from one to another.

Provide the student with empty detergent bottles and plastic spray bottles. Assist the child to fill the bottles with water (add a small amount of nonstinging detergent to the bottles to make bubbles), screw on the tops, and encourage the child to squeeze the water out of the bottles. Assist the child with drying and putting away the materials.

Provide a variety of objects. Discuss with the student what sinks and what floats. Have the student push objects into the water and observe those that float to the top and those that sink to the bottom.

Primary Level. Arrange for a field trip to the local YMCA or community center and schedule a week of swimming as part of the physical education program available through the school. Many instructors are trained to adapt swimming lessons for children with disabilities. Pair the students with buddies and devise water games that are suitable to the student's developmental age, including ring toss, ball games, water polo, and water basketball. Provide additional supervision through parent volunteers.

Add salt to water and discuss what will float in the salt water and what will sink. Compare wet and dry materials, such as paper or aluminum foil, comparing what happens to each when wet.

Intermediate and Secondary Levels. Provide swimming opportunities that are commensurate with the student's abilities, such as swimming lessons or junior lifesaving classes through the local YMCA or community center.

Conduct classroom experiments by boiling, freezing, and coloring water. Discuss the attributes of each.

Have the student assist in the school cafeteria with dishwashing and floor washing as part of a transitional program, if appropriate. Be sure to instruct the student in washing and putting away materials.

Family Interventions

Infant and Toddler/Preschool Level. Even the youngest infant can be provided water play activities, including gently pouring water on their stomachs while bathing or encouraging the baby to splash gently in the bath.

Using a bath seat in the tub to support the young child, encourage the parents to provide and demonstrate the use of toys and containers in the tub. Toy stores sell a variety of safety approved bath toys that promote play in the tub. Caution the parents to *never* leave their child unattended in the tub, regardless of the emergency.

During warmer weather small wading pools, including those with slides or animal shapes, can provide opportunities for water play. Also, most parents have hoses and sprinklers that can be turned on to provide water play opportunities for children.

Primary Level. With supervision, floats and other small rafting devices can provide hours of fun in pools or lakes for the child with the parents.

Suggest to parents that their young child assist in dishwashing with lots of bubbles. Have the parent demonstrate how to make shapes from the bubbles and blow them. Remind parents to instruct their child specifically regarding the use and cleaning of electrical appliances and the dangers associated with using them around water.

Intermediate and Secondary Levels. Encourage the parents to involve their youngster in community pools and other organized swimming-related activities, such as swim lessons or pool days for community or association groups. Many pools offer summer passes, which include a variety of options for water-related activities.

Summer camp programs for children with disabilities provide opportunities for organized water activities and lessons.

Specific Objective D

The student plays low-activity games.

Teacher Interventions

Infant and Toddler/Preschool Level. By the age of 6 months, infants can be offered ring stacks or shape boxes to manipulate. As the child develops more skills, demonstrate additional uses for these toys.

Provide the child with age-appropriate activities (e.g., stationary swing, nontoxic modeling dough, stacking toys, picture bingo), and demonstrate how to play with each. If the game requires two players, play at least one time as the second player. Involve another child, when appropriate.

Primary Level. Teach the student a variety of hand games (e.g., Cat's Cradle, Scissors–Rock–Stone).

Assist the student to make his or her own book. Have the student make pages using single sheets of paper for two pages (front and back). Staple along one edge or punch holes, using yarn to bind the book through the holes. Provide the student with a theme for the project and have the student write or dictate the story and illustrate the book.

Intermediate Level. Have the students bring in a variety of disposable household objects and create mobiles for their rooms.

Implement a classroom unit to make plants grow. Have the students bring in avocado pits, grass seeds, and celery tops. Provide the students with paper cups that can be used as plant containers. Instruct the students to punch holes in the bottoms of the plant containers and fill with soil, or use toothpicks to suspend an avocado pit partially in water. Teach the students to test the soil or observe the water level to determine if the plant requires water.

Secondary Level. Discuss the concept of timelines with the student and the importance of planning and understanding life's events. Have the student either bring in old photographs or draw pictures on index cards and arrange them in order. Have the student string these along a modified clothesline, and then discuss his or her life, acting out each picture.

Family Interventions

Infant and Toddler/Preschool Level. Encourage the parents to take a walk with their child and play I Spy (e.g., "I spy something tall with leaves."). This game can be played in a variety of settings, such as the grocery store or street.

Have the parent play What's Wrong? Encourage them to use things in their child's immediate environment (e.g., pouring milk from an unopened carton, attempting to put on a shoe without untying it, eating soup with a fork).

Primary Level. Suggest to the parents that they play a guessing riddle game with their child (e.g. "What has four wheels and moves?" "What has numbers and rings?" "What animal is furry and meows?").

Ask the parents to provide their child with a magnifying glass. Ask them to help their child take a closer look at his or her hand, a leaf, a flower, hair, spiders, or any other available small object with texture. Ask the child questions about the object, such as about color, texture, and movement.

Have the parents take their child to a miniature golf course or arcade room in a mall or sports center. Remind the parents to encourage their child to attempt a variety of games to keep the child interested and to practice eye–hand coordination.

Intermediate and Secondary Levels. Ask the parents to set up a croquet set or tetherball on the lawn. Encourage the parents to engage the youngster in discussions of safety and game rules.

Have the parents participate with the youngster to make a family tree using photographs. Assist the youngster to understand the concepts of family and shared characteristics, if appropriate. (This may not be applicable to adoptive or blended families.) Discuss the appropriateness of the selection of low-activity games when their youngster is ill or when a quiet activity is relevant, such as during limited space or time.

Specific Objective E

The student plays high-activity games.

Teacher Interventions

Infant and Toddler/Preschool Level.   Engage the infant in crawling or rolling games on the floor by placing favorite objects slightly out of reach and encouraging the infant to grasp them.

Demonstrate the game Red Light/Green Light by having the student stand in the playground with his or her back to the group of children. Have the student call, "1–2–3–4 green light," and the other students begin to run toward his or her back. Have the student then call "red light" and turn around to see if the other students have stopped.

Primary Level.   Engage the student in a game of animal imitations, encouraging the child to imitate as many animal movements as possible (e.g., deer, spider, frog, horse).

Create an obstacle course on the playground that requires the student to jump, run around, and crawl under. Have the student participate in games of dodge ball, four square, Greek dodge, and tetherball.

Intermediate and Secondary Levels.   Take the student to a gym to engage in a game of one-on-one basketball. Invite other students to join so that a neighborhood game of basketball can be played.

Engage the student in a variety of racing games, such as Keep Away and relays. Discuss the benefits of strenuous exercise but caution the student to avoid high-activity games when tired or recovering from an illness.

Family Interventions

Infant and Toddler/Preschool Level.   Ask the parents to combine exercise and song by singing with their child, "Head and Shoulders, Knees and Toes." Have them demonstrate naming and touching the body parts as they sing, increasing the pace.

Ask the parents to pair activity words to movements with their child, such as jump, hop, skip, run, walk.

Primary Level. Ask the parents to provide their child with a radio or tape player with tapes. Encourage them to give their child opportunities to dance spontaneously to the radio or rhythmic tapes.

Intermediate and Secondary Levels. Ask the parents to enroll their youngster in organized recreational activities, such as soccer or baseball, through the school, community or recreation council, or local YMCA. If available, request that the parents arrange for their youngster to participate in intramural sports after school.

 ## Specific Objective F

The student plays target games.

Teacher Interventions

Infant and Toddler/Preschool Level. Provide the child with a soft ball and gently toss the ball back and forth. When the child can respond to "throw," give him or her a stationary stand-up ring. Demonstrate how to toss the ball into the ring. Reinforce the child for each attempt.

Purchase a standing bean bag toss board with strategically placed holes. Provide the young child with bean bags and demonstrate tossing the bags through the holes. Encourage the young child to try the activity.

Primary Level. Use chalk to draw a circle on the floor. Provide the student with marbles and assist him or her to learn to shoot the marbles.

Using darts with suction cups and a soft target with numbers, assist the student to throw the darts at the target. Have the student keep score and assist other students to participate. Assist the student to understand the scoring rules.

Intermediate Level. Set up horseshoes on the playground. Use plastic horseshoes to ensure the safety of the students. Demonstrate how to toss the horseshoe at the stake. Assist the student to toss the horseshoe and provide encouragement for each attempt. Teach the student to observe all safety rules.

Secondary Level. Locate a gym or recreational facility with a shuffleboard court. Provide the student with an opportunity to observe the game being played. Instruct the student in the scoring rules and procedures for playing. Assist the student to play the game.

Family Interventions

Infant and Toddler/Preschool Level. Describe for the parents how to use a turned-over cardboard box (with holes cut in the bottom) as a target and have them help their child to push clothespins into the holes. Then the parents can assist the child to toss jar rings over the pins. As the child gets older, the parents can label the pins with color or numbers. The parents can ask the child to aim for the pin colored blue or red or numbered 1, 2, or 3.

Encourage the parents to provide opportunities for blindfold games, with adult supervision, such as blind man's bluff and pin the tail on the donkey.

Primary Level. Ask the parents to show their child how to play tiddlywinks. This game can combine color concepts with estimation of distances to the target.

Ask the parents to get Velcro target games, such as those that use Velcro balls and a Velcro paddle. Have the parents demonstrate how to throw the balls with underhand and overhand throws and encourage their child to keep an eye on the target.

An easy indoor game is the cup and ball game, which can be played by one person. The cup and ball are made of wood, joined by a length of cord. The player holds the cup at the base with the ball hanging toward the ground. The child swings the ball and tries to catch the ball in the cup.

Ask the parents to provide their child with marbles. Demonstrate how to play and partner with the child to play a game. Remind the parent to monitor the child to keep the marbles in a drawstring bag or other container.

Intermediate Level. Provide the parents with sandbags and ask the parents to create targets in their child's room that are consistent with their child's interests (e.g., basketball hoop, animal shapes, planets).

Suggest to the parents that marbles have been popular for years and that the objective of the game is to develop skills that teach the child to aim the marbles. The marbles are rolled into a circle. The knuckle of the forefinger is placed on the ground and the marble held in balance with the thumb behind the forefinger. If one player hits another's marble, he or she may keep or "capture" the marble.

Secondary Level. Encourage the parents to take their youngster to a mall arcade with a variety of electronic target games. The computerized games keep score, which can assist and motivate the youngster to concentrate on the skills of the target game.

Encourage the parents to play ball with their youngster regularly using a large catcher's mitt. The youngster can develop target skills and improve his or her catching ability.

Specific Objective G

The student plays balance games.

Teacher Interventions

Infant and Toddler/Preschool Level. Play Simon Says with the child, giving commands that require the child, for example, to stand on one foot or to bend over at the waist.

   Turn on active music and ask the child to dance. Explain that once in a while, the sound will go off and the child must stand like a statue.

Primary Level. Use the floor game Twister and assist the students to adapt the game as appropriate. Remind the students to balance carefully so as not to fall on another student.

Intermediate Level. Engage the student in a game of building a house of cards. Provide the student with instructions and assist him or her in following the instructions. As the student gains skills, assist him or her to build alternative structures.

Secondary Level. Provide the student with a balance beam that can be adjusted for progressively increasing heights. For students with certain physical difficulties, provide bars to support their bodies. Play music and encourage the student to attempt to safely walk from one end to the other.

Family Interventions

Infant and Toddler/Preschool Level. Ask the parents to demonstrate to their child how to play donkey kick. Tell them to get on their hands and knees with arms straight. Have them lower their head and bring their leg up to touch their nose and kick the leg behind. Alternate legs.

   Have the parents place a board, at least 1 foot wide, with one end on the floor and one raised off the floor. Have them assist their child to walk from the low end to the high end and turn around and walk back down.

Primary Level. Have the parents teach their child to play hopscotch. Tell them to adapt the game to the child's ability, with the goal to be independent in tossing and hopping.

Intermediate Level. Ask the parents to teach their child to play dominoes. Explain that, although the game involves matching and joining dominoes end to end, the game can be combined with balancing the dominoes.

Secondary Level. Jenga is an inexpensive game that can be used for many age groups. The game contains wood blocks that are initially stacked to form a tower. The parents and youngster then take turns removing blocks from the bottom, one by one, and placing them on top to build the tower higher, seeing how high the tower can be constructed without falling.

Specific Objective H

The student plays table games.

Teacher Interventions

Infant and Toddler/Preschool Level. As a lead-in to table games, provide the young child with opportunities to play a version of a floor game that involves whole body movements (e.g., Twister). These games provide activities that keep the young child's interest and move the child through the game while teaching turn-taking and basic rules.

Preschool children can participate in shuffleboard with adult assistance. Shuffleboard is available in table and floor versions. It is ideal for young children because it involves full body movement and can be played with adult assistance.

Primary Level. Provide the student with a wide range of board games that are appropriate to the student's developmental level. Some games (e.g., Monopoly and Clue) are available in nonreading versions that can be played readily by children this age. Provide time during the class to encourage the student to choose a partner and play the game, observing the rules and playing until there is a winner.

Intermediate and Secondary Levels. Obtain a versatile table version of air hockey, foosball, or soccer. Provide the student with simple instructions and time within the class to play the games as a leisure activity.

Family Interventions

Infant and Toddler/Preschool Level. Encourage the parents to provide opportunities for their child to participate in and observe the family playing board games. Ask the parents to partner with their young child in a game of floor checkers, using a checker mat with large pieces.

Primary, Intermediate, and Secondary Levels. Ask the parents to take their child to a community recreational facility or sports complex to teach their child how to play table hockey and table shuffleboard.

Specific Objective I

The student plays card games.

Teacher Interventions

Infant and Toddler/Preschool Level. Select a variety of larger sized card games for matching of pictures, dots, colors, shapes, or large numbers. Partner with the student and demonstrate the game.

As the child begins to understand the concept of putting cards down and making pairs, introduce other more complex games, such as Go Fish and Old Maid.

Primary Level. Provide the student with a regular 52-card deck, using large-print numbers when appropriate. Discuss the games of War and Solitaire. While playing with the student, demonstrate the variety of strategies used in playing these games.

Intermediate and Secondary Levels. Show the student card games that can be played when alone. In addition, for students this age, computer software packages are available that can increase the student's interest in playing card games.

Students can be engaged in group card games, such as bridge and simple games of chance.

Family Interventions

Preschool and Primary Levels. Ask the parents to teach their child simple card games using a regular 52-card deck (e.g. War, Go Fish, Hearts). Encourage the parents to assist their child to identify numerals and letters and the suit to which a card belongs.

Intermediate and Secondary Levels. Ask the parents to purchase card games that require special cards and to teach the games to their youngster.

Using a regular deck of cards, ask the parents to teach their youngster to play Solitaire, assisting with the placement of cards in rank order and scoring. Another fun game for youngsters to play with the family is Euchre, which has many variations and can keep the family's interest for quite a while.

Parents need to caution their youngster that there are people who might exploit them by playing cards for money.

Specific Objective J

The student plays games of chance.

Teacher Interventions

Primary Level. Show the student how to use dice as part of games in which the throw of the dice determines the order of play and the number of spaces moved.

Fifty is a simple dice game that involves throwing two dice and the winner is the first player to score 50 points. Each player rolls the two dice, but scores only when identical numbers are thrown.

Intermediate and Secondary Levels. Show the student how to play Yahtzee and Double Yahtzee. These games can be purchased and provide hours of fun.

Hearts is a game for two or more players. Six dice are used, and the objective is to score more than your opponents over a series of rounds.

Family Interventions

Primary Level. Ask the parents to show their child how to play games such as bingo. Many children this age become aware of lottery games, and some parents may choose to purchase the scratch-off versions. Caution the parents to talk to their children about games of chance and the impact on their lives if they risk money needed for regular life-sustaining activities.

Intermediate and Secondary Levels. Encourage the parents to introduce their youngster to games of chance, such as those described in Teacher Interventions and Primary Level Family Interventions.

Specific Objective K

The student plays strategy games.

Teacher Interventions

Primary Level. Purchase specially designed lotto games (e.g., Lotto, Memory). Teach the student to select games and play them during leisure periods in class.

Demonstrate tic–tac–toe and assist the student to identify ways to block the completion of a line.

Intermediate Level. Show the student how to play Sorry, Trouble, and Chinese Checkers, explaining the different strategies to be used in playing the game.

Secondary Level. Introduce the student to games such as backgammon and chess. These games require a higher level of understanding and the ability to plan strategies several moves ahead.

Family Interventions

Primary Level. Ask the parents to show their child how to play checkers. With children with fine motor problems, large floor mats and pieces can be used.

Chinese Checkers is another game that can be played by parents and their children of all ages.

Intermediate and Secondary Levels. Ask the parents to purchase and play with their youngster such strategy games as Battleship, Monopoly, and Stratego. Encourage them to assist their child in comprehension of the scoring rules and procedures, which come with the games. When appropriate or if needed, they may modify the rules.

Specific Objective L

The student plays real-life games.

Teacher Interventions

Infant and Toddler/Preschool Level. Engage the young child in games of musical chairs and magic carpet. When the music stops assist the child to sit on the chair or the magic carpet piece.

Provide adult clothing in the room and play stations which encourage young children to dress up and act out a variety of roles and activities. Discuss with the child the kinds of people in homes and communities and what they do.

Primary, Intermediate, and Secondary Levels. Games such as Monopoly and the Game of Life can be used to discuss with the student the problems and issues of contemporary life, such as the cost of housing, the process of banking, loss of funds, and planning for future expenses.

Family Interventions

Infant and Toddler/Preschool Level Encourage parents to play games such as those described for Teacher Interventions.

Primary, Intermediate, and Secondary Levels. Ask the parents to engage their children in a variety of real-life games, such as Monopoly. Encourage them to reinforce skills necessary to the game, such as the exchange of money and taking turns.

Specific Objective M

The student plays knowledge and word games.

Teacher Interventions

Primary Level. Give each student a treasure hunt map with word clues. The theme for the game can be names of objects in the room, colors, nouns, verbs, or math problems, with the answers located in strategic spots in the room or building. Provide prizes to the students finding each answer and object.

Intermediate Level. Introduce the student to the game Go to the Head of the Class. The game may need to be modified by simplifying the questions to provide opportunities for the student to be successful.

Secondary Level. Play academic games, such as Presidents, if they are within the student's ability.

Family Interventions

Infant and Toddler/Preschool Level. Ask the parents to sing songs to their babies whenever the occasion is appropriate (e.g., when changing diapers, sing "This Little Piggy," gently wiggling each toe).

Encourage parents to sing the ABC song when driving in the car with their young child. As the child learns the ABCs, introduce the concept of singing words with the letter, such as "A is for apple, B is for bear, C is for candy, D is for dog, . . ." The library has video and audio tapes that can demonstrate such songs.

Primary Level.   Ask the parents to play games such as Concentration and Password if their child is able to play these games with some success.

Intermediate and Secondary Levels. Ask the parents to play Scrabble and Spill and Spell with their youngster, assisting him or her with the scoring rules and procedures if necessary.

Specific Objective N

The student chooses a variety of toys and games.

Teacher Interventions

Infant and Toddler/Preschool Level. Provide a wide range of toy boxes and learning stations in the room that encourage the student to select toys and games. These toys should be kept at eye level and need to represent a wide range of developmental levels.

Primary Level. Delegate specific times of the day for free play. Encourage the student to choose from a cupboard of toys and games of interest. If the student selects the same game or toy each time, guide the student to choose a different one by demonstrating it in a fashion that engages the student to play.

Intermediate and Secondary Levels. Post a check-out chart on the shelf of games or toys. Have the student mark down the item selected for classroom free play. Explain to the student that the goal is to have a different game or age-appropriate toy for each day.

Family Interventions

Infant and Toddler/Preschool Level. Encourage the parents to select a variety of toys and games that are appropriate and safe for their child. Remind them that children learn best through interaction and modeling.

Ask the parents to arrange play dates and alternate going to other children's homes to increase the variety of different toys and games for their child.

Primary Level. Ask the parents to provide their child with a variety of toys and games. Explain that, although it is natural for a child to play exclusively with a new toy, they should encourage their child to play with all their toys and games.

Intermediate and Secondary Levels. Parents of older youngsters may need suggestions for the types of games and toys that will be appropriate. Suggest that parents ask their youngster about specific interests and select games that will stimulate fun and reinforce the importance of leisure activities within the home.

 ## Specific Objective O

The student plays multiple types of video games.

Teacher Interventions

Primary, Intermediate, and Secondary Levels. Obtain a video game machine by visiting yard sales or through the PTA, if possible. Used games can be purchased inexpensively at second-hand stores and yard sales or can be rented at the local library. Be very careful to preview all video games to be used in the classroom setting for violence or sexual content. Games can be used in the classroom in conjunction with a regular lesson plan if the game relates to the content material.

In addition, during designated leisure times, the student can be provided with opportunities to play video games if class work is completed, behavior is appropriate, and parental permission has been granted.

Family Interventions

Primary, Intermediate, and Secondary Levels. Parents can be encouraged to select a wide range of video games that reinforce learning and provide leisure opportunities for their youngster. Games can be borrowed through the public library or rented from video stores. Develop and provide parents with a list of educational games that are appropriate to the youngster's age and grade level. Caution parents to monitor the content and the amount of time spent on video games.

If the youngster needs adaptations to the equipment, provide the necessary referrals or information that would enable the youngster to be accommodated.

GOAL II.

The student will engage in sports and activities of physical fitness.

Sports activities are an opportunity for fun and exercise. Special attention must be given to the individual's physical and cognitive limitations, ensuring that the emphasis is on enjoyment and fitness rather than on competition. Prior to involving a student in a sport, an analysis of the skills needed to participate should be completed. Special adaptations and other modifications in structure may need to be included for the student with cognitive and physical disabilities. The nature of participation will vary with the nature of the activity. The functional context of games should be the emphasis on combining socialization with the importance of physical fitness.

Any program involving sports activities must also include an assessment of the student. This may include a consideration of how he or she functions as part of a team, whether or not the student enjoys competitive activities, and the student's tolerance of physical exercise. Any program of physical exercise should be medically cleared, and include components of total conditioning and balanced exercises. Students should be encouraged to include warm-up and cool-down periods.

SPECIFIC OBJECTIVES

The student:

❑ A. Rides a tricycle or bicycle.

❑ B. Participates in roller or in-line skating activities individually, with friends, and/or as part of a team.

❑ C. Participates as a spectator or active participant in water sports.

❑ D. Participates in boating activities.

❑ E. Participates in snow sports.

❑ F. Participates in mountain sports activities.

❑ G. Participates in exercise and physical fitness activities.

❑ H. Participates as a spectator at sports events.

❑ I. Participates in two-person sports.

❑ J. Participates in team sports.

❑ K. Participates in aerobics.

SUGGESTED ACTIVITIES

Specific Objective A

The student rides a tricycle or bicycle.

Teacher Interventions

Infant and Toddler/Preschool Level Young children enjoy being pushed in strollers and other rolling equipment. A variety of adaptive devices are available to provide the sensation of riding in order to familiarize the young child with bicycle movement.

During playtime provide a variety of supine tricycles and bicycles with training wheels on a surfaced area. Assist the child with grasping the handles with both hands, using the palmar grasp. Purchase the foot holder peddles so the child's feet can be stabilized on the peddles.

Primary Level. Assist the student to balance and steer the bicycle using the handlebars. Adaptive support bars are available for the back of the bike for teachers to assist with balance and steering. As part of the lesson, discuss safety rules for riding, including hand signals and the appropriate side of the road for riding versus walking. Always require a helmet, and if you are biking with the student wear a helmet as well.

Intermediate and Secondary Levels. Students are usually able to ride a bicycle independently by this age. The important information at this point is related to safety and the possible dangers of riding on roads and negotiating traffic. Discourage riding at night and make safety issues an important part of each lesson. For older students with physical limitations, consult with a physical therapist about using a large adult tricycle instead of a bicycle to minimize balance problems and provide opportunities for participation.

Family Intersventions

Infant and Toddler/Preschool Level. For the very young child, ask the parents to use a safety approved child seat on the back of an adult bike and provide opportunities for riding together as a family. Stress caution and safety when doing this activity.

Encourage the parents to set aside time for tricycle and bicycle riding on a regularly scheduled basis, depending on the weather and the child's health and physical condition.

Primary Level. If the parents have a stationary bike, suggest that their child use it to practice the bicycling motion, adjusting speed of rotation and foot technique. Many stationary bikes are listed for sale in the newspaper and are usually inexpensive.

Intermediate Level. Ask the parents to locate an approved bike path and take their child on a family outing to ride and enjoy the physical activity in the environment. If the child has a severe physical disability, provide the parents with information on using an adaptive device to pull the child.

Secondary Level. Provide the parents with information on charity bike rides to raise money for charities. Encourage the parents to participate as a family to emphasize the responsibility of good citizenship. For students in states with school service learning hour requirements, the youngster may wish to earn service hours.

Specific Objective B

The student participates in roller or in-line skating activities individually, with friends, and/or as part of a team.

Teacher Interventions

Primary Level. Engage the student in skating activities that are appropriate to his or her developmental age. For the student with good balance and strong ankles, arrange for a field trip to a skating rink, involving roller skates or roller blades. If possible, arrange for instruction and provide one volunteer per student. Emphasize safety rules and procedures prior to the skating activities.

Students who may not be able to skate can be pushed in wheelchairs around the rink if prior arrangements have been made with the management to provide them with an opportunity to participate. The severely physically limited student can select the music or arrange for refreshments as alternative activities.

Intermediate and Secondary Levels. See the activity described for the Primary Level. At this age safety concerns need to be emphasized. Remind the students that helmets should be worn when skating outside. If the student is participating in in-line skating, review the need for wrist, elbow, and knee protection, in addition to the helmet.

Family Interventions

Primary Level. Encourage the parents to purchase training skates and to assist their child by first physically supporting him or her while the child is learning. After the child has acquired adequate balance and some of the rhythm of skating, encourage the parent to glide slowly while holding the child in front of the parent. As the child gains confidence, suggest that the parent release the child and skate behind him or her as a safeguard.

Suggest that the parent plan parties and gatherings at local skating rinks where both roller and in-line skates are allowed. On Saturday mornings, many rinks limit skating to parties with young children.

Intermediate and Secondary Levels. Ask parents to emphasize safety concerns, as discussed in Teacher Interventions.

Specific Objective C

The student participates as a spectator or active participant in water sports.

Teacher Interventions

Infant and Toddler/Preschool Level   Waterplay tables provide younger students with opportunities to get used to water activities. As the weather warms, wading pools can be used. Be sure that there is adequate supervision to ensure the safety of all children. Introduce water games in the pool and encourage participation. Never leave children unattended.

Primary Level.   Ask a lifeguard or recreation and parks instructor to visit the classroom to speak to the students about water sports and safety. When working with a specific student, advise the speaker about the student's disability and functioning level.

Intermediate Level.   Ask the local health club or hotel with an indoor pool if your student may have access to the pool. Obtain parental permission and arrange for instruction at the pool for the student. Stress water safety and responsible behavior in the pool and swimming areas.

Secondary Level.   Once the student can swim, arrange for supervised instructional units for physical education at the community pool. Provide adaptations for students who are unable to float independently. Form teams for water relay races, water volleyball, or simplified water polo.

Family Interventions

Infant and Toddler/Preschool Level.   Some parents will already have introduced their children to the water through water-babies classes. Discuss with parents the use of a wading pool and the necessary safety issues.

Primary Level.   Encourage the parents to have their child participate in community swimming opportunities that are appropriate to his or her level of functioning. Many parks and recreation pools offer a variety of adaptive water programs.

Intermediate and Secondary Levels. Water safety remains an important issue for adolescents. Encourage the parents to teach their youngster to avoid unsafe places (quarries) or unhealthy places (polluted water).

When appropriate, ask the parents to have their youngster participate in swimming lessons. When their youngster knows how to swim, encourage the parents to have him or her participate in a variety of water sports.

Specific Objective D

The student participates in boating activities.

Teacher Interventions

Primary Level. Ask the parents or guardians for permission and arrange to take the student to a place where rowboats or paddleboats can be rented. Be sure the student uses a lifejacket, even if he or she can swim. Demonstrate how to row the boat or to use the legs in a cycling motion on the paddle boat.

Some harbor resorts or lakeside parks have a variety of boating activities that groups can use.

Intermediate and Secondary Levels. When appropriate, take the student to a sailing or canoeing school. Many of these schools provide one-on-one instruction and adaptations for individuals with disabilities.

Some large sailboats provide back-to-nature adventures with overnight opportunities for students and sailing instruction at a wide range of levels.

Family Interventions

Primary Level. Tell the parents about the advantages of psychomotor skill development through paddling or rowing. Encourage them to take their child to a park that rents boats or other watercrafts, so they can view various activities in which they might wish to participate.

Intermediate and Secondary Levels. If possible, ask the parents to plan a family outing on a large motorized boat, such as a harbor cruise ship.

Specific Objective E

The student participates in snow sports.

Teacher Interventions

Infant and Toddler/Preschool Level. During the winter, discuss the weather and what will happen if the air is cold and precipitation falls. If the local climate is too warm, demonstrate to the children how to put water in a tray, which has a snowman mold, and put it in the freezer. Unmold the snowman and talk about winter and snow.

In areas of the country that routinely have cold weather and snow, encourage parents to provide snow clothing for their child. When the climate is appropriate, allow the students to go outside to feel, smell, and play with the snow. Develop a thematic unit about the seasons. Have the student participate in developing an experience story about winter and create three-dimensional displays based on the story.

Primary Level. Discuss the types of equipment that can be used to participate in winter sports. Select a video that shows a wide range of snow-related sports. If no snow is available to actually go sledding, demonstrate the use of a sled or toboggan in school, and ask the students to bring in any sports equipment that can be used during the winter months (e.g. skis, snowboards, ice skates).

On a snowy day, take the student outside to build a snowman and igloo. Emphasize the need to walk carefully on snow and ice to avoid falling.

Intermediate and Secondary Levels. In addition to the Primary Level activities, provide the student with a block of ice and demonstrate how to do ice sculpting. Provide the student with a chisel and rubber-handled hammer and assist him or her to make a geometric shape or more representative creation. Practice safety procedures while using the chisel and hammer.

Family Interventions

Infant and Toddler/Preschool Level. Encourage the parents to take their child outside to make snow angels by gently falling back in the snow and waving their arms. Ask the parents to assist the child to make snow balls and throw them up in the air and watch them fall.

Primary Level. Ask the parents to help their child make a snowman. Encourage the parents to have the child select a favorite hat and scarf, a carrot for the nose, and other decorations.

Ask the parents to take their child skiing or snowboarding, if possible. If the parents would prefer to go to an ice skating rink, ask them to consider having a birthday party with an instructor present.

Encourage the parents to have their child take off wet clothing and hang it to dry, and to build in time for hot chocolate and a hot bath.

Intermediate and Secondary Levels. Ask the parents to involve their youngster in any family-related activities that include snow sports. Provide the parents with information on community skiing trips or nearby toboggan trails. Physical activities can provide the youngster with the benefits of physical exercise as well as social contacts.

Remind parents to encourage their child to follow safety rules in all snow sports. Especially with adolescents, who are not always well supervised, the parents need to emphasize the dangers of throwing snow balls, particularly at cars and people.

Specific Objective F

The student participates in mountain sports activities.

Teacher Interventions

Infant and Toddler/Preschool Level. Young children enjoy strolling or walking along nature trails. Plan interclass activities that include older children and young children to encourage the buddy system and provide for interaction around nature themes.

Primary Level. Discuss the variety of settings where the student can walk and enjoy the outdoors. Plan a walk or nature hike on a local park trail. Many areas provide bike paths through wooded areas. Plan an outing to a local nature path that allows mountain biking, providing sufficient supervision.

Intermediate and Secondary Levels. Plan a day-long outing with the student, asking the student to pack a lunch, including drinks, as well as other important items such as sunscreen, bug repellent, and sunglasses.

Family Interventions

Infant and Toddler/Preschool Level. Ask the parents to take their young child in a backpack on a nature walk, protecting the child from the sun and insects.

Ask the parents to provide their child with a plastic bucket and encourage the child to collect nature items for a collage to be made when the family returns home. Encourage the parents to identify the various objects by name and discuss their importance in the natural environment.

Primary, Intermediate, and Secondary Levels. If available, ask the parents to take their youngster mountain biking at an area that has a ski lift or cable car to the mountain or hilltop. If their youngster has a physical limitation, contact the local sports association for the disabled and determine if adaptations are available.

If the youngster is able, the parents can involve their child in more challenging sports, such as rappelling or mountain climbing. Many areas offer indoor rappelling facilities and climbing walls, with safety devices that permit climbing by participants of varied ability levels.

Specific Objective G

The student participates in exercise and physical fitness activities.

Teacher Interventions

Infant and Toddler/Preschool Level. Very young children can be placed on a floor pad and engaged in a wide range of crawling activities, using puppets and balls.

Using a pillow, coax the student to crawl over the pillow while you support the child's shoulders as he or she crawls over. The pillow crawl enhances the strength and coordination of the young child.

Play Simon Says with the student, using a wide range of physical movements and calisthenics (e.g., touch forehead to toes, raise the flag, squat).

Primary, Intermediate, and Secondary Levels. Initiate a program of calisthenics, using a variety of movements, including steppers (i.e., benches) and other supporting equipment to engage the student. Have the student keep a record of the daily exercise period. Include peer reinforcement and other incentives to reward the student.

Family Interventions

Infant and Toddler/Preschool Level. Ask the parents to play music while holding their infant and moving the child gently to the rhythm. Young babies enjoy body massage and gentle leg manipulation and stretching. Many infant books have sections on the importance of touching and handling the infant.

If there are local recreation programs for tots, encourage the parents to participate.

As the child gets older, encourage the parents to have the child exercise in time with the music. Have the parents take the child for a fast hike around the neighborhood.

Primary, Intermediate, and Secondary Levels. Encourage the parents to participate in the local YMCA or health clubs and to take their youngster to participate in physical fitness activities. Ask the parents to involve their youngster in activities such as gymnastics, tumbling, weight lifting, and rope jumping, when appropriate.

Specific Objective H

The student participates as a spectator at sports events.

Teacher Interventions

Primary Level. Read the student a book about a variety of spectator sports that are age appropriate. Discuss the types of sports that spectators go to see and the role of spectators at sporting events. Discuss whether the student has been to any spectator sports and the behaviors of the spectators.

Intermediate and Secondary Levels. Ask the student to bring in the sports section of the newspaper. Review the spectator sports events of the day and scoring, as well as the concept of professional and amateur sports and team standings.

Obtain a stadium seating chart for a major sporting event. Review possible seating locations with the student. Purchase tickets and take the student to the event.

Identify spectator sports in which the student has an interest, including individual and team sports. Arrange for the student to attend school events, discussing appropriate spectator behaviors.

Family Interventions

Primary Level. Encourage the parents to provide the child with opportunities to watch major sporting events. Ask the parents to take their child to local sports events, such as baseball and soccer. If the child is interested, encourage the parent to involve their child in activities that have spectators to reinforce the concept of participating as a spectator.

Intermediate and Secondary Levels. Ask the youngster to keep a calendar of sporting events based on the newspaper and those listed in the local TV guide. Encourage the youngster to watch the events and report the scores.

Specific Objective I

The student participates in two-person sports.

Teacher Interventions

Infant and Toddler/Preschool Level. Take the child to an indoor playground designed for young children. Engage the child in two-person activities, such as playing catch, see-sawing, and two-person swinging.

Primary Level. Organize a game of tether ball for two students, demonstrating the strategy and scoring. Provide two students with Velcro throwing paddles and balls. Demonstrate how to play catch.

If appropriate, take the students to a game center or purchase an expensive sports table. Arrange for the student to pair with another student to play soccer or air hockey.

Intermediate and Secondary Levels. Arrange for the students to have physical education instruction in sports table tennis, golf, racquetball, handball, and squash. For some sports, the emphasis should be on special equipment and clothing that would protect the student.

Family Interventions

Infant and Toddler/Preschool Level. Ask the parents to arrange the child and another family member with their legs stretched out and their feet touching. The two people then roll a large ball back and forth.

Ask the parents to provide the child with a soft ball and demonstrate with another person how to throw the ball back and forth.

Primary, Intermediate, and Secondary Levels. Encourage the parents to involve their youngsters in sports activities with a friend or through a program at the recreational council (e.g., badminton, tennis, catch). Frequently health clubs have courts for racquetball and paddle ball, games that are easily learned by a beginner.

Ask the parents to play one-on-one basketball with their youngster. Even with a youngster in a wheelchair, the net can be adjusted to accommodate shots.

 ## Specific Objective J

The student participates in team sports.

Teacher Interventions

Infant and Toddler/Preschool Level. Engage the students in group activities such as sitting on a floor and rolling the ball to specific students and Duck–Duck–Goose.

Young children enjoy activities such as sack walks and wheelbarrow drives (i.e., holding the child's feet while he or she walks on hands), which develop an understanding of interdependence in physical activities. These activities can be adapted for children with varying levels of physical development and skill.

Primary Level. Students at this age are usually interested in higher levels of physical activity for leisure periods and will begin to organize themselves into teams for informal games, such as tag and kick ball.

Soccer has become very popular in recent years and offers a variety of positions for students with varied skills. Basketball and baseball also provide students with the skills to play on teams of players with varied skill levels.

Some physical education classes take students bowling. Neighborhood bowling alleys can provide bumpers and other assistance for students with physical needs.

Intermediate and Secondary Levels. Form teams for sports in the appropriate season (e.g., soccer and football in the fall; basketball, indoor soccer, lacrosse, and volleyball in the winter; baseball, tennis, and softball in the spring; swimming in the summer). Initiate intramural sports between classes if organized school sports are not available. Emphasize sportsmanship and use of appropriate equipment. It is also important that youngsters develop an understanding of physical fitness as a lifetime endeavor.

Family Interventions

Infant and Toddler/Preschool Level. Encourage parents to engage their child in activities such as those described in Teacher Interventions.

Primary, Intermediate, and Secondary Levels. Encourage the parents to join bowling, swimming, and softball teams through community facilities. For the youngster with disabilities that have an impact on his or her ability to participate, recreational therapists through recreation councils can provide adapted opportunities.

Specific Objective K

The student participates in aerobics.

Teacher Interventions

Infant and Toddler/Preschool Level. Very young children have different levels of energy and coordination. Most, however, enjoy crawling, walking, and running. Some days, the child will welcome organized exercise and participate for long periods of time. Other days, 10 minutes will seem too long.

Sit on the floor with the young child and do arm crossovers, swings, and raises; touch head to toes; and do modified roll-downs (sit-ups). Stand and bend over and do monkey walks, rabbit hops, duck walks, and jumping jacks. These can be combined with the game Simon Says, and music with an energetic rhythm can be played.

Primary, Intermediate, and Secondary Levels. Appropriate aerobic activities for older students include jumping rope, walking, jogging, skating, and swimming. Students can participate at their own level, and variations of the activities will keep the student interested.

Many team sports, such as basketball, offer aerobic benefits. Students can be encouraged to participate and may engage in them as lifetime leisure activities.

Family Interventions

Infant and Toddler/Preschool Level. Encourage parents to engage their child in activities such as those described in Teacher Interventions.

Primary, Intermediate, and Secondary Levels. Ask parents to encourage their youngster to participate in activities such as those described in Teacher Interventions.

Many families have exercise equipment available, such as treadmills, stairclimbers, and stationary bicycles. Parents should be encouraged to provide their youngsters with opportunities to use the equipment with the necessary instruction and supervision.

GOAL III.

The student will participate in camping and diverse outdoor activities.

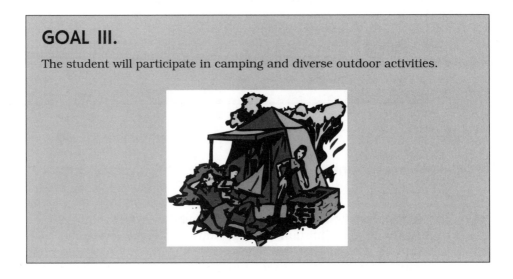

SPECIFIC OBJECTIVES

The student:

❑ A. Engages in a variety of activities using park and playground facilities and equipment.

❑ B. Goes fishing and/or catches shellfish.

❑ C. Goes camping.

❑ D. Engages in outdoor cooking activities.

❑ E. Engages in diverse outdoor activities, including operating a lantern and camp stove; using utensils, a knife, an ax, and a compass; and tying ropes.

SUGGESTED ACTIVITIES

Specific Objective A

The student engages in a variety of activities using park and playground facilities and equipment.

Teacher Interventions

Infant and Toddler/Preschool Level. Plan an outing to a local restaurant that has a play area. Ball pits provide a safe play environment for young children.

Locate a preschool playground and identify equipment that the child can use independently or with assistance, depending on his or her needs or limitations. Identify the equipment by name and explain the use of each piece. With toddlers, provide assistance and monitor the use of the equipment. Be sure the playground has appropriate padding on the ground, such as bark chips or rubberized mats.

Primary Level. During recess, encourage the student to use the playground equipment. Caution the student to use the equipment carefully and demonstrate the safe way to use it.

Set up "obstacle" courses on the playground. Include swinging on a swing, climbing on a jungle gym, and other age-appropriate activities. Lead the student through the obstacle course a few times, emphasizing safety. Leave the obstacle course set up and encourage the student to use it at recess.

Intermediate and Secondary Levels. A park can provide an opportunity for older students to explore the terrain and participate in nature activities. Some areas offer outdoor facilities with rope swings and outdoor challenges.

Family Interventions

Infant and Toddler/Preschool Level. Encourage the parents to take their child to a park or playground. Ask the parents to play Follow the Leader, stopping at each piece of equipment while explaining its safe and correct use (e.g., climb on the jungle gym, swing on a swing, slide down the slide).

Primary, Intermediate, and Secondary Levels. Remind the parents of the importance of building lifetime habits of good physical and mental health through the use of outdoor activities. During inclement weather, parents can take youngsters to indoor jungle gyms and arcade facilities that are appropriate for all ages. These facilities offer both leisure and socialization opportunities.

 ## Specific Objective B
The student goes fishing and/or catches shellfish.

Teacher Interventions

Infant and Toddler/Preschool Level. Provide a waterplay area within the class setting. Using plastic fishing equipment available in toy stores, allow young children to simulate the fishing experience. Provide supporting activities and books to read that have fishing as a theme.

Also available for young children are magnetic games that provide opportunities for young children to "catch" the fish and place them on the gameboard.

Primary, Intermediate, and Secondary Levels. If appropriate, plan and take a variety of fishing trips, discussing and implementing units around the types of fishing and the locations in which the fishing is done (e.g., saltwater fishing at the beach; freshwater fishing in streams, lakes, or rivers). If possible, include catching shellfish, such as crabs, clams, and lobsters.

Provide the students with a variety of bait and instruct and demonstrate baiting a hook. Encourage the student to cast the fishing line, wait patiently, and reel it in carefully and slowly to attract fish.

If feasible, take the student icefishing, reviewing the necessary equipment and clothing needs.

Family Interventions

Infant and Toddler/Preschool Level. Encourage parents to engage their child in activities such as those described in Teacher Interventions.

Primary, Intermediate, and Secondary Levels. Encourage the parents to take their youngster on fishing trips. Include the youngster also in the cleaning and cooking of the fish. Many resort areas have piers and boating trips that can offer a variety of activities for family members.

Specific Objective C

The student goes camping.

Teacher Interventions

Infant and Toddler/Preschool Level. In the classroom, set up small "toy" tents and have the child nap in the tent during the rest period. Read stories about camping, discussing and acting out the various activities, including setting up the tent and using a sleeping bag.

Primary Level. As part of a discussion that focuses on outdoor science, contact local or state parks and recreation councils and ask a forest ranger to speak to the class about the natural environments. Continue the discussion with a lesson focusing on preserving the environment and enjoying the outdoors for leisure activities. Focus on camping and camp safety.

Contact the local chapter of Boy and Girl Scouts or Indian Guides and invite a representative to the school to discuss their camping and nature activities. If agreeable, ask the Scouts or Guides to allow your class to accompany them on a hike and camping trip.

Intermediate and Secondary Levels. Ask the parents to identify groups that would provide opportunities for camping experiences for youngsters with a variety of disabilities (e.g., physical limitations, visual impairments, hearing impairments). In certain cases parents may be requested to participate, but families should be encouraged to identify peer companions if supervision is necessary.

Family Interventions

Infant and Toddler/Preschool Level. Encourage the parents to allow their child to "camp out" in the home, using a sleeping bag or indoor tent. Frequently siblings and neighborhood children can be included to provide opportunities for socialization and storytelling.

Primary Level. Ask the parents to take their child on weekend or overnight camping trips and nature walk activities. Provide them with camp songs and suggested outdoor activities. Encourage them to roast marshmallows and keep a "camping journal" to share with the class.

Intermediate and Secondary Levels. Ask the parents to take their child to a sporting goods store and point out the various camping equipment and explain the function of each piece of equipment. They might ask the salesperson to demonstrate select pieces of equipment. Encourage the parents to involve their youngster with a scout troop or other group that goes camping.

Many schools are now sponsoring "camp-outs" in the school to raise money and to provide supervised sleep-over opportunities. Ask the parents to organize a similar activity with their youngster and friends.

Specific Objective D

The student engages in outdoor cooking activities.

Teacher Interventions

Primary, Intermediate, and Secondary Levels. As an end-of-the-year activity, plan a class barbecue. Help the students to select the menu and plan the preparation of the meal. Determine a menu that includes grilling vegetables and a variety of meats. Discuss how this can be accomplished, including the preparation and clean up.

Family Interventions

Primary Level. Ask the parents to plan a family barbecue party during the warmer weather. The child can be responsible to the degree possible for the barbecue activities. After the meal, provide long sticks for roasting marshmallows.

Intermediate and Secondary Levels. Encourage the parents to plan a camping trip. Ask them to involve the child in safely building a campfire, cooking on it, and extinguishing the fire.

Specific Objective E

The student engages in diverse outdoor activities, including operating a lantern and camp stove; using utensils, a knife, an ax, and a compass; and tying ropes.

Teacher Interventions

Primary, Intermediate, and Secondary Levels. Involve the student in a class sleepover at the school building, focusing on activities typical of camp-outs. To the extent feasible, involve the student in using battery-operated lanterns, electric camp stoves, utensils, and a compass.

Invite a representative of the Navy, a nature club, or a Boy or Girl Scout troop to the class for a lesson in knot tying. Schedule a knot-tying activity in the class. Ask each student to select a knot and have the student describe in step-by-step detail how the knot is tied and the purpose of the knot. Have the student prepare a lesson for the class with either written or pictorial plans.

Family Interventions

Primary, Intermediate, and Secondary Levels. Ask the parents to take their youngster camping and demonstrate how to safely operate a camp lantern and camp stove. To the extent the parents are comfortable, ask them to instruct their youngster in the use of a variety of camping equipment.

Encourage the family to take their child to a local park and involve them in survival activities. Ask the parents to demonstrate how to use a knife and ax safely to gather wood and to participate in various camping tasks.

GOAL IV.

The student will use information from the study of nature to engage in relevant leisure activities.

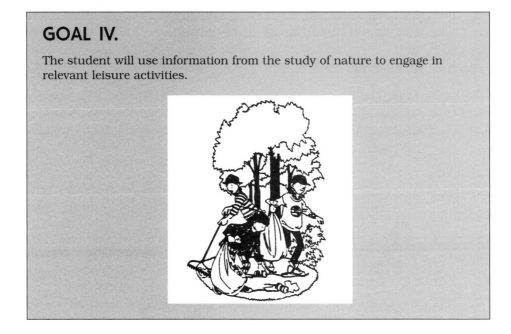

SPECIFIC OBJECTIVES

The student:

- ❏ A. Plans and goes on walks and hiking trips.
- ❏ B. Participates in nature exploration activities.
- ❏ C. Raises and cares for plants.
- ❏ D. Raises and cares for pets.
- ❏ E. Collects leaves, rocks, and shells for a collection, crafts, and/or decorating projects.
- ❏ F. Engages in photography and other art experiences based on natural themes.

SUGGESTED ACTIVITIES

 ### Specific Objective A

The student plans and goes on walks and hiking trips.

Teacher Interventions

Infant and Toddler/Preschool Level. Take the young child on a treasure trip around the outside of the building, making a game of finding insects and natural items to bring back to the classroom to make a collage. Assist the child to identify and to arrange and glue each item.

Primary Level. Take the student on a community walk, pointing out landmarks and other sights. Give the student a list of items to find (or pictures if the student is a nonreader).

Plan a trip to a nearly park or wildlife trail. Discuss the plants and animals that are indigenous to the area; discuss the issue of safety and review behavior appropriate to hiking and walking.

Intermediate and Secondary Levels. Plan a nature trip and review the types of plants and wildlife indigenous to the area. Identify certain items to be collected and plan a classroom display.

Family Interventions

Infant and Toddler/Preschool Level. Encourage the parents to plan a walking trip outdoors, using a stroller or backpack for the younger child. With preschoolers, a wagon can be used to carry both the child and the items gathered along the trail.

Primary, Intermediate, and Secondary Levels. Ask the parents to involve the youngster in preparing for a walk or hike on a trail. Remind the parents to review safety practices with the youngster, particularly if the family hikes in an area with abundant wildlife or poisonous plants. Stress the importance of proper footwear and clothing. When appropriate, sunscreen and insect repellent may be necessary.

 Specific Objective B

The student participates in nature exploration activities.

Teacher Interventions

Infant and Toddler/Preschool Level. Provide the child with a backpack and take the student on a trip to the park. Assist the child in identifying and selecting a variety of items commonly found in a park (e.g., leaves, rocks, acorns). Help the child to construct a diorama to display the nature scene. Invite the parents to see the display.

Primary Level. Take the student on a bird watching trip, preferably to a wildlife sanctuary. As part of the preparation for the trip, provide a unit on bird species, identifying specific characteristics that the student can use to distinguish types of birds. Discuss migratory patterns and the types of birds that will be observed during the specific season of the trip.

Have the student prepare a booklet to identify the birds, and assist the student to include summary information. During the trip, have the student check off each bird seen. Provide the student with binoculars, if available, demonstrating their use and care.

Intermediate and Secondary Levels. Arrange for a cave-exploring trip for the student. In most areas of the country, there are caves that are open to the public and provide guides and routine safety precautions. For the student with a physical difficulty, check to see if elevators and handicap access are available. Review the types of rock formations that the student will observe, including the formation and composition of the rocks.

Family Interventions

Infant and Toddler/Preschool Level.   Encourage the parents to take their child for a trip to the beach. Young children particularly enjoy the opportunity to pick up seashells and other beach-related artifacts.

Publicly operated aquariums frequently have touch rooms that provide opportunities for preschool children to touch and hold a variety of anemones, turtles, seagrass, and shells. In addition, a guide will provide an age-appropriate program to acquaint children with nature exploration.

Primary, Intermediate, and Secondary Levels.   Share the activities described in Teacher Interventions with the parents.

Also encourage the parents to involve their youngster in organizations and community groups that provide group outdoor activities. If needed, a peer companion can help the youngster to participate in age-appropriate activities.

Specific Objective C

The student raises and cares for plants.

Teacher Interventions

Infant and Toddler/Preschool Level.   As an introductory lesson to plant care, provide the child with an avocado pit suspended halfway into a jar of water by toothpicks. Place near a sunny window and watch it sprout roots and topleaf greenery. Assist the student to keep it watered.

Keep easy-care classroom plants (e.g., philodendron, snake plant) on the window sill and include their care in the classroom job list for students. Teach the student to provide care for each plant and the specific needs for lighting.

Provide the child with easily grown seeds, such as coleus plants or peas. Provide the child with sterile dirt and vermiculite in two large containers. Measure 1 scoop each of soil and vermiculite, and mix them in a Styrofoam cup. Explain that the soil needs drainage and nutrients to grow the plant. Assist the child to place the seed into the mixed soil. Assist the child in testing the soil for dryness and providing water when needed. As the seed germinates, discuss each stage with the child.

Primary Level.   As a holiday gift, especially around Mother's Day, plan to grow plants and make planters for mothers. Combine this activity with a plant identification lesson. Provide the student with fact cards about a variety of easily grown plants. Discuss the lighting, soil and nutrients, and watering required for the different plants. Assist the student to understand the difference between low maintenance plants (little water or leaf drop) and higher maintenance plants (draft sensitive, careful watering, flowering leaf drop).

Assist the student to make a plant care chart (see example in Figure 3.1). Draw a picture of the plant or plants the student is caring for and indicate the appropriate plant care needs and conditions. Review the chart during the time of the day the student cares for the plant.

Take a field trip to a local gardening shop. Explain the difference between annuals, perennials, and vegetable plants. In addition, explain the care needs for houseplants, flowers, garden, and a lawn.

Intermediate and Secondary Levels. If a plot is available, assist the students to establish a vegetable garden and assist in planting and caring for the plants. Have the students harvest and prepare a vegetarian luncheon for the class.

Have the student plan a trip to a botanical garden. Before the trip identify the foliage and plants that will be found there. The student can prepare a notebook with questions to be answered about each plant and garden as part of the trip.

Family Interventions

Infant and Toddler/Preschool Level. Ask the parents to take their child to a farm, preferably one frequented by school groups. If possible, have the guide or the farmer describe the planting cycle and related agricultural activities.

Suggest that the parents purchase seedlings of vegetables that can be planted in a small plot of land or a strawberry planter to encourage the child's understanding of the growth process and the need for water and light.

Primary Level. If the family has space available, ask the parents to assist their child in selecting and planting a variety of seeds or seedlings. Encourage them to provide the child with the necessary tools and plant care products, such as fertilizer and soil testing materials. Remind them that the child may need to be supervised when using any products that may be poisonous.

Encourage the family to select house plants that can be easily maintained by the child. Ask them to develop a checklist for care that the child can use as a guide.

Intermediate and Secondary Levels. Ask the parents to plan trips to area home shows and special botanical events to interest their youngster in plants and plant-related studies.

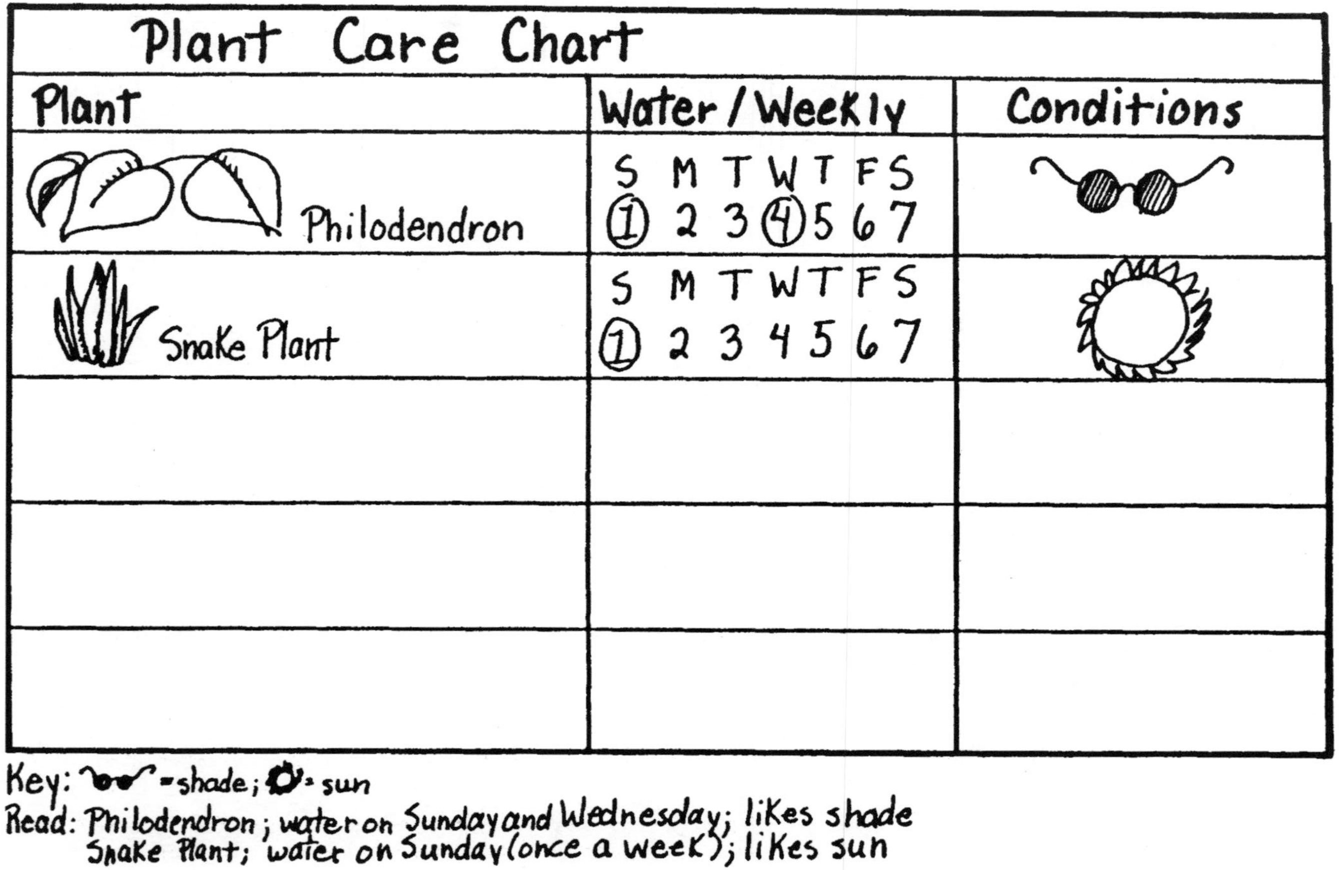

Plant Care Chart

Plant	Water/Weekly	Conditions			
Philodendron	S M T W T F S ① 2 3 ④ ⑤ 6 7	(sunglasses)			
Snake Plant	S M T W T F S ① 2 3 4 5 6 7	(sun)			

Key: (eyeglasses) = shade; ☀ = sun
Read: Philodendron; water on Sunday and Wednesday; likes shade
Snake Plant; water on Sunday (once a week); likes sun

FIGURE 3.1. Plant care chart.

If the family has a computer with a CD capacity, software can be purchased providing a combination of video and voice to teach the youngster about plants and plant science.

Specific Objective D

The student raises and cares for pets.

Teacher Interventions

Infant and Toddler/Preschool Level. For very young children, stuffed animals can provide the opportunity for guided play and learning related to animals and their care. Classroom petting "zoos" can be set up, and children can have many hours of fun and learning by arranging and touring the zoo.

Arrange for a class trip to a real petting zoo within the community. Prepare for it by learning about the animals and discussing the foods they eat and their care.

Purchase a goldfish and keep it in the classroom. Feeding the fish can be a classroom job. Demonstrate to the child how the water needs to be changed and the proper temperature for the water.

Primary Level. Bring into the classroom a variety of small pets, such as hamsters, gerbils, and guinea pigs. Discuss the food and water each animal consumes, stressing the amount and type of each. Demonstrate how to care for the pets and assist the student in learning to handle the pets.

Set up an aquarium in the classroom. Have the student identify the types of fish that could be purchased to keep in the aquarium. Assist the student to identify fish that live in fresh versus salt water. Select the type of food that will be needed and other items that may be added to the aquarium. Plan a trip to the fish store and purchase the fish and food. Set up a schedule for the care and feeding of the fish, stressing the importance of cleaning the filtering systems and not overfeeding.

Intermediate and Secondary Levels. Plan a trip to a regional zoo. Before the trip discuss the types of animals that may be pets and in what setting each type of animal would be a pet. For instance, a snake or guinea pig might be appropriate for someone living in an apartment and a pig may be a pet on a farm.

Have the students identify their pets and investigate their pets' lineage. If the student has a cat, for example, at the zoo he or she can find the lions and tigers and see the characteristics that are similar to their pet cat. Discuss the eating and care needs of all of the animals in the zoo and the similarities of caring for pets in their home.

Family Interventions

Infant and Toddler/Preschool Level. Ask the parents to provide their child with opportunities to learn about and interact with pets, with adult supervision. Many areas have children's zoos that offer interactive experiences for young children. In addition, many children's videos have pets or animals as their story theme.

Primary Level. If the family is able, ask the parents to provide their child with a pet that can be cared for independently by the child, such as a bird, fish, hamster, or reptile. Ask them to review the pet's needs with their child and develop a chart for care (see example in Figure 3.2). Provide supervision as needed.

Intermediate and Secondary Levels. Youngsters at this age can be assigned the care and maintenance of the family pet, particularly feeding the cat or walking the dog. If the family has land, domestic animals such as horses and goats can be cared for by the youngster. Be sure the parents supervise the process periodically to be sure the care is adequate for the animal's needs.

Specific Objective E

The student collects leaves, rocks, and shells for a collection, crafts, and/or decorating projects.

Teacher Interventions

Infant and Toddler/Preschool Level. Take the child on a walk outside with a bag to collect leaves, acorns, and pinecones. Assist the child in making a nature collage or covering a shoe box with these items. Describe the beauty in these natural decorations, discussing what they are and their origins in nature. To the extent available, assist the child to press leaves from each season to create a seasonal tree chart.

Primary Level. Take the student on a field trip to a nearby park. Make the trip a treasure hunt by creating a list of natural objects to be collected during the nature walk (e.g., specific leaves, nutshells, seed pods, evergreens).

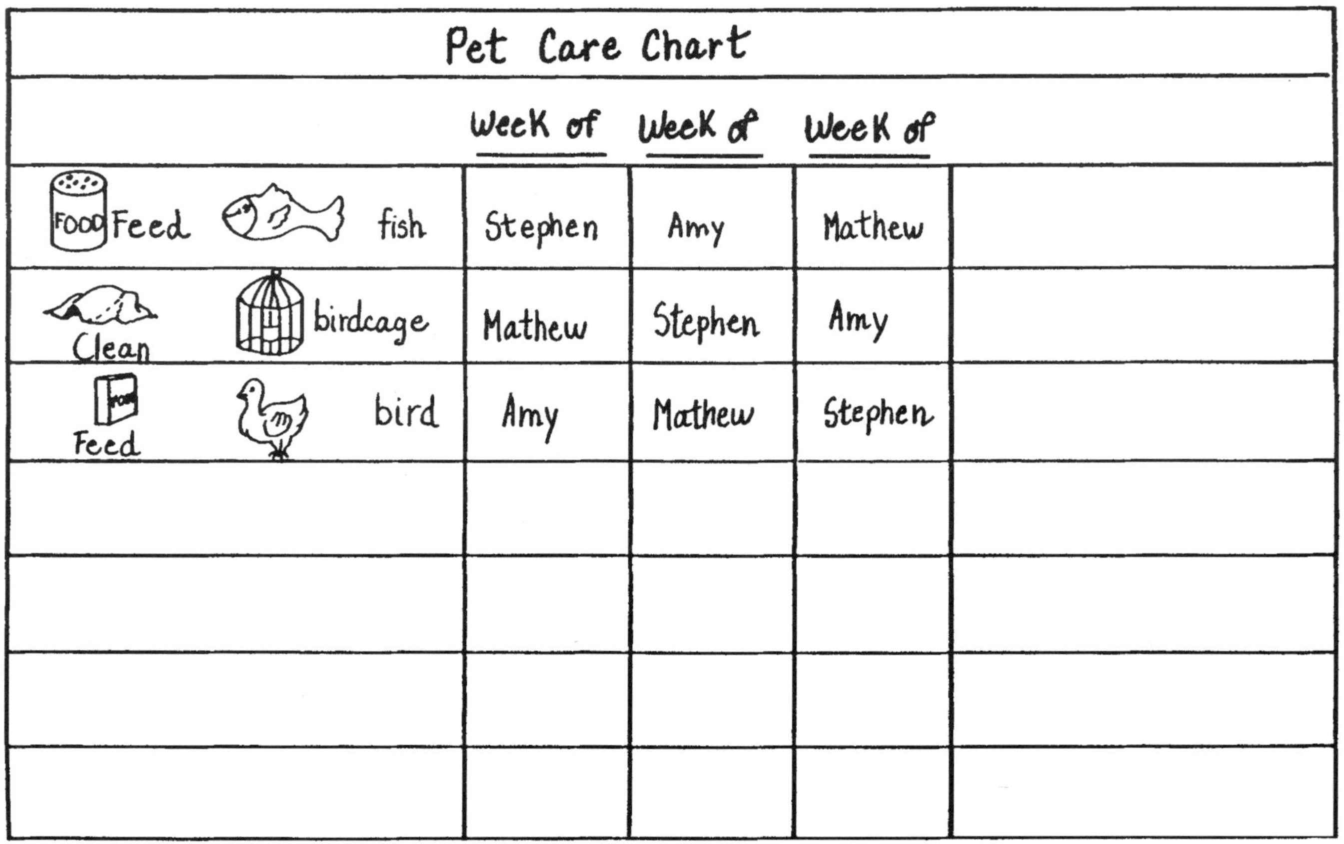

Pet Care Chart

	week of	week of	week of				
Feed fish	Stephen	Amy	Mathew				
Clean birdcage	Mathew	Stephen	Amy				
Feed bird	Amy	Mathew	Stephen				

FIGURE 3.2. Pet care chart.

Intermediate and Secondary Levels. Have the student design a decorative natural project and list the items that will be needed. Discuss where these items can be obtained and have the student plan outings to collect them. Emphasize the necessity to avoid collecting specimens that are poisonous or dangerous. In addition, discuss rare or endangered specimens that should not be collected.

Family Interventions

Infant and Toddler/Preschool Level. Ask the parents to take their child to the beach with a bucket to collect shells and other beach items. Encourage the parents to have their child cover a wooden or cardboard box to create a shell treasure box in which to store the special shells.

Primary Level. Encourage the parents to take their child on a beach walk to collect driftwood and shells. Parents can then provide the child with the necessary items to create a table decoration.

Intermediate and Secondary Levels. Suggest that the parents take their youngster on a rock climb appropriate to his or her ability. Identify the various types of rocks and collect rocks to be used at home to create a rock design. Depending on the size of the rocks, the decorative products can be used as book supports, paperweights, or doorstops.

Specific Objective F

The student engages in photography and other art experiences based on natural themes.

Teacher Interventions

Infant and Toddler/Preschool Level. Provide the child with books and pictures about nature themes. For example, the *Berenstain Bears* story series and a "how nature works" series teach about these themes. Many museums carry preschool-level books on artists who focus on nature.

Primary Level. When appropriate, request that each student bring in a disposable camera. Demonstrate how to use the camera and assist the student to understand the limits of distance and lighting. Take the student on a nature walk, pointing out opportunities to photograph natural themes, such as trees with colorful foliage in the fall, natural collections of rocks and wood, streams, flowering bushes, or drifts of snow.

Intermediate and Secondary Levels. Show the student slides of various photographers' and artists' works, explaining different styles and periods of art.

Take the student on a photography outing, instructing the student in how to select a subject and frame the picture. Assist the student to plan a pictorial record around a specific theme. Take the student to have the film developed and ask the student to lay out the photographs and place them in an album with captions and explanation.

Family Interventions

Infant and Toddler/Preschool Level. Ask the parents to provide their child with familiar photos, assisting the child to name the person or object. The child should be encouraged to identify those photos that were taken outdoors.

The parents can assist the child to identify photos in magazines that have a natural theme and cut them out. They can be pasted into a collage and hung in the child's room at eye level.

Ask the parents to cut up old sponges and provide their child with nontoxic, washable tempera paints. The parents can pour the paint in plastic cups and provide their child with a sponge cube for each color. Then the child can sponge paint on the sidewalk, creating various designs that can be washed away with a garden hose.

Primary Level. Ask the parents to provide their child with pictures of land- and seascapes, discussing the setting and the attributes. Encourage the parents to have their child photograph natural landscapes. Hang the child's photographs on a bulletin board.

Intermediate and Secondary Levels. Ask the parents to provide their child with various options to explore natural themes when on vacation. These include sketch pads and charcoal, disposable cameras, and collections of various objects to create a collage.

GOAL V.

The student will identify activities and opportunities to use as hobbies.

SPECIFIC OBJECTIVES

The student:

❑ A. Selects and pursues a hobby involving the creation of tangible objects and items.

❑ B. Selects and pursues a hobby involving the acquisition of collections and collectibles.

SUGGESTED ACTIVITIES

 Specific Objective A

The student selects and pursues a hobby involving the creation of tangible objects and items.

Teacher Interventions

Primary Level. Provide the student with a selection of hobby magazines. Encourage the student to look through the magazines. If the student expresses an interest in a particular craft or hobby, discuss the activities involved and answer any questions. Assist the student to make a list of the items needed to pursue the hobby or craft.

Assist the student to identify resources (e.g., hobby club members, friends) for information on specialty hobbies and to select materials and supplies.

Intermediate and Secondary Levels. Select a variety of hobbies, setting them up in stations around the classroom. Encourage the student to select a variety of craft materials (e.g., paints, decoupage, clay, jewelry making, leather-craft). Assist the student to design a project, identifying the steps and materials needed. Teach the student to order materials from a catalog. Supervise and praise the student.

Provide opportunities to complete crafts and hobby activities at school. Plan a hobby and craft show so that the crafts can be displayed.

Family Interventions

Primary Level. Suggest that the family take their child to a hobby or craft store. Ask the parents to encourage the youngster to identify a variety of hobbies and crafts. Explain that pursuing a hobby or craft is a fun way to use leisure time.

Ask the parents to share any hobbies or crafts that they pursue in their leisure time. Encourage the parents to share these activities as a family activity.

Intermediate and Secondary Levels. Ask the parents to encourage their youngster to identify ways of acquiring the materials for certain hobbies, including understanding the time, cost, and space requirements for specific types. Encourage the parents to use different media and to join related hobby groups.

 ## Specific Objective B

The student selects and pursues a hobby involving the acquisition of collections and collectibles.

Teacher Interventions

Primary, Intermediate, and Secondary Levels. Identify collections that exist in the school, such as sports trophies or other classroom collections. Explain the pleasure the student may gain from displaying his or her collection and classification system.

Provide the student with magazines that contain information on the various types of collectibles and antiques. Discuss with the student the range of specialty activities that can be found in brochures and catalogs.

Include in the discussions of collectibles the common items that are possible collectibles for the student (e.g., dolls, buttons, coins, stamps, magazines, comic books, baseball cards). Ask the student to identify the collections that exist in his or her home.

Family Interventions

Primary Level. Ask the parents to share any collections they have with their child. Encourage the parents to involve their child in locating items to add to their collections by going to flea markets or community fairs.

Encourage parents to take their child to a museum and identify a wide range of collections, including pictures, ceramics, and animals.

Intermediate and Secondary Levels. Ask the parents to provide opportunities for their child to attend events related to collectibles and antiques. Of interest to many older children are baseball card sales, comic book events, train meets, stamp collector meetings, or specific doll or dollhouse events.

Taking children to flea markets can provide an inexpensive opportunity for children to begin collecting items of specific interest (e.g. china plates, ceramic figurines, doll clothes, tweezers, cups, bottles).

GOAL VI.

The student will select craft activities to engage in leisure and hobby activities.

SPECIFIC OBJECTIVES

The student:

- ❏ A. Engages in food crafts.
- ❏ B. Engages in craft activities involving various materials, such as fibers, wood, plastics, and fabrics.
- ❏ C. Engages in craft activities for gift making and/or home decorating.
- ❏ D. Engages in model and craft making involving the use of kit materials.

SUGGESTED ACTIVITIES

 ## Specific Objective A
The student engages in food crafts.

Teacher Interventions

Infant and Toddler/Preschool Level. Assemble a variety of food items, including apples, grapes, raisins, oranges, and carrots. Young children will enjoy watching you create food people using food items cut in a variety of shapes and secured by toothpicks.

Cut oranges and apples into a variety of geometric and animal shapes. Provide the child with nontoxic and washable tempera paint. Assist the child to dip the fruit into the paint and use it to "sponge" paint a picture.

Primary Level. Bring pasta of different shapes, sizes, and colors into class. Assist the student to string macaroni to make bracelets, necklaces, and belts, or to make a picture by gluing different pasta shapes onto cardboard. Encourage the student to select a family member for whom to create an item for a special occasion.

Intermediate and Secondary Levels. Bring a completed gingerbread house into school for display or for a gift that can be earned.

Purchase a precut gingerbread kit and encourage the student to create a unique house of his or her own. Encourage the student to use unique icing patterns and arrangements of food decorations.

Family Interventions

Infant and Toddler/Preschool Level. Ask the parents to make a dough of flour, salt, and water. The parents can assist their young child to create a bread sculpture of a face or animal, which can be dried and enjoyed by the child.

Primary Level. Ask the parents to provide their child with a large russet potato and the facial features from a Mr. Potato Head game. Ask the parents to assist their child in making a real Mr. Potato Head.

Ask the parents to make popcorn and purchase fresh whole cranberries. Using string or fishing line, the parents can demonstrate how to string the popcorn and cranberries, alternating the popcorn and cranberries in a specific pattern. Remind the parents to supervise the activity closely since the cranberries should not be swallowed whole and use of a needle can be dangerous. The garlands can be used during the holidays to decorate trees and doorways.

Intermediate and Secondary Levels. Ask the parents to provide their youngster with a variety of dried beans and pasta. The youngster can create a drawing, which can be used as the basis for a mosaic created from a variety of small food items glued onto the design.

 ## Specific Objective B

The student engages in craft activities involving various materials, such as fibers, wood, plastics, and fabrics.

Teacher Interventions

Primary Level. Provide the student with a pot holder kit that has a variety of cloth loops and a pot holder frame. Ask the student to select his or her preferred colors. Demonstrate how to make a simple pot holder and assist the student to complete one of his or her own.

During various holidays provide materials that are appropriate to the season for the student to create unique crafts.

Intermediate and Secondary Levels. Provide the student with a selection of large remnants. Encourage the student to choose a preferred fabric. Provide the student with a selection of simple patterns, such as an apron, dish-cloth, carry-bag, or bandanna. Demonstrate how to cut the pattern out of the remnant and sew it by hand or with a simple machine. Students who have difficulty sewing may use bonding glue.

Family Interventions

Primary Level. Ask the parents to provide their child with a variety of items, including fabric pieces, braid pieces, rickrack, and sequins. The parents can provide the child with a variety of surfaces (e.g., cardboard, paper plates) and glue so that the child can create a collage that can be hung up in the child's room or the family room.

Intermediate and Secondary Levels. Encourage the parents to engage their youngster in a craft activity that the family enjoys. If the youngster has the ability, encourage the parents to demonstrate knitting, crocheting, quilting, or needlepoint. If the youngster has physical limitations, assist the parents to modify the activity so he or she can participate.

 Specific Objective C

The student engages in craft activities for gift making and/or home decorating.

Teacher Interventions

Primary Level. Assist the student to fold paper and to make cuts to create snowflakes for seasonal decorations in the classroom.

Provide the student with strings of varying lengths and glue that dries clear. Provide the student with a model and assist the student to create string art pictures.

Bring in a selection of magazines. Ask the student to cut out pictures around a theme, such as favorite animals, fruits, landscapes, or faces. Demonstrate to the student how to make a collage (see Figure 3.3).

Intermediate and Secondary Levels. Demonstrate the art of origami, paper folding. Assist the student, if able, to make a simple bird figure to provide as a gift to another student or family member.

Ask the student to bring in old candles to melt down. Purchase wicks to create candles. Supervise the student as he or she safely pours the

FIGURE 3.3. Making a collage by pasting overlapped pictures onto construction paper.

melted wax into small paper containers of varying sizes, and let the wax cool. Assist the student to remove the container and to wrap the candles for a family gift.

Family Interventions

Primary Level. Ask the parents to provide their child with a bar of soap. The parents can provide their child with a small blunt tool to carve the soap into a simple animal shape. If the child enjoys the activity, he or she can carve a small collection of soap animals as a gift.

Intermediate and Secondary Levels. Identify community fairs and encourage the parents to take their youngster to booths where home decorating crafts are displayed. If the child expresses an interest in a craft, the parents can determine if it is suitable and provide the necessary materials.

Specific Objective D

The student engages in model and craft making involving the use of kit materials.

Teacher Interventions

Primary Level. Request that other teachers bring to your class models and crafts that have been made from kits. Ask the students in the class to bring in similar models and crafts from their homes. Discuss how these were completed and the types of models and crafts represented. With this variety of examples, discuss with the student the wide range of options.

Purchase a wide range of kits and simple models (e.g. leather, airplane, string art, needlework, paper crafts). Provide time in the class for the student to complete a model or craft kit, with assistance and supervision.

Intermediate and Secondary Levels. Ask the students to participate in a class fundraising effort for a special purchase for the school, a neighborhood child care center, or a home for the elderly. Purchase model and craft kits that are appropriate to the various students' functioning levels. Assist the students to complete the kits, create a class display, and make advertisements. Invite other students, teachers, parents, and community members to the "art show" and sell the crafts and models. Have the students count the money and take a community field trip to purchase the identified item for the school or community cause.

Family Interventions

Primary Level. Ask the parents if the family has any particular craft hobbies. If the parents are able, ask them to take their child to a craft fair and assist the child to identify a model or craft that can be purchased in a kit. Ask the parents to assist the child to complete the kit as a family-supported project, praising the child for his or her efforts.

Intermediate and Secondary Levels. Ask the parents to check with the local YMCA or recreation council to identify a community class in crafts or model making. After talking with the instructor to determine if the youngster can function in the class, ask the parents to provide the opportunity to their youngster.

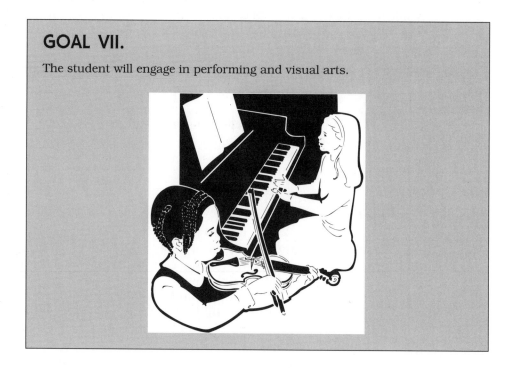

GOAL VII.

The student will engage in performing and visual arts.

SPECIFIC OBJECTIVES

The student:

- ❏ A. Engages in fine arts activities.
- ❏ B. Engages in musical activities as a participant.
- ❏ C. Engages in musical activities as a listener–spectator.
- ❏ D. Participates in creative dramatics and in plays and play productions.

SUGGESTED ACTIVITIES

 Specific Objective A

The student engages in fine arts activities.

Teacher Interventions

Infant and Toddler/Preschool Level. Provide the child with a variety of pictures with large objects. Help the child to name the colors and familiar objects in the pictures.

Provide the child with a large sheet of paper and a variety of finger paints. Make sure the child's clothing is protected by using an oversized old shirt, and assist the child to select colors and to finger-paint. Help the child to use his or her hands, including fingertips, palms, and nails to create patterns and shapes on the paper.

Primary Level. Give the student paints and sponges cut into a variety of geometric shapes and animal figures. Discuss the shapes and figures and ask the student how he or she would use the shapes. Provide nontoxic tempera paint and demonstrate how to dip the sponges into the paints and press onto construction paper to create designs and pictures.

Intermediate and Secondary Levels. Provide the student with a variety of sculpting activities, including wood, soap, ceramics, and metal.

Plan a trip to a local museum, providing the students with a walking tour and discussing the wide range of options for design and sculpture.

Encourage the student to suggest new materials that can be sculpted; provide directions and models.

Family Interventions

Infant and Toddler/Preschool Level Ask the parents to provide their child with nontoxic modeling dough. Ask the parents to demonstrate rolling and pulling the dough apart and making shapes.

Encourage the parents to provide their child with a variety of materials, including nontoxic and washable paints and felt-tip markers, crayons, and sponges. Ask the parents to provide a protected surface and paper so that their child can explore the use of these materials and have creative opportunities.

Primary Level. Suggest to parents that they take their children to touch-and-feel museums that encourage the interaction of children with the exhibits.

Encourage parents to take their child to a variety of stores that carry inexpensive art supplies and purchase materials the child selects to encourage his or her self-expression in a wide range of mediums.

Intermediate and Secondary Levels. Ask the parents to request that their youngster create a fine arts display for the family room or bedroom. Tell them to have the child prepare a list of supplies, design the project, and consult with the parent. Have the parents assist him or her with a timeline and identify a place to work. Remind the parents to provide reinforcement at each stage of the project.

Specific Objective B

The student engages in musical activities as a participant.

Teacher Interventions

Infant and Toddler/Preschool Level. Provide a musical background in the room during any periods of free time, varying the tempo and type of music. Sing along with the music, facing the young child and providing exaggerated facial expressions.

Structure opportunities for the child to participate in a group sing, including hand and foot movements so that the child can develop an awareness of rhythm and sequence.

Provide a variety of music-producing toys, such as a musical viewing box with wind-up handles and a children's tape recorder with built-in buttons for selecting brief musical songs. Encourage the child to manipulate these music-producing toys.

Primary Level. Provide a variety of rhythm band instruments (e.g., maracas, tambourine). Demonstrate each instrument and encourage the student to play each one.

In a group setting, provide each student with a rhythm instrument that can be manipulated using a hand, foot, or any part of the body that can vibrate the appropriate instrument. Select a simple musical piece and have the students prepare a performance for other students and family members.

Intermediate and Secondary Levels. Provide the students with selections of current popular music and discuss the variety of musical styles and the role of certain instruments. Ask the student to bring in a recording of a favorite musical piece.

Family Interventions

Infant and Toddler/Preschool Level. Encourage the parents to integrate music and singing as part of their daily activities. "This is the Way We Wash Our Clothes" can be changed to reflect any household activity (e.g., empty trash, load dishwasher, fold clothes, sweep floor, take bath). Even conversational activities with young children can become a song. Younger children will imitate the sounds and rhythm.

Children this age often enjoy singing commercials that have recognizable lyrics. Have a class activity in which each student sings, hums, or plays an instrument to the tune of a selected jingle and the other students identify the commercial.

Primary Level. Ask the parents to involve their child in a musical creative arts program in the community. Recreational programs and community colleges are particularly good resources for parents. Suggest that the parents select a program where the purpose is to develop musical interests rather than to train a musician. The child can benefit from involvement in a band or choral group activity. The child may also benefit from participating in a sign language group that performs locally and provides for a wide range of abilities.

Intermediate and Secondary Levels. Ask the parents to provide opportunities for their youngster to participate in dance activities. The youngster can participate in a line dancing class through the recreation council, school dances, classes for ballroom dancing, and family dance activities. The youngster should be encouraged to select a variety of music, and family members and friends can each demonstrate the varied styles of dance, engaging the youngster at each level.

Ask the parents if family members or friends play musical instruments. A musical group can be formed in which the youngster can try a variety of instruments and participate with family and friends.

 ## Specific Objective C

The student engages in musical activities as a listener–spectator.

Teacher Interventions

Infant and Toddler/Preschool Level. Provide many opportunities within the group setting to play music for listening to rhythms of the sounds and songs. In addition, many children's musical videos are available that can be used to entertain young children while providing exposure to a wide range of educational activities and varieties of musical performances.

Provide a field trip for the young child to a "tot concert" sponsored by a local symphony orchestra.

Primary Level. Encourage the student to select a musical performance to video-tape. Assist the student to tape the performance, and have the student lead a class discussion about the musical aspects.

Arrange with a nearby middle school to have their band, string orchestra, dance group, and/or chorus perform at the school so students can develop an interest in a specific music performance style.

Intermediate and Secondary Levels. Ask the student to select a musical performance from the entertainment section of the newspaper and discuss what a spectator could expect if attending. Encourage each student in the class to select a wide range, including ballet, musical theater, symphonies, rock concerts, opera, large stage productions, and instrument recitals.

Family Interventions

Infant and Toddler/Preschool Level. Encourage the parents to make music a part of their everyday life, playing the radio in the car, listening to a wide range of music in the home, and singing to their young child.

Primary Level. If the parents or a family member has a musical skill, encourage them to have a "family recital," emphasizing the entertainment value as well as appropriate behavior.

Encourage the family to include their child in a wide range of listening experiences, such as community concerts, church music, local school recitals, and musical performances of particular interest to the child.

Intermediate and Secondary Levels. Ask the parents to have their youngster select a musical performance to attend as a family. Have the youngster identify performance times and ticket costs. Ask them to take the youngster to the ticket office and purchase the tickets, selecting the seating location and ticket cost that are appropriate to the funds available for the activity. Have the youngster be responsible for keeping the tickets in a safe location until the performance. Discuss the time needed to get to the performance, allowing for traffic, parking, and seating.

Specific Objective D

The student participates in creative dramatics and in plays and play productions.

Teacher Interventions

Infant and Toddler/Preschool Level. Using hand puppets, play games with the very young child, such as peek-a-boo and activities stimulated by TV programs. Engage the child in reaching for the puppets and physical interplay, such as tickling and stroking on the arm and leg.

Provide the young child with finger and hand puppets. Arrange the child so that each of you has a puppet and can act out a common activity, such as walking, dancing, or jumping, all the while encouraging the child to talk about what is happening.

Engage the child in creative dramatics such as taking a language experience story, making straw puppets, and acting out the story for the group.

Provide a dress-up corner in the room with a wide range of clothing available. Have the child select this learning area during story time and encourage experimentation with clothing and roles.

Primary Level. Arrange for a puppeteer group to come for a class performance. Ask them to engage the student in a discussion of how the puppets are manipulated and the voice production.

As a class project, develop the concept for a one-act play, write the script, and create the props, scenery, and costumes. Depending on the student's individual strengths and abilities, assist the student to select a role in the production. If the student selects a speaking role, assist the student to develop the dialogue, practicing to learn it to the extent the student is able. In an integrated setting, encourage the student to work with peers to obtain assistance. Invite another class or the parents to be the audience.

Intermediate and Secondary Levels. Plan a class field trip to a creative dramatic arts performance. Provide an opportunity for the student to select the type of performance, ranging from a school play, local theater production, or professional performance. Discuss with the student the aspects of the performance and have the student clarify expectations of type and quality of performance.

Family Interventions

Infant and Toddler/Preschool Level. Encourage the parents to engage their young child in creative play opportunities, reminding them that early language development is dependent on frequent and stimulating interactions.

Provide the parents with examples of ways (e.g., puppets, videos, recreational activities) in which they can stimulate their toddler for creative play.

Primary Level. Ask the parents to take their child to puppet performances and encourage them to ask the child to recreate the activity at home, with the parent's support and involvement.

Encourage the parents to identify television viewing for the child that includes creative performances of interest to children and sit with their child during the performance to enhance the experience.

Intermediate and Secondary Levels. Remind parents that their older youngster will be more interested in dramatic activities if the subject matter is age appropriate. Assist the parents in locating creative performances that are of interest to adolescents.

Encourage the parents to provide their youngster with opportunities to participate in community performances, either through auditioning for a role, acting as a stage hand, building props, or doing publicity.

GOAL VIII.

The student will seek a variety of entertainment and cultural opportunities.

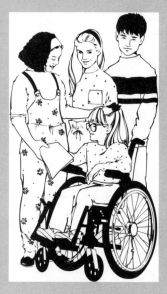

SPECIFIC OBJECTIVES

The student:

❑ A. Engages in quiet activities, such as looking at picture books and magazines, playing electronic games, and listening to the radio or stereo.

❑ B. Watches television, videotapes, and discs.

❑ C. Plays games on computer, television, or hand-held machines.

❑ D. Plans and hosts a party.

❑ E. Goes to fast food restaurants, cafeterias, snack shops, and other restaurants.

❑ F. Attends movies, puppet shows, concerts, and plays.

❑ G. Plans and participates in picnics, outings, and excursions.

❑ H. Participates in special events, such as holiday parties, programs, dances, and the Special Olympics.

❑ I. Locates and participates in clubs, special-interest groups, and events sponsored by schools, recreation councils, and community groups, such as scouts/Indian Guides, 4-H clubs, and garden clubs.

❑ J. Takes vacations and goes on other trips.

❑ K. Visits relatives, friends, and neighbors.

SUGGESTED ACTIVITIES

Specific Objective A

The student engages in quiet activities, such as looking at picture books and magazines, playing electronic games, and listening to the radio or stereo.

Teacher Interventions

Infant and Toddler/Preschool Level. During rest times, play relaxing music for the young child. Children can learn to respond to a variety of musical styles by listening to background music during other activities.

Provide the toddler with big books with stiff covers that can be easily grasped. For children with physical disabilities that affect the hand, fluff the pages by inserting small pieces of sponge or drops of dried glue between the pages.

Primary Level.   If available, provide the students with educational electronic games to be used in the classroom. Many programs available for these electronic games provide educational material in a game format that makes the learning high interest and fun.

Have a corner in the room with a carpet, beanbag seats, and low bookshelves filled with a wide range of high-interest books appropriate to the age range and ability of the student. Encourage the student to use this area for quiet time during the day or after completing his or her work.

Intermediate and Secondary Levels.   Have each student identify his or her favorite quiet activity. Encourage the student to describe activities that can be done while not distracting or disturbing others. Create an area in the room with these options available. Tell the student to listen to music with headphones when his or her regular classwork is completed.

Family Interventions

Infant and Toddler/Preschool Level.   Encourage the parents to provide a very young infant with a teething ring to chew or big rings to swing.

Ask the parents to provide a variety of small stuffed animals and encourage the very young child to play with them to the extent the child is able. Ask the parents to play quiet music or sing quietly to calm a young child.

Ask the parents to keep a variety of large books and out-of-date magazines in their child's room and in the family area. When the child finishes an activity and has time available, encourage the parents to direct the child to the books and magazines.

Primary Level.   Ask the parents to provide the child with a project and, when complete, ask the child to select a quiet activity until the parent is available for interaction.

Tell the parents to encourage their child to select quiet activities during the early morning while the parents are sleeping or engaged in other activities.

Remind the parents to engage in a routine nighttime activity with the child, such as listening to music or reading a story prior to bed to relax and calm the child.

Intermediate and Secondary Levels.   Ask the parents to discuss with their youngster the types of quiet activities that can be used in the home during the late night or early morning hours. Encourage the parents to provide the youngster with access to these activities for relaxation and quiet times.

 ## Specific Objective B

The student watches television, videotapes, and discs.

Teacher Interventions

Infant and Toddler/Preschool Level.   During appropriate programming for young children, even the youngest child can be stimulated by sitting and watching television or videotapes with singing and colorful action.

Keep a selection of interactive videotapes available during classroom periods when the child's interest may be waning or during a period of relaxation. Engage the child to the extent he or she is able to attend and understand the theme and appropriate interaction.

Primary, Intermediate, and Secondary Levels.   Bring in the various forms of television guides, such as *TV Guide*, local cable guide, or newspaper TV sections. Talk about the variety of programming and the options for selecting suitable programming. If specific keys to programs include symbols or ratings, familiarize the student with the reference guide and assist the student to select age-appropriate programs.

Ask the student to keep a viewing diary and have a discussion about the types of programs the student is viewing and the amount of time spent watching television.

Bring in a variety of videotapes for a discussion of different viewer ratings. Discuss what the G, PG, PG-13, and R ratings mean, and what is considered to be the viewing content of the videotapes. If appropriate, have the students view programs or videotapes and discuss the content and ratings.

Family Interventions

Infant and Toddler/Preschool Level.   Parents can be encouraged to assist their child in developing healthy television viewing habits by being given a listing of programs that are appropriate for young children. In addition, many children's groups are publishing literature that describes and provides information on the quality and quantity of television viewing for young children.

Parents may choose to use television and videotapes as a family hour in the household. Provide parents with videotapes from school on a checkout basis if they do not have access to a neighborhood library or video store. Many outlets have a wide range of appropriate children's shows available for viewing.

Primary, Intermediate, and Secondary Levels. Ask the parents to encourage their child to watch suitable television programs during leisure time and in the evening when outdoor play is not possible. Remind the parents to stress educationally oriented and nonviolent programming. Certain televisions may come equipped with the capacity to block X-rated programs, and parents should be alerted to these controls.

Remind parents to review television listings with their child and to monitor their child's viewing. Parents should encourage the substitution of other leisure activities when possible.

Specific Objective C

The student plays games on computer, television, or hand-held machines.

Teacher Interventions

Primary, Intermediate, and Secondary Levels. Students in these age ranges are beginning to develop the eye–hand coordination to be able to effectively play a wide range of electronic games. Ask the PTA or other parent groups for access to these games in the classroom. These can be used as rewards and can be educationally relevant with careful selection of games.

For students with emotional and behavioral problems, controlled access to computer games as part of a behavioral contract may result in improved behavior during learning activities if supervised by the teacher.

For students with physical disabilities who require modifications, many options for adaptive technology are available for the school setting. Local engineering groups, disability organizations, and resource libraries have access to volunteers who can modify equipment for individual students.

Family Interventions

Primary, Intermediate, and Secondary Levels. Encourage parents to make a variety of computer and electronic games available. Playing these games assists children to develop eye–hand coordination and provides an alternative leisure-time activity.

In addition, encourage parents to allow their children to participate as a social activity with other children at a game room in a mall or at home, and to assist their child to be able to effectively play a wide range of electronic games with other children. These opportunities can be used as rewards and can be educationally relevant with careful selection of games by the parents.

Parents should be told that, for children with physical disabilities who require modifications, many options for adaptive technology are available in the community setting. Parent and disability organizations and disability resource libraries have access to volunteers who can provide information and help to modify equipment for individual children.

Specific Objective D

The student plans and hosts a party.

Teacher Interventions

Preschool and Primary Levels.   Younger children enjoy participating in the planning and preparations for a party. During the school year many holidays can be occasions for parties. Involve the student in planning the menu, making the decorations, selecting the music, and choosing games or activities. Emphasize the importance of cleanup as part of the complete activity.

During a month without a specific event, ask the student to select a party theme and develop the plan for the party. Have the student solicit volunteers from the class to assist in implementing the party plans.

Intermediate and Secondary Levels.   Ask the student to choose a small group of other students and together they can select a specific occasion and plan a small party. They can determine whom to invite; make the invitations; determine the costs; establish a menu; purchase foods, decorations, supplies, and party activities; and arrange the cleanup.

Family Interventions

Preschool and Primary Levels.   Ask the parents to involve their child in the planning and preparation of his or her birthday party. Depending on the child's age, suggest the child do the following: develop the list of invitees, prepare the invitations, make the decorations, assist in food preparation, and help with cleanup.

Intermediate and Secondary Levels. Encourage the parents to provide occasions, perhaps on Friday nights, when friends can be invited over and the child can plan for the visits. Pizza is a simple menu and results in easy cleanup. The youngster can plan the activities to include music, games, videos, and other quiet leisure activities.

Specific Objective E

The student goes to fast food restaurants, cafeterias, snack shops, and other restaurants.

Teacher Interventions

Primary Level. Many schools have cafeterias. Review with the student the process for accessing, ordering, and paying for food. Some schools use a debit card process. Assist the student to understand how to add money to the account and keep track of the card.

Plan a field trip to include a visit to a fast food restaurant. Review with the student the food options available and the cost of the food. Have the student preselect the food and calculate the cost. Discuss with the student restaurants he or she has been to and the process of ordering food. Clarify how to pay for the food and calculate the change due.

Intermediate and Secondary Levels. Many students will have a wide range of experience with cafeterias and fast food restaurants. Review with the student the types of eating situations that may be encountered in various restaurants. Review how to select a restaurant from the Yellow Pages, and how to call for information. Review the process for ordering, calculating the cost, tipping, and disposing of the food tray in self-serve restaurants.

Family Interventions

Infant and Toddler/Preschool Level. Encourage parents to take their child to a fast food restaurant. Many restaurants have entertainment options for young children, including outside playground equipment and ball pits.

Primary Level. Encourage parents to involve their child in activities such as those discussed in Teacher Interventions.

Intermediate and Secondary Levels. Encourage parents to involve their youngster in restaurant activities. Suggest that they do the things mentioned in Teacher Interventions.

Specific Objective F

The student attends movies, puppet shows, concerts, and plays.

Teacher Interventions

Preschool and Primary Levels. Provide an opportunity in the classroom for the student to select and view a movie with a group. Review with the student the types of behavior appropriate to the setting, and stop the movie to deal with problem behaviors. Remind the student to be quiet and seated so that others may view the movie. If the student has vision problems, adapt the experience to be similar to the public setting to provide an opportunity for the student to understand what to expect. This can be done by arranging chairs, creating aisles, and so forth, in the classroom.

Include the student in school cultural events (e.g., concerts, plays, puppet shows, movies). Review the appropriate behaviors and be available to intervene, if necessary.

Intermediate and Secondary Levels. Provide the student with the opportunity to select a movie to attend in the community. Include a discussion of movie ratings and content in the selection process.

Attend a classical concert as a field trip. Many symphonies have school discounts and special programs of interest to students of all ages. Discuss appropriate dress and behavior with the student. Remind the student of the type of music that will be presented and discuss the program and interesting facts prior to the trip.

Family Interventions

Preschool and Primary Levels. Ask the parents to take their child to a community puppet show or children's theater. Opportunities may exist for birthday parties at children's musical theaters. Performers often relate to young children and may involve them in the performance.

Intermediate and Secondary Levels. Encourage the parents to provide an opportunity for their youngster to select concert events of interest (e.g., rock, folk, classical music). With other parents, plan an outing to the concert.

Ask the parents to review the appropriate behaviors for concert goers and the need to stay with the group or to let an adult know when leaving the group.

Specific Objective G

The student plans and participates in picnics, outings, and excursions.

Teacher Interventions

Infant and Toddler/Preschool and Primary Levels. Plan a group outing, discussing with the students where the picnic should be. Ask for suggestions for the menu and activities. Involve the other teachers and parents in the plans for transportation. Ask the student to help you make the shopping list, either by selecting pictures, naming, or writing the items. When appropriate, assign team leaders and have the student plan and lead the group activities at the picnic. (Note: With young students picnics and outings need to be well planned, with ample supervision and adult hands.)

Intermediate and Secondary Levels. Ask the student to bring in the section of the newspaper or magazines that provides information on area amusements. Develop a list of information the student needs to make a decision about what is a reasonable option (e.g. interest level, price, age limit, transportation options, date and time, whether reservations are necessary). Have the student complete the list for several functions and discuss with the student which options are feasible. Ask the student to select the function and make plans to attend. Go on the excursion with the student or group of students.

Family Interventions

Infant and Toddler/Preschool and Primary Levels. Ask the parents to involve their youngster in planning a weekend camping trip or day excursion. Identify how the child can help (e.g., list food, select clothing, make reservations, pack, choose activities).

Intermediate and Secondary Levels. Ask the parents to encourage their youngster to identify and participate in neighborhood functions (e.g., trip to shopping center, community fair, flea market, nature walk). When possible, encourage the parents to include the youngster's friends in the outing.

Specific Objective H

The student participates in special events, such as holiday parties, programs, dances, and the Special Olympics.

Teacher Interventions

Preschool, Primary, Intermediate, and Secondary Levels. (See also Objective D.) When appropriate, ask the physical education teacher to make arrangements for the student to participate in the Special Olympics. Plan the training necessary to prepare the student. Hold events at the school that prepare the student to be a participant. An important part of the preparation is discussion related to why the Special Olympics offers an important opportunity for individual achievement and team building.

Family Interventions

Preschool, Primary, Intermediate, and Secondary Levels. (See also Objective D.) Ask the parents to include their child in family parties and excursions. If the parents need assistance in making arrangements for special accommodations, provide them with the information or resources to facilitate the process.

Remind the parents to discuss community events that may be occurring and their significance (e.g., Fourth of July parade, Rose Bowl, Labor Day picnics, holiday sales at the mall).

Specific Objective I

The student locates and participates in clubs, special-interest groups, and events sponsored by schools, recreation councils, and community groups, such as scouts/Indian Guides, 4-H clubs, and garden clubs.

Teacher Interventions

Primary, Intermediate, and Secondary Levels. Compile a list of age-appropriate clubs and events in which the student may participate. Discuss personal interests and the type of organization involved in such activities as scouts, school clubs (e.g., yearbook, chess, photography), the YMCA and YWCA, recreational sports, and special-interest camps. Encourage the student to select one of the activities as a school-related project. Discuss how to contact the group or event and the responsibilities of being a member.

Family Interventions

Primary, Intermediate, and Secondary Levels.   Share information about organizations and events with the parents. This is particularly important for families with children who have disabilities who require very specific accommodations. For example, special interest groups, such as those for individuals who are blind, are deaf, or have physical or mental retardation, can be a support for many families.

Encourage the parents to include their youngster in community events and clubs that will provide the youngster with age-appropriate peers and activities that can be shared by the entire family.

Specific Objective J

The student takes vacations and goes on other trips.

Teacher Interventions

Infant and Toddler/Preschool Level.   Involve the child in planning a field trip that is age appropriate. Encourage the child to express his or her personal interest (e.g., parade, playground, park, musical event). With younger children, provide adequate adult supervision and contact to ensure that the child is both safe and actively involved in the trip. If possible, include the parents as chaperones so that they may carry over the activity into the home.

Primary, Intermediate, and Secondary Levels.   Plan a field trip to a travel bureau or invite a travel agent into the classroom. Ask the visitor to bring brochures of the many travel opportunities. Initiate a discussion of the type of travel necessary, the provision of food, types of clothing, and the cost.

Go to the library and check out travel videos and tapes. Provide an opportunity for the student to watch and/or listen to a variety of travel opportunities (e.g., a cruise to a warmer climate and one to Alaska, a hiking trip, a sightseeing bus or train ride).

Family Interventions

Infant and Toddler/Preschool Level. Encourage the parents to plan family outings and vacations that include their child. Provide the family with age-appropriate suggested outings as part of a class newsletter.

Primary, Intermediate, and Secondary Levels. Ask the parents to involve their youngster in identifying family vacation options within the family budget. Encourage the parents to provide the youngster with the necessary materials or the opportunity to research the vacation on his or her own. The youngster can then present the family with a "tourbook" and keep a daily diary of the family vacation.

 ## Specific Objective K

The student visits relatives, friends, and neighbors.

Teacher Interventions

Infant and Toddler/Preschool Level. As part of the daily routine, take the child to other group settings and include the child in small group activities. Younger children can benefit from changes in the routine, which can prepare them for the process of visiting.

Read stories to the young child about going to visit relatives and friends, and ask the child to respond to simple questions related to preparation for the visit and what was fun about the event.

Primary Level. Engage the student by providing a book appropriate to his or her reading level about visiting. Ask the student to read the book or read it to the student.

Ask the student about visits to relatives and friends. Engage the student in a discussion about the types of behavior that occurred and about the way the time was spent (e.g., conversation, games, eating).

Develop an experience chart titled "Good Manners for Visiting" (see Figure 3.4), with the student providing ideas. Review the chart with the student and remind him or her to practice these behaviors when visiting in the school to other classrooms, the office, or the cafeteria.

Intermediate and Secondary Levels. Students in these age ranges may have independent access to public transportation or may drive. Many also may be able to walk to neighbors or friends on their own. Review the appropriate behaviors for visiting.

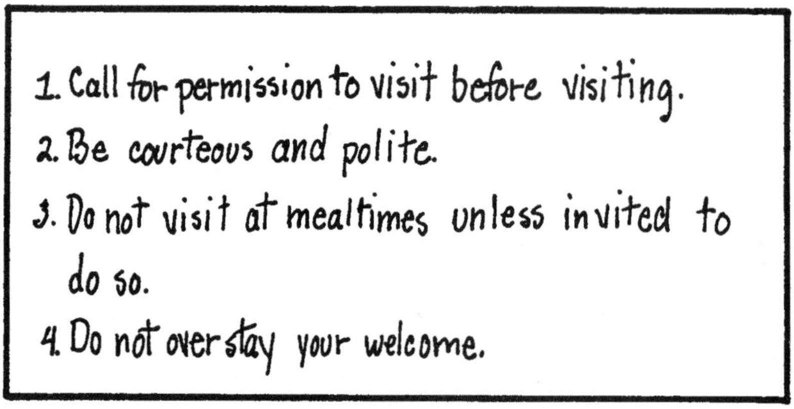

1. Call for permission to visit before visiting.
2. Be courteous and polite.
3. Do not visit at mealtimes unless invited to do so.
4. Do not overstay your welcome.

FIGURE 3.4. Good manners for visitors chart.

Ask the student about the types of situations that may arise when visiting friends, relatives, and neighbors. Role-play a variety of situations and the appropriate behaviors (e.g., calling before visiting, taking a small gift if appropriate, arriving after or leaving before mealtimes).

Family Interventions

Infant and Toddler/Preschool Level. Encourage the child's family to include the child on family visits and outings. Make a checklist of suggested activities that are appropriate for young children when traveling or visiting. Remind parents of the need for snacks and other distractions for the young child if quiet behavior is desirable during the visit.

Primary Level. Encourage the parents to make arrangements for the child to visit friends on weekends and vacations. Ask if it is appropriate for the child to invite other children to the home. Remind parents that the child can benefit from a wide variety of playmates and interactions with others outside of the family. Always provide adequate supervision.

Intermediate and Secondary Levels. Parents of youngsters in these age ranges may need to more closely monitor the activities of their children since they may have independent access to public transportation or drive. With many parents working, youngsters may also be walking to visit neighbors or friends on their own. Ask the parents to review with their youngster the appropriate behaviors for visiting and the importance of informing parents of his or her whereabouts at all times.

Encourage the parents to talk with their youngster about the types of situations that may arise when visiting friends, relatives, and neighbors, including drugs, sex, or aggressive behaviors. Ask the parents to role-play a variety of situations and the appropriate behaviors (e.g., calling before visiting, taking a small gift if appropriate, arriving after or leaving before mealtimes, calling the parent for a ride home, learning to say no when necessary).

Sample Lesson Plan 1

Topic Area: Leisure Skills

Designed by: Sarabeth Sharkster

Time Recommended: 45 Minutes

Student Involved: Dwight (Secondary Special Class)

Background Information:

> The student has attentional difficulties and fluctuates in behavior problems and school interest. He demonstrates strong math skills but does not complete written reading assignments and has been diagnosed with a learning disability in the area of written expressions. He is peer oriented and listens to contemporary music.

General Goal *(Leisure Skills VII)*:

> The student will engage in performing and visual arts.

Specific Objective *(Leisure Skills VII-C)*:

> The student engages in musical activities as a listener–spectator.

Lesson Objective:

> The student will select a particular musical performance and videotape the performance.

Materials and Equipment:

> - Schedule of community and school musical performances
> - Videotape
> - Camcorder
> - Tripod

Motivating Activity:

Plan a class party as a reward for having completed a unit and accumulating class points for behavior and time on task.

Instructional Procedures:

Initiation—Ask the student to identify varieties of music that would be appropriate for a class party. Provide the student with the schedule of performances and ask the student to select the performance to videotape.

Guided Practice—Instruct the student verbally and assist the student to operate the camcorder. Demonstrate to the student how to set up the camcorder on the tripod. Have the student explain how to turn it on and operate the various functions of the camcorder.

Independent Practice—Ask the student to tape a school activity and to play it back for the class. Discuss how to focus, frame the picture, keep the camera steady, and fade out.

Closure—Ask the student to plan what is needed to tape the musical performance and supervise the taping of the actual performance.

Assessment Strategy:

Ask the student to play the videotape for the class and discuss what is enjoyable about the performance. Discuss what improvements can be made in the process.

Follow-Up Activity or Objective:

The student will lead a class discussion regarding the musical aspects of the performance and what he enjoys about the particular music.

Sample Lesson Plan 2

Topic Area: Leisure Skills

Designed by: Tommy Tailgate

Time Recommended: 45 Minutes

Student Involved: Laurel (Primary Special Class)

Background Information:

The student is at the primary level with some cognitive delays and gross motor problems. Although the student can follow simple directions, supervision is required to ensure task completion. The student has some memory deficits and requires repetition and simple task analysis.

General Goal *(Leisure III)*:

The student will participate in camping and diverse outdoor activities.

Specific Objective *(Leisure III-B)*:

The student goes fishing and/or catches shellfish.

Lesson Objective:

Given a fishing pole with a hook, the student will bait the hook and cast the line into the water.

Materials and Equipment:

- Fishing rod
- Fishing line
- Earthworms
- Safety fishhook
- Fishing area

Motivating Activity:

Plan a class outing that will include cooking and eating at a park with a fishing area. Discuss the benefits of outdoor activities for health and leisure.

Instructional Procedures:

Initiation—Explain to the student that, although fish can be purchased at a store, many people go fishing as a leisure activity. Discuss how the hook is baited with worms and the process of throwing the line into the water. Label each of the pieces of equipment and discuss the sequence of activities.

Guided Practice—Use a pipe cleaner bent into the shape of a hook and grapes to replace the bait. Have the student practice with these until the process is understood and she can recite and perform the steps.

Using the actual bait, demonstrate how to reach down into the bait bucket, palm face down with thumb and index finger extended to pick up the worm. Ask the student to apply gentle pressure to pick up the worm and how to position the worm directly over the point of the large safety hook or paperclip bent like a hook, held in the other hand.

Assist the student to throw the line into the water. Have the student stand several feet from the water and curl the fingers of her dominant hand around the pole. Bend the elbow and assist the student to rotate the wrist so the pole extends backward and then is able to flex forward, casting the fishing line into the water.

Independent Practice—Provide the student with verbal instructions while watching the student bait the hook and throw the fishing line into the water. Assist as needed until the student can perform the activity independently.

Closure—If the student catches a fish, discuss whether the student wants to throw it back and why that would be helpful to the environment and how other people might enjoy catching the fish.

Assessment Strategy:

Have the student demonstrate how to bait the hook and cast the line. Observe the student casting the line and how the student is able to safely perform the activity.

Follow-Up Activity or Objective:

Have the student draw a picture and write a short story describing the activity. Suggest to the family that the student be included in a family outing to fish or catch crabs.

References

Adkins, J., & Matson, J. L. (1980). Teaching institutionalized mentally retarded adults socially appropriate leisure skills. *Mental Retardation, 18,* 249–252.

Allen, J. I. (1980). Jogging can modify disruptive behaviors. *Teaching Exceptional Children, 2,* 63–70.

Beasley, C. R. (1982). Effects of a jogging program on cardiovascular fitness and work performance of mentally retarded adults. *American Journal of Mental Deficiency, 86,* 609–613.

Bedeni, L. A., Bullock, C. C., & Driscoll, B. (1993, Second quarter). The effects of leisure education on factors contributing to the successful transition of students with mental retardation from school to adult life. *Therapeutic Recreation Journal,* pp. 70–82.

Bender, M. (1994). Learning disabilities: Beyond the school years. In A. Capute, P. Accardo, & B. Shapiro (Eds.), *Learning disabilities spectrum: ADD, ADHD, & LD.* (pp. 241–254). Baltimore: New York Press.

Brannan, S. (1979). *Project Explore: Expanding programs and learning in outdoor recreation and education for the handicapped.* Washington, DC: Hawkins and Associates.

Compton, D. M., & Iso-Ahola, S. (Eds.), *Leisure and mental health* (Vol. 1). Park City, UT: Family Development Resources.

Frith, G. H., & Mitchell, J. W. (1983). Art education for mildly retarded students: A significant component of the special education curriculum. *Education and Training of the Mentally Retarded, 18,* 138–140.

Giangreco, M. F. (1983). Teaching basic photography skills to a severely handicapped young adult using simulated materials. *Journal of The Association for the Severely Handicapped, 8,* 43–49.

Hanley, P. E. (1979). Handmade games for home and school. *Day Care and Early Education, 7,* 38–40.

Havens, M. D. (1992). *Bridges to accessibility.* Dubuque, IA: Kendall/Hunt.

Joswiak, K. F. (1979). *Leisure counseling program materials for the developmentally disabled.* Washington, DC: Hawkins and Associates.

Kingsley, R. F., Viggiano, R. A., & Tout, L. (1981). Social perception of friendship, leadership, and game playing among EMR special and regular class boys. *Education and Training of the Mentally Retarded, 16,* 201–206.

Louis Harris & Associates. (1986). *The ICD Survey of Disabled Americans: Bringing disabled Americans into the mainstream.* New York: International Center for the Disabled.

Marchant, J. A. (1979). Teaching games and hobbies. In P. Wehman (Ed.), *Recreation programming for developmentally disabled persons.* Austin, TX: PRO-ED.

Mathews, P. (1977). Recreation and normalization of the mentally retarded. *Therapeutic Recreation Journal, 11,* 17–21.

McCarron, L., Kern, W., & Wolf, C. S. (1979). Use of leisure time activities for work adjustment training. *Mental Retardation, 17,* 159–160.

Moon, M. S. (1994). The case for inclusive school and community recreation. In M. S. Moon (Ed.), *Making school and community recreation fun for everyone* (pp. 1–13). Baltimore: Brookes.

Nietupski, J., & Svoboda, R. (1982). Teaching a cooperative leisure skill to severely handicapped adults. *Education and Training of the Mentally Retarded, 17,* 38–43.

Salzberg, C. L., & Langford, C. A. (1981). Community integration of mentally retarded adults through leisure activity. *Mental Retardation, 19,* 127–131.

Sparrow, W. A., & Mayne, S. C. (1990, Third quarter). Recreation patterns of adults with intellectual disabilities. *Therapeutic Recreation Journal,* pp. 45–49.

Sternlight, M., & Hurwitz, R. (1981). *Games children play: Instructive and creative play activities for the mentally retarded and developmentally disabled child.* New York: Van Nostrand-Reinhold.

Voeltz, L. M., Wuerch, B. B., & Wilcox, B. (1982). Leisure and recreation: Preparation for independence, integration and self-fulfillment. In B. Wilcox & G. T. Bellamy (Eds.), *Design of high school programs for severely handicapped students* (pp. 175–209). Baltimore: Brookes.

Wehman, P., & Schleien, S. (1980). Assessment and selection of leisure skills for severely handicapped individuals. *Education and Training of the Mentally Retarded, 15,* 50–57.

Winnick, J. P. (Ed.). (1995). *Adapted physical education and sport* (2nd ed.). Champaign, IL: Human Kinetics.

York, J., & Rainforth, B. (1995). Enhancing leisure participation by individuals with significant intellectual and physical disabilities. In S. J. Schleien, L. H. Meyer, L. A. Heyne, & B. B. Brandt (Eds.), *Lifelong leisure skills and lifestyles for persons with developmental disabilities* (pp. 113–131). Baltimore: Brookes.

Suggested Readings

Adkins, J., & Matson, J. L. (1980). Teaching institutionalized mentally retarded adults socially appropriate leisure skills. *Mental Retardation, 18,* 249–252.

Allen, J. I. (1980). Jogging can modify disruptive behaviors. *Teaching Exceptional Children, 2,* 63–70.

Amary, I. (1975). *Creative recreation for the mentally retarded.* Springfield, IL: Charles C Thomas.

Aveno, A. (1987, June). A survey of leisure activities engaged in by adults who are severely retarded living in different residence and community types. *Education and Training in Mental Retardation,* pp. 121–127.

Beasley, C. R. (1982). Effects of a jogging program on cardiovascular fitness and work performance of mentally retarded adults. *American Journal of Mental Deficiency, 86,* 609–613.

Bender, M., Brannan, S., & Verhoven, P. (1984). *Leisure education for the handicapped.* San Diego: College-Hill.

Bergman, J. S. (1991). *How to position people with severe disabilities.* St. Paul, MN: Governor's Planning Council on Developmental Disabilities.

Bohm, H. (1972). *Making simple constructions.* New York: Watson-Cuptill.

Breuning, S. E., Davis, V. J., & Lewis, J. R. (1981). Examination of methods of selecting goal-directed activities for institutionalized retarded adults. *Education and Training of the Mentally Retarded, 16,* 5–12.

Brown, F., & Lehr, D. (1993). Making activities meaningful for students with severe disabilities. *Teaching Exceptional Children, 25*(4), 61–70.

Byers, E. S. (1979). Wilderness camping as a therapy for emotionally disturbed children: A critical review. *Exceptional Children, 45,* 628–635.

Crawley, S. B., & Chan, K. S. (1982). Developmental changes in free-play behavior of mildly and moderately retarded preschool-aged children. *Education and Training of the Mentally Retarded, 17,* 234–239.

Dattilo, J., & Light, J. (1993). Setting the stage for leisure: Encouraging reciprocal communication for people using augmentative communication systems through facilitator instruction. *Therapeutic Recreation Journal, 27*(3), 156–171.

Datillo, J., & Schleien, S. J. (1994). Understanding the provision of leisure services for individuals with mental retardation. *Mental Retardation, 32*(1), 53–59.

Day, R., & Day, H. M. (1977). Leisure skills instruction for the moderately and severely retarded: A demonstration program. *Education and Training of the Mentally Retarded, 12,* 128–131.

Deyrup, A. (1972). The complete book of tie dyeing. New York: Lancer Books.

Elium, M. D., & Evans, B. (1982). A model camping program for college students and handicapped learners. *Education and Training of the Mentally Retarded, 17,* 241–242.

Ellis, G. D. (1993). *Leisure efficacy interview.* Salt Lake City, UT: Western Laboratory for Leisure Research.

Fairchild, E., & Neal, L. (1975). *Common-unity in the community—A forward looking program of recreation and leisure services for the handicapped.* Eugene: University of Oregon, Center of Leisure Studies.

Farina, A. M. (1976). Implementing play activities for the mentally retarded. *Physical Education, 33,* 180–185.

Favell, J. E., & Cannon, P. R. (1976). Evaluation of entertainment materials for severely retarded persons. *American Journal of Mental Deficiency, 81,* 357–361.

Frith, G. H., & Mitchell, J. W. (1983). Art education for mildly retarded students: A significant component of the special education curriculum. *Education and Training of the Mentally Retarded, 18,* 138–140.

Funk, D. (1980). *Guidelines for planning travel for the physically handicapped: A handbook for travel agents, tour wholesalers, and recreation/travel personnel.* Washington, DC: Hawkins and Associates.

Giangreco, M. F. (1983). Teaching basic photography skills to a severely handicapped young adult using simulated materials. *Journal of The Association for the Severely Handicapped, 8,* 43–49.

Gould, E., & Gould, L. (1978). *Arts and crafts for physically and mentally disabled: The how, what and why of it.* Springfield, IL: Charles C Thomas.

Halle, J. W., Silverman, N. A., & Regan, L. (1983). The effects of a data-based exercise program on physical fitness of retarded children. *Education and Training of the Mentally Retarded, 18,* 221–225.

Halloran, W., & Ward, M. J. (1988). *Improving transition programming: Bringing disabled Americans in the mainstream.* New York: International Center for the Disabled.

Hanley, P. E. (1979). Handmade games for home and school. *Day Care and Early Education, 7,* 38–40.

Harvey, J. R. (1979). The potential of relaxation training for the mentally retarded. *Mental Retardation, 17,* 71–76.

Hedberg, S. (1980). Outdoor education can help the handicapped. *Today's Education, 2,* 54–56.

Heyne, L., & Schleien, S. (1994). Leisure and recreation programming to enhance quality of life. In E. Cipani & F. Spooner (Eds.), *Curriculum and instructional approaches for persons with severe disabilities* (pp. 213–240). Needham Heights, MA: Allyn & Bacon.

Hill, J. W., Wehman, P., & Horst, G. (1982). Toward generalization of appropriate leisure and social behavior in severely handicapped youth: Pinball machine use. *Journal of The Association for the Severely Handicapped, 6,* 38–44.

Hopper, C., & Wambold, C. (1978). Improving the independent play of severely mentally retarded children. *Education and Training of the Mentally Retarded, 13,* 42–46.

Joswiak, K. F. (1979). *Leisure counseling program materials for the developmentally disabled.* Washington, DC: Hawkins and Associates.

Kingsley, R. F., Viggiano, R. A., & Tout, L. (1981). Social perception of friendship, leadership, and game playing among EMR special and regular class boys. *Education and Training of the Mentally Retarded, 16,* 201–206.

Leisure today: Selected readings. (1975). Washington, DC: AAHPER.

Let's play to grow. (1980). Washington, DC: Joseph P. Kennedy, Jr. Foundation.

Li, A. K. F. (1981). Play and the mentally retarded child. *Mental Retardation, 19,* 121–126.

Mahon, M. J., & Bullock, C. C. (1992). Teaching adolescents with mild mental retardation to make decisions in leisure through the use of self-control techniques. *Therapeutic Recreation Journal, 26*(1), 926.

Marion, R. L. (1979). Leisure time activities for trainable mentally retarded adolescents. *Teaching Exceptional Children, 11,* 158–160.

Mathews, P. (1977). Recreation and normalization of the mentally retarded. *Therapeutic Recreation Journal, 11,* 17–21.

Matson, J. L., & Marchetti, A. (1980). A comparison of leisure skills training procedures for the mentally retarded. *Applied Research in Mental Retardation, 1,* 113–122.

Maynard, M. (1976). The value of creative arts for the developmentally disabled child: Implications for recreation therapists in community day service programs. *Therapeutic Recreation Journal, 10,* 10–13.

McCarron, L., Kern, W., & Wolf, C. S. (1979). Use of leisure time activities for work adjustment training. *Mental Retardation, 17,* 159–160.

Moon, M. S., & Renzaglia, A. (1982). Physical fitness and the mentally retarded: A critical review of the literature. *Journal of Special Education, 16,* 269–287.

Museums and handicapped students—Guidelines for educators. (1977). Washington, DC: Smithsonian Institution.

Nietupski, J., & Svoboda, R. (1982). Teaching a cooperative leisure skill to severely handicapped adults. *Education and Training of the Mentally Retarded, 17,* 38–43.

Odom, S. L. (1981). The relationship of play to developmental level in mentally retarded preschool children. *Education and Training of the Mentally Retarded, 16,* 136–141.

Pope, L., Edel, D., & Hakley, A. (1979). *Special needs: Special answers—A resource of reproducible exercises and activities for special education and early childhood programs.* New York: Book-Lab.

Putnam, J. W. (Ed.). (1993). *Cooperative learning and strategies for inclusion: Celebrating diversity in the classroom.* Baltimore: Brookes.

Sable, J. (1992). Collaborating to create an integrated camping program: Design and evaluation. *Therapeutic Recreation Journal, 26*(3), 38–48.

Salzberg, C. L., & Langford, C. A. (1981). Community integration of mentally retarded adults through leisure activity. *Mental Retardation, 19,* 127–131.

Santomier, J., & Kopczuk, W. (1981). Facilitation of interactions between retarded and non-retarded students in a physical education setting. *Education and Training of the Mentally Retarded, 16,* 20–23.

Schleien, S. J., Kiernan, J., & Wehman, P. (1981). Evaluation of an age-appropriate leisure skills program for moderately retarded adults. *Education and Training of the Mentally Retarded, 16,* 13–19.

Schleien, S., & Ray, T. (1988). *Community recreation and persons with disabilities: Strategies for integration.* Baltimore: Brookes.

Schleien, S., Wehman, P., & Kiernan, J. (1981). Teaching leisure skills to severely handicapped adults: An age-appropriate darts game. *Journal of Applied Behavior Analysis, 14,* 513–520.

Sengstock, W., & Jens, K. G. (1974). Recreation for the handicapped: Suggestions for program adaptations. *Therapeutic Recreation Journal, 8,* 172–178.

Shea, T. M. (1977). *Camping for special children.* St. Louis: Mosby.

Shields, E. W. (1979). Intramurals: An avenue for developing leisure values. *Journal of Physical Education and Recreation, 50,* 75–77.

Sliney, M. A., & Geelen, K. E. (1977). *Manual of alternative procedures—Recreational activities.* Medford: Massachusetts Center for Program Development and Education.

Sports skills instructional program. (1980). Washington, DC: Special Olympics.

Stein, A., & Sessoms, H. D. (1977). *Recreation and special populations.* Boston: Holbrook Press.

Sternlight, M., & Hurwitz, R. (1981). *Games children play: Instructive and creative play activities for the mentally retarded and developmentally disabled child.* New York: Van Nostrand–Reinhold.

Sussman, E. J. (1976). *Art projects for the mentally retarded child.* Springfield, IL: Charles C Thomas.

Switzky, H. N., Ludwig, L., & Haywood, H. C. (1979). Exploration and play in retarded and nonretarded preschool children: Effects of object complexity and age. *American Journal of Mental Deficiency, 83,* 637–644.

Verhoven, P., & Goldstein, J. (1976). *Leisure activity participation and handicapped populations: An assessment of research needs.* Arlington, VA: National Recreation and Park Association.

Voeltz, L. M., Wuerch, B. B., & Bockhaut, C. H. (1982). Social validation of leisure activity training with severely handicapped youth. *The Journal of The Association for the Severely Handicapped, 7,* 3–13.

Voeltz, L. M., Wuerch, B. B., & Wilcox, B. (1982). Leisure/recreation: Preparation for independence, integration and self-fulfillment. In B. Wilcox & G. T. Bellamy (Eds.), *Design of high school programs for severely handicapped students* (pp. 175–209). Baltimore: Brookes.

Wahler, R. G., & Fox, J. J. (1980). Solitary toy play and time out: A family treatment package for children with aggressive and oppositional behavior. *Journal of Applied Behavior Analysis, 13,* 23–29.

Wambold, C., & Bailey, R. (1979). Improving leisure-time behaviors of severely/profoundly mentally retarded children through toy play. *AAESPH Review, 4,* 237–250.

Wehman, P. (1976). A leisure time activities curriculum for the developmentally disabled. *Education and Training of the Mentally Retarded, 11,* 309–313.

Wehman, P. (1977). *Helping the mentally retarded acquire play skills.* Springfield, IL: Charles C Thomas.

Wehman, P. (Ed.). (1978). *Recreation programming for developmentally disabled persons.* Baltimore: University Park Press.

Wehman, P. (1979). Instructional strategies for improving toy play skills of severely handicapped children. *AAESPH Review, 4,* 125–135.

Wehman, P. (1979). Teaching table games to severely retarded children. *Mental Retardation, 17,* 150–151

Wehman, P., & Schleien, S. (1979). *Leisure skills curriculum for the severely handicapped* (Books 1, 2, 3, and 4). Richmond: Virginia Commonwealth University.

Wehman, P., & Schleien, S. (1980). Assessment and selection of leisure skills for severely handicapped individuals. *Education and Training of the Mentally Retarded, 15,* 50–57.

Wuerch, B., & Voeltz, L. (1982). *Longitudinal leisure skills for severely handicapped learners: The Hoonanea curriculum component.* Baltimore: Brookes.

Selected Materials/Resources

KITS/CURRICULAR MATERIALS

- *Child Development Inventory*
  Behavior Science Systems, Inc.
  Box 580274
  Minneapolis, Minnesota 55458
  (612) 929-6220

- *Discovering Me & My World*
  American Guidance Service
  4201 Woodland Road
  PO Box 99
  Circle Pines, Minnesota 55014-1796
  (800) 328-2560

- *I Can: Speech, Leisure, Recreational Skills*
  PRO-ED
  8700 Shoal Creek Boulevard
  Austin, Texas 78757-6897
  (512) 451-3246

- *Tips from Tots*
  VORT Corporation
  PO Box 60880
  Palo Alto, California 94306

VIDEOS

- *Forever Fit Video, Forever Fit 2*
  S & S Worldwide Games
  PO Box 517
  Colchester, Connecticut 06415-0517
  (800) 243-9232

- *Gentle Fitness—Yes! Videos* (80 minute/close captioned)
  S & S Worldwide Games
  PO Box 517
  Colchester, Connecticut 06415-0517
  (800) 243-9232

- *Shape Up 'n Sign*
  Harris Communications
  6541 City West Parkway
  Eden Prairie, Minnesota 55344
  (612) 946-0921

- *Wheelchair Javelin*
  Benchmark Press
  PO Box 3068
  Carmel, Indiana 46032
  (317) 253-3763

- *Young and Special 30 Video Set*
  American Guidance Service
  4201 Woodland Road
  PO Box 99
  Circle Pines, Minnesota 55014-1796
  (800) 328-2560

ASSISTIVE DEVICES

- *Bowling and Bowling Assistance Ramp*
  S & S Worldwide Games
  PO Box 517
  Colchester, Connecticut 06415-0517
  (800) 243-9232

- *Braille: Scrabble*
  Independent Living Aids, Inc.
  27 East Mall
  Plainview, New York 11803
  (800) 537-2118

- *Cards: Maxi-Rack*
  Therapro, Inc.
  225 Arlington Street
  Framingham, Massachusetts 01701
  (508) 872-9494

- *Chess Set: Deluxe*
  Maxi Aids
  42 Executive Boulevard, PO Box 3209
  Farmingdale, New York 11735
  (800) 522-6294

- *Croquet: Softouch*
  Hammatt Senior Products
  PO Box 727
  Mount Vernon, Washington 98273
  (206) 428-5850

- *Texture Dominoes*
  S & S Worldwide Games
  PO Box 517
  Colchester, Connecticut 06415-0517
  (800) 243-9232

- *"Thistle" Tri-Lo Hand Propelled Tricycles*
  Jesana Ltd.
  PO Box 17
  Irvington, New York 10533
  (800) 443-4728

ORGANIZATIONS

- *American Athletic Association of the Deaf (AAAD)*
  3607 Washington Boulevard, Suite 4
  Ogden, Utah 84403-1737
  (801) 393-8710

- *American Camping Association*
  5000 State Road 67N
  Martinsville, Indiana 46151
  (317) 342-8456

- *American Wheelchair Archers*
  RD #2, Box 2043
  West Sunbury, Pennsylvania 16061
  (412) 735-4359

- *Dwarf Athletic Association of America (DAAA)*
  418 Willow Way
  Lewisville, Texas 75607
  (214) 317-8299

- *Indoor Sports Club*
  1145 Highland Street
  Napolean, Ohio 43545
  (419) 592-5756

- *National Wheelchair Athletic Association (NWAA)*
  3595 East Fountain Boulevard, Suite L-1
  Colorado Springs, Colorado 80910
  (719) 574-1150

- *Special Olympics International (SOI)*
  1350 New York Avenue, NW, Suite 500
  Washington, DC 20005
  (202) 628-3630

- *United States Association for Blind Athletes (USABA)*
  33 North Institute Street
  Brown Hall, Suite 015
  Colorado Springs, Colorado 80903
  (719) 630-0422

Notes

Notes

Notes

Notes

Notes

Notes